NEWCASTLE UNITED
MATCH
OF MY LIFE

NEWCASTLE UNITED
MATCH
OF MY LIFE

ALEX CROOK
& JAKE RUSBY

First published by Pitch Publishing, 2023

Pitch Publishing
9 Donnington Park,
85 Birdham Road,
Chichester,
West Sussex,
PO20 7AJ

www.pitchpublishing.co.uk
info@pitchpublishing.co.uk

A CIP catalogue record is available for this book
from the British Library.

ISBN 978 1 80150 641 0

Typesetting and origination by Pitch Publishing
Printed and bound in Great Britain by TJ Books

Contents

Acknowledgements

Thank you to Jane at Pitch Publishing for commissioning and putting together this book, and for helping to bring to life so many amazing stories, and to all of the contributors who so kindly gave up their time and memories.

We are also indebted to Chris Upfield, Neil Allen and Olly Clink for their painstaking proofreading, and to Mark Hannen, Graham Courtney and Jamie Docherty for opening their contacts books to enable us to reach out to so many Newcastle United legends.

Jake expertly managed to shoehorn his family into his 'about the author' bio, but would like to say thank you again to them here for their constant love and support, and to pay tribute to his parents, Amanda and Tim, for always encouraging him to pursue his passion of writing and for endlessly indulging his love of the beautiful game.

Alex would also like to thank his wife Emma and children Annabelle, Jamie, Oscar and Rosie for their unwavering support and patience.

Finally, and most importantly in many ways, thank you to the journalistic giant that was Pat Symes, whose memory this book is dedicated to. It was at Pat's funeral that we came up with the idea for this book to continue the great man's writing legacy.

Foreword by Rafa Benitez

The potential of the club and the city is what made me want to come to Newcastle United. They were a sleeping giant, you could see a city behind the team a bit like I had witnessed with Liverpool. I could see that we could create something, we could build something there. The fans have always been behind the team, and now the club has some money, which means they can sign top-quality players. I think they have done so, giving them a more competitive squad, which is helping them compete on another level. I believe they have the potential to keep on improving. How much? I don't know. But they have the belief and the support, so the sky is the limit.

In 2021, I was waiting to hear if Newcastle wanted me back, but the Premier League were being slow at giving permission for the new ownership to take over. Then I had a difficult decision to make: Everton approached me with a project. Would I wait for Newcastle or take them up on their offer? In the end I decided to stay close to my family in Liverpool. I still follow Newcastle United and the relationship with the fans is still really good, so I am very happy to see them doing well, but I had to make a decision, and the timing was not right for me. Everton approached me with some ideas and I thought it would be a good move, but unfortunately it didn't turn out for the best for me at Everton. It was not until two or three months after I had been appointed that permission was given to buy Newcastle.

I am very proud of the time that I spent at Newcastle. We stabilised the team in the Premier League without money, making a profit for the club, and signing players that went on to have good careers there. I loved living in Newcastle too. In Liverpool I have problems with the accent, and I had that too in Newcastle, but usually I would talk about football with people and then I could understand them. I find it very difficult to understand my daughter when she speaks to me fast with a Scouse accent – and with the Geordie accent it's the same. Obviously it was very different to my time in Spain because of the weather and the conditions, but I liked Newcastle. I didn't mind the rain or the cold, for me it is just important to be somewhere you can do your job, and then people will appreciate that.

The first match that comes into my head when I think about my time with Newcastle United is our 5-1 win over Tottenham Hotspur in May 2016. Tottenham were playing for second position, and we were relegated already, but the stadium was full of people supporting, singing and cheering my name. It was a great game where we played with intensity and you could feel the passion everywhere, and that atmosphere, the support of the fans and their commitment to me on that final day of the season was one of the key things that made me want to stay, even though we had been demoted. It was a massive turning point.

I was given the job as manager with 12 games to play, which was a little too late – we had to play Leicester, who went on to be champions, and Sunderland and Norwich, our relegation rivals, in our first three games, and had 13 injuries. We didn't have a holding midfielder or a left-back. Little by little we managed to bring players back, and then had six games in a row where we were unbeaten. We had some positives at the end of the season, but time was against us. It was a risk to go to Newcastle because we could get relegated, but this game was the difference, in terms of the feeling that I could do something important at the football club, with the whole city behind me.

An important thing for me always is to analyse things in their context. When I went to Newcastle they were desperate for something different, and behind me from day one. It was very similar to the Liverpool fans – they wanted a change, they wanted to improve, they wanted to be competitive, and we did compete.

In this case we did it without the resources, but we were able to improve things because the fans were behind the team. It is not like you have two or three teams in the city; you have one and everybody follows that team, everybody loves that team and they are fully committed in terms of support.

The Tottenham game was crucial: the atmosphere was crucial, and the support was crucial. Having a city behind you is something every manager wants.

At that time it was very difficult to go to the Championship, but in the end I think it was the right decision to go down with the club because I could show my loyalty to the people who had been supporting me from the beginning.

To still have the full support from the fans was amazing. We did what we had to do, and the fans appreciated that. In the end, my decision to stay was 100 per cent justified. As a manager, as a coach, people can talk about trophies or the style of football, but when you go to a different country, different divisions and still succeed as a manager and as a professional, you feel right, you feel happy within yourself. People can criticise whatever they want, but I proved I could do my job in a different league, in different conditions, like I have now done in England, Italy and Spain.

When we went down to the Championship, we signed players with experience in that division, for example Grant Hanley, Matt Ritchie and Dwight Gayle, and then put them together with the Premier League players and that's how we created a successful team. Some of the players who left when we got relegated were important players, and them leaving meant we had to adapt. The Championship is a very difficult league, and the players we signed were very important in terms of performance and also mentality. Ritchie was a player with massive experience, Gayle scored a lot of goals, and these kinds of players were specifically signed to go up.

It was not difficult to create a good team spirit – everybody wanted to get promotion and then to do well in the Premier League, so the atmosphere in the dressing room was very good. We played 4-2-3-1, we were attacking, we were pressing, we were aggressive. Sometimes you need time to adapt to a new division and a team with lots of new players, but little by little we managed, we developed, and earned ourselves promotion back to the Premier League.

There are some games from that Championship season I remember very well: the 4-3 victory over Norwich in September 2016, where we scored two late goals. It was such an important match because we were coming back to the belief that we could succeed in the Championship that season. When we beat Brighton 2-1 away at the Amex that was another big game that season, because Brighton were close to us, so to win with late goals from Mo Diamé and Ayoze Pérez was massive in our push for promotion, which we eventually achieved.

In terms of the Premier League, in February 2018 we beat Manchester United 1-0, in Martin Dúbravka's first game, where he made a lot of outstanding saves. It was so important in terms of belief and confidence. I look back with a smile at when we beat Manchester City 2-1 in January 2019. Sergio Agüero scored in the first minute, but we fought back and Salomón Rondón equalised in the 66th minute, before Ritchie got a late penalty. It is not very often that you beat Manchester City, and the atmosphere was absolutely amazing. I also have fond memories of my last game, when we beat Fulham 4-0.

Initially, when we were in the Premier League, Mo Sissoko was a very important player for us, because he could manage the group very well, but then after relegation to the Championship, Jonjo Shelvey and later Jamaal Lascelles were key men in the dressing room, and players like Diamé. They were characters that everybody liked and respected. They were not too vocal, but everybody followed and trusted them. Dúbravka took on that role later on, too.

We had Christian Atsu in our squad as well. He was a Chelsea player that I knew and had very good references about him. He was a nice lad and a very good professional. Everybody loved him. He was training well and was excellent technically. He was very skilful, could go past players and could make the difference in the final third. He knew exactly what I wanted and what we needed from him, and he did it. I was trying to contact him and to check if he was okay when the earthquake happened in Turkey in February 2023, and then it was very bad news. He's a big loss.

In the Championship, we spent around £16m and recovered £90m by selling players like Sissoko, Daryl Janmaat, Andros Townsend and Georginio Wijnaldum, so we made a big profit. I was expecting that, the year afterwards when we got promoted back to the Premier League, with all of the additional TV revenue, we'd have some money to spend, but sadly it was not the case. We had to continually match our player targets with the money we had, which was not very much. I think our spending when we were back in the Premier League was less than almost everyone else.

If you want to buy a car and you have more money, you can buy a better car and you can go faster, it's that simple. We had the right car in the Championship, but when we got back into the Premier League we just had to manage the same car in the best way possible; we didn't have the engine to go faster.

We tried to bring players through from the academy that fitted the owner's model who would also help us compete – like Sean Longstaff, who we promoted to the first team – but we didn't really have the possibility to do that with many players, unfortunately.

I remember when we signed Joelinton for £42m. He was a good player but maybe not the striker we needed. He was scoring around ten goals a season for his previous club, and we were talking about making a record signing. I told Mike Ashley that I didn't think he was a £42m striker – we paid £16m for Miguel Almirón, with add-ons that could make it £21m – and that was a record fee for the club. You are talking about £42m for a player that was not scoring too many goals, even though I liked the player, and his work rate and ability were excellent; I didn't see Joelinton as a £42m striker. I told Mike Ashley they could spend less money and get someone else, but he didn't listen. I tried to protect the club in one way, and they ignored me. What Joelinton has proved since is that he's a very good player, but not a striker! He has excelled under Eddie Howe as an attacking midfielder, or winger. That is the right position for him.

As for Almirón, we knew him and that he was doing well in the MLS (Major League Soccer), and I had lots of information on him from my contacts in America. We knew he was a nice lad, a good professional and a hard worker, scoring goals. The MLS is different, but now he's doing well in the Premier League and I am very pleased for him.

I was happy to recruit the players that we signed, and with the performances they gave us, but some of the players we signed were not even in the top-five players on our list. In the end we tried to adapt to the resources of the club, and tried to find the players to match the money we had available, like with Almirón.

We gave everything. We improved the training ground a little and then we wanted to improve other things, but it was impossible. From my last meeting with Mike Ashley in 2019, it was very clear from him that he would not be spending money – he would not invest in the academy, nor the training ground, and obviously not the squad, so I was expected to manage with the resources we had. There was no point in staying there when I would not be able to compete year after year. You could see the investment was not there.

That is when I decided it was not the time to stay – suffering trying to be tenth in the league. That was not the idea, especially for a city and club like Newcastle United with the potential they had.

I look back at my time at the club with pride and still feel a bond with the supporters and the city. While I was there, the fans needed someone who could give them a little bit of hope and belief, and I think I did that. I knew what they wanted and tried my best to give it to them.

Rafa Benitez,
28 March 2023

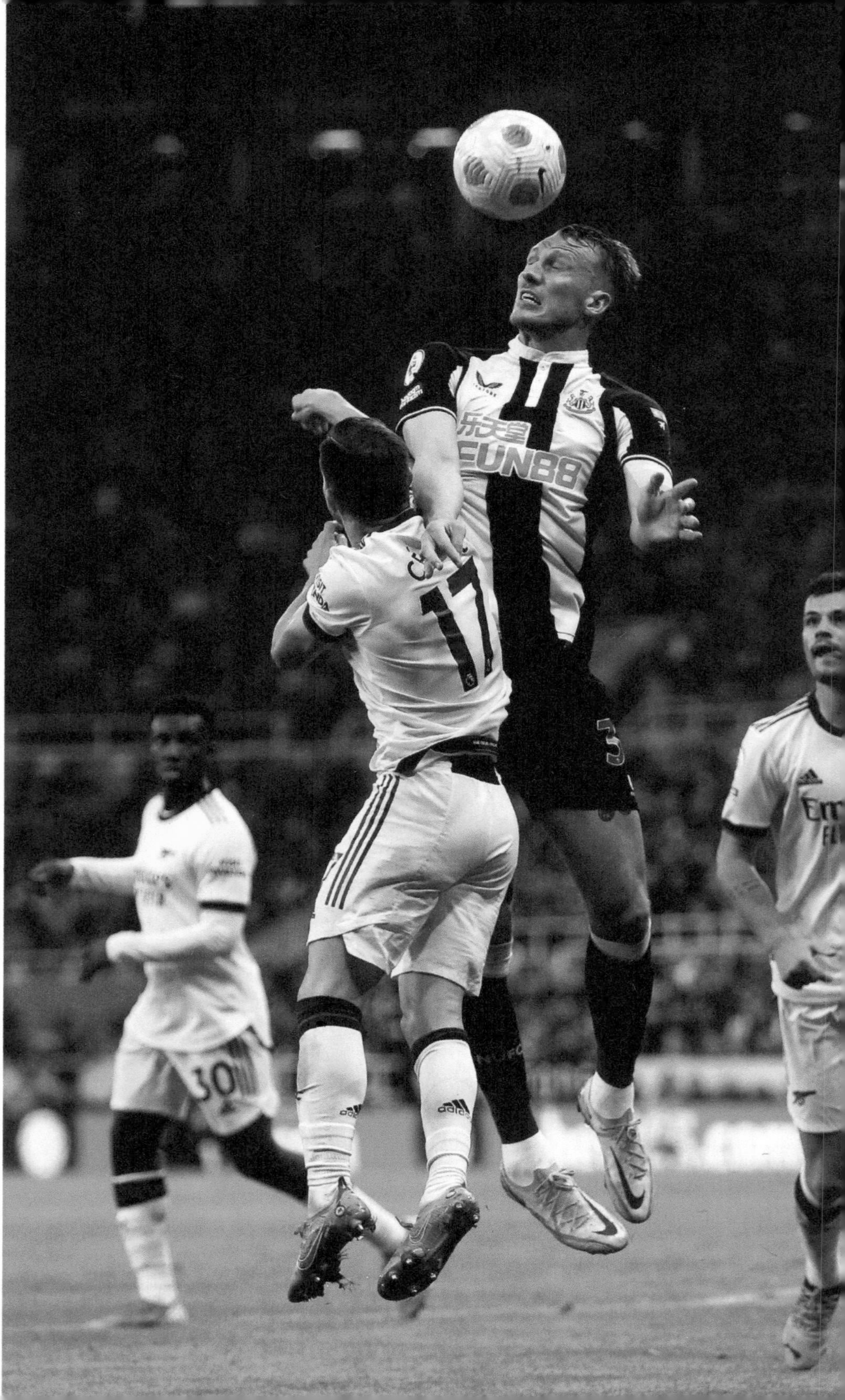
FUN88

Dan Burn
Defender
2022–present

When Newcastle became one of the world's richest football clubs following their Saudi Arabian-led takeover in 2021, few people, even Dan Burn himself, would have predicted the 6ft 7in defender would be one of their first signings. Burn, who famously turned up for one of his early training sessions driving a Smart Car, is as far removed as can be from some of the more glamorous names like Neymar and Cristiano Ronaldo, who were being linked with a move to St James' Park. But the Blyth-born friendly giant – who grew up idolising Alan Shearer and was released by Newcastle as a schoolboy – quickly established himself as a hero among the Toon Army he used to be part of with his wholehearted displays.

After signing from Brighton in January 2022, Burn played a key part in Newcastle avoiding relegation before going on to establish himself as first-choice left-back in the team that would finish fourth in the Premier League in 2022/23 to bring Champions League football back to the North East for the first time in nearly two decades. It's the quarter-final of that season's Carabao Cup en route to facing Manchester United in the final at Wembley that Burn has chosen as the match of his life.

Newcastle United 2-0 Leicester City

Carabao Cup, quarter-final
Tuesday, 10 January 2023
St James' Park, Newcastle
Attendance: 52,009

Newcastle	**Leicester**
Pope	Ward
Trippier	Castagne
Schar	Amartey
Botman	Faes
Burn	Thomas (Iheanacho)
Longstaff	Ndidi
Guimarães	Tielemans
Willock (Murphy)	Albrighton
Almirón (Saint-Maximin)	Pérez (Mendy)
Wilson (Isak)	Barnes
Joelinton	Daka (Vardy)

Managers

Eddie Howe	Brendan Rodgers

Goals

Burn

Joelinton

I remember my goal vividly because I still replay it every few nights on the television. I broke into the box, took a good second touch, and thought to myself, *I'm just going to hit this.* The moment I struck the shot I knew it was going in and then it was just pure joy, scoring at the Gallowgate End, what I'd dreamed of doing since I was a kid. I've got a box in that exact corner of St James' Park as well, so to do it down there and be able to run over and celebrate in front of all my friends and family was amazing and still feels very surreal.

I do sort of regret the celebration in the dressing room afterwards. After some of the games, the gaffer tries to get people up and dancing and it's only really Jacob Murphy that ever does because he can move. Everyone was telling me to dance and then the gaffer urged me to get up – I thought he wanted me to dance, but he actually wanted me to make a speech. I thought I'd just throw a dance in and then it went viral on social media. I was a bit gutted because it deflected away from how good the goal was, but I think people appreciate that anyway. Wherever I go now people come up to me and say, 'Can you do the dance?' but I save it for goals and, luckily, I don't score that many, so don't have to do it very often.

Later that season I scored my first Premier League goal, against my old club Brighton, which was another great feeling. I was most shocked because I'd scored with my head, as that's something I've always struggled with. It's not for the lack of trying so I don't know if it's about timing or whatever, but, given my height, you'd expect me to score more headers.

People have asked whether I considered not celebrating in front of Brighton, but I didn't really think about that until after and I don't score enough goals to not celebrate.

To be fair to Brighton, they were great with me when I left. They really didn't want me to go but understood it was my boyhood club and didn't want to stand in the way. I wouldn't have left for anyone apart from Newcastle, barring a Manchester City, but that was never going to happen. It was always going to be Newcastle or no one. I actually remember saying to my dad just as the takeover happened that my chances of playing for Newcastle were gone – then, three months later, there I was signing. It's crazy how these things work out.

I was in Dubai when I first started to hear a few rumours and there were loads of players being touted for Newcastle because everybody knew what was happening with the new owners coming in. The two clubs were speaking to each other, trying to agree a fee, and I wanted to speed it up a little bit, so I ended up ringing Graeme Jones, one of the coaches who my agent had a bit of a relationship with, and spoke to him about it. As it was going through so many different people, I didn't really know what was happening, so I spoke to Graeme and then the gaffer and both said similar things. I knew they were looking at a few other options but, luckily, I managed to get it done. I didn't plead my case as such, but wanted to say that I thought I could help a lot on the pitch in terms of experience, but also off the pitch with the standards I demand of myself and the players around me. Within the space of a week, it went from nothing to me driving up to Newcastle on transfer deadline day to sign the contract.

Signing was really emotional because I had my wife and both my parents there. Seeing how choked they all were brought out the emotion in me as I've had a lot of ups and downs in my career, including being let go by Newcastle as a kid, which was the right decision because I was crap at football back then and not even that into it until I got a bit older!

To know that I was getting the chance to sign for Newcastle and running out a local hero, wearing a black-and-white shirt was really emotional. I was very nervous stepping out for my debut against Aston Villa, but that's something that will live with me forever.

My first impressions of Eddie Howe were really good, particularly the attention to detail he puts into everything and the intensity he works at. It's not just that but also the fact he really wants to build a relationship with you as a person and not solely as a footballer. He wanted to know about my family, kids and my background in order to work out how he could get the best out of me. I've only got good things to say about the training, which took a little while to get used to just because of the intensity. What you see on a Saturday, the way we press, that's us every single day of the week. I had to get used to long sessions and it was like a sort of mini pre-season for me, not that the training at Brighton wasn't good, but it was a lot more relaxed in the way we went about it. Straight away I saw a lot of similarities between Eddie and Graham Potter, but it's just a lot more intense with the gaffer and we reaped the rewards.

Eddie and his assistant Jason Tindall are very much a team, very similar, and work well together. Jason does a lot of work with the defenders and we went through a stage where we kept ten clean sheets in a row. A lot of that was down to him and the stuff he drilled into us every single day. It just becomes a habit. Jason is a great guy and the impression you get of him is not the reality. Everyone laughed about the stuff that appeared on social media and all the photos about him wanting to be the centre of attention. We gave him a bit of stick and printed out pictures of his face and put them around the training ground, but he took it well.

There are a lot of clubs where the staff and the players are separate, but we're all one big group. Our mentality has always been that no one person is bigger than the team, and that really helped because everyone was pushing towards the same goal. I saw that when I first signed and we were battling to stay up, because I'd been in relegation battles before where I felt people had gone into self-defence mode and ended up deflecting a lot by saying, 'He should have done this,' or 'You should have done that,' but here we were all pulling in the same direction. Even the guys not playing were all getting behind the lads and trying to push them. I looked at that and thought we stood a good chance of avoiding relegation just because of how tight the group was. That goes a long way and there was no sort of bitterness towards players who had been playing from those who hadn't.

A lot has been made of the post-match team celebration photos we take after wins. I'd seen it a few times from afar when I was at Brighton, and Newcastle did it after picking up the first win with Eddie Howe as manager against Burnley, and it went from there. Sometimes when you're winning games, you can take it for granted, but I've been on the other side where you're losing games constantly so, to look at the photo, it helps remind you what you've done it for. It's a good thing to do and we put them up on the walls around the training ground, so every time you win they're always put up so you can walk past them.

I think that's a reflection of a real change in mentality, because normally in football you'll do training drills and there's a forfeit for the loser, so you're always just not wanting to be the loser, whereas we take photos of the winning team and at the end of the season there's a prize for whoever has won the most games. That keeps training really competitive and little things like that improve the mentality and raise standards.

When I first arrived, a few of the players took me out to welcome me to the club, even though I'm a local, which was nice. As for the manager, he does try to get everyone on a level playing field, so we do these things called 'timelines' where you stand up and talk for 10–15 minutes about anything from your life growing up to how you got into football, where you've been and what your ambitions are. It's good because when you see each other every day you only really talk about football at a very surface level. Once you get into learning about people's backgrounds, it helps you understand them all and understand their different moods. I think being up there, being vulnerable and speaking in front of the lads, brings everyone closer together and it's something Eddie is really passionate about, so maybe why we're such a tight-knit group.

I get on with and speak to everyone, but you tend to gravitate towards people who are similar to yourself, so that's always what I do. I got on with Sean Longstaff and Mark Gillespie straight away and am really close to Jacob Murphy as well. You'll always get little cliques in football, mostly because of the language that you speak and similar interests you have. I'm in my 30s now and have kids and stuff, so I can't relate as much to someone who's in their

20s. You also get people like Bruno Guimarães, Miguel Almirón and Joelinton, who spend a lot of time with each other, and then there are the younger lads – Sven Botman, Alexander Isak and Joe Willock are always together.

Almirón had a brilliant 2022/23 for us, but that ability has always been there and with him it's just a confidence thing. Miggy is a great player and every full-back in the league would struggle to play against him. It seemed everything he hit was going in and he obviously gained confidence from that, but people don't see how much work he puts in off the ball as well, with the way he leads the press. I was really happy for him as he had a tough start here when he first arrived, similar to 'Big Joe', who had a really tough start, so it was great to see them both thrive and do so well.

Isak possesses amazing ability. His pace is obviously a big factor, but also the way he can move the ball and how he glides. He's going to be a top player and even more popular with the fans than he is now. He's also a very good finisher and, as a defender, you wouldn't want to play against him.

Eddie is a very grounded manager, and I don't think he really spoke about us challenging for the top four until the last six or seven games of the season, once we were within touching distance. For me I think it was a couple of games after we lost the cup final. We had hard games against Manchester City and Liverpool and then started picking up some results. We needed things to go for us, but I thought we stood a chance, and it was just about consistency. We went out every single game with the same mindset, that we're going to play our way and attack, and if you were good enough to beat us, you were good enough to beat us. We were so consistent and that helped us pick up some big results against some of the top teams, which you need, and our home form was really good.

When things are going well at the club, there's a real connection between the fans and the team and, for me, there isn't a better place to play. The stuff 'Wor Flags' do gives us that extra bit of push and I think you feed off each other as well; the fans feed off the players and vice-versa. When I used to watch as a kid, you just wanted the players to work hard and if they lost you could accept it as long as you thought they put it all out there. I think the way we played, the fans responded to that.

One of the games that really stands out for me was when facing Arsenal at home in May 2022 and we battered them, winning 2-0. The fans were electric that night and I think Arsenal were shocked at how much of a big night it was for us and how big the fans were. Another amazing atmosphere was Southampton at home in the League Cup semi-final second leg in January 2023. Before the game, I remember looking around the stadium and actually getting emotional at just how hyped everyone was for it; you could feel the energy in the crowd and it was amazing.

We'd claim Wembley wasn't a distraction to our league form, but I think it was, not only for us as players, but the city in general. There was such a lot of hype before the match, and it was all anyone was talking about. We did as much as we could to take the emotion out of it and just play it like another game, but that did affect us a bit and if we were to get to another final we'd have a totally different mindset of 'this is what we've got to do and we're going to win', rather than it just being a great weekend. I was gutted after the game, but I wasn't inconsolable because it was still an amazing achievement just to get there. It was a great day out for every generation of Newcastle fans and didn't really sink in until a few days later that we could have won – then you imagine how different it would have been if we had. It did hurt and, in general, it was a bit weird because I could sense how nervous the fans were. I thought we played well, but games are won in both boxes and you could just tell that Manchester United had been there and done that so many times, whereas we hadn't.

We tried to keep the build-up as normal as possible because we had been so good at taking every game as it came and being consistent with it. We had a leadership group made up of Callum Wilson, Kieran Trippier, Jamaal Lascelles, Matt Ritchie and me, who came up with a few things we thought would help. We wanted to see Wembley the day before the final, just to get a feel for it because I'd been there before and knew what it was like. You want to see where your family will be sitting, and it's only when you get there that you realise the size of the stadium and how big the pitch is. You don't want to be doing that on the day of the game, so we did that and then I decided I wanted to speak. I'd written a speech, so gathered all the lads in the changing room, sat everyone down and delivered it as best I could. That was quite emotional for me, but I just felt like I was at that stage in my career where I had that experience and, being a local lad, wanted to let everyone know what it meant to me and to the club in general.

I wouldn't change anything we did, but, on the morning of the game, some letters from loved ones of the players were released on The Athletic's website and I remember people reading them and getting quite emotional. It was lovely and I'm not knocking it, but everyone was very emotionally charged.

Callum is a great guy, you can tell he's a striker as he has that swagger about him, but he's just one of these people always in the right place in the box and scored a lot of important goals for us. Trips is another great guy. That was a big help with our mentality, seeing someone who has played in a Euros final, a Champions League final, a World Cup semi-final and won La Liga and how he goes about his day-to-day business. There were a lot of clubs he could have joined but, when the takeover happened, we needed a big name to come and make other people want to do it. He set the tone for the likes of Bruno and Sven Botman to come in.

It's only natural that we get linked with pretty much every player in the world, but I think you've got to be a certain type to play in this team. I remember from when I came in, the gaffer is very strong on getting in touch with people from your hometown, to ask how my mates were, to see whether they'd be a bad influence on me and things like that, which seems ridiculous, but you want to make sure you've got the right characters who aren't going to upset the chemistry in the dressing room. Even when Alex Isak came in, he didn't play a lot at the start because you've got to get used to the way we play – and the same with Anthony Gordon. Bruno never played when he first came in and it took him nine or ten games to sort of get used to it. You have to really buy into the way we work.

Bruno probably didn't know as much about the club as other people did, but he really invested in that and built a brilliant relationship with the fans. He loves the passion, and a lot of the South American lads are like that because they're quite similar to Geordies in that they're working class and want to work hard. The fans reciprocate that and have always loved the South American players who have come over.

After losing at Wembley, we had a few team meetings where we said we were quite happy to get the final out of the way. The manager said he didn't feel distracted, but he could sense that maybe we were a little. We always had this mentality where it was us against the world because nobody outside the club really wanted us to get into the top six or top four, so we had to fight against that and switch our focus back to the Premier League because that's all we could concentrate on.

We went on a really good run of form after that and needed to because Liverpool were coming up on the rails. As a team, we never really spoke about it and you always say, 'I'm not going to look at the league table,' but I'd sit there every night working out what we needed to do and what Liverpool required because I knew they were a team capable of stringing a run of wins together, so we just needed to get over the line. It's a different type of pressure because I've been the other way around, when you're in a relegation scrap and just praying for another win, but I knew we were playing well and picking up points.

We cemented ourselves in the top four in our last home game by drawing 0-0 with Leicester. It was nice to get it done before the end of the season, otherwise there would have been a lot of pressure going to Chelsea on the last day and needing a result.

It felt like Leicester came just not to lose, which was strange because it could have been an opportunity for them to get the win and save themselves from relegation. It would have helped us if they'd played for the victory because we were better suited to teams coming on to us so we could attack them. It was a really strange game and I remember, with about two minutes left, we were standing with the ball for about 20 seconds at one point, just waiting for someone to come and press us, and then they nearly scored right at the end with their only attack of the game.

It was a bit surreal even after the match because we did the lap of honour with our families and everyone went back into the dressing room at different times, so didn't really get the chance to celebrate the achievement of qualifying for the Champions League. It was a bit of an anticlimax going home that night and, with hindsight, I think we could have done things a little bit better by just coming in five minutes earlier to congratulate each other.

That was the Monday night and some of us, but not everyone, went out for a little while on the Tuesday for a few drinks. We still had Chelsea to come and could mathematically take third place, but knew we couldn't drop out of the top four.

It was a great feeling for me personally because watching Newcastle play in the Champions League as a kid inspired me to be a footballer, seeing all those big teams come to St James' Park on a Tuesday or Wednesday night under the floodlights, the atmosphere was absolutely electric. I remember Andy Griffin scoring against Juventus and watching the Feyenoord game at home with my dad when we'd lost three matches in a row and had to win the next three to go through to the next round. Those were special games that stand out for me, so to know a whole new generation were going to get the chance to see that was really exciting.

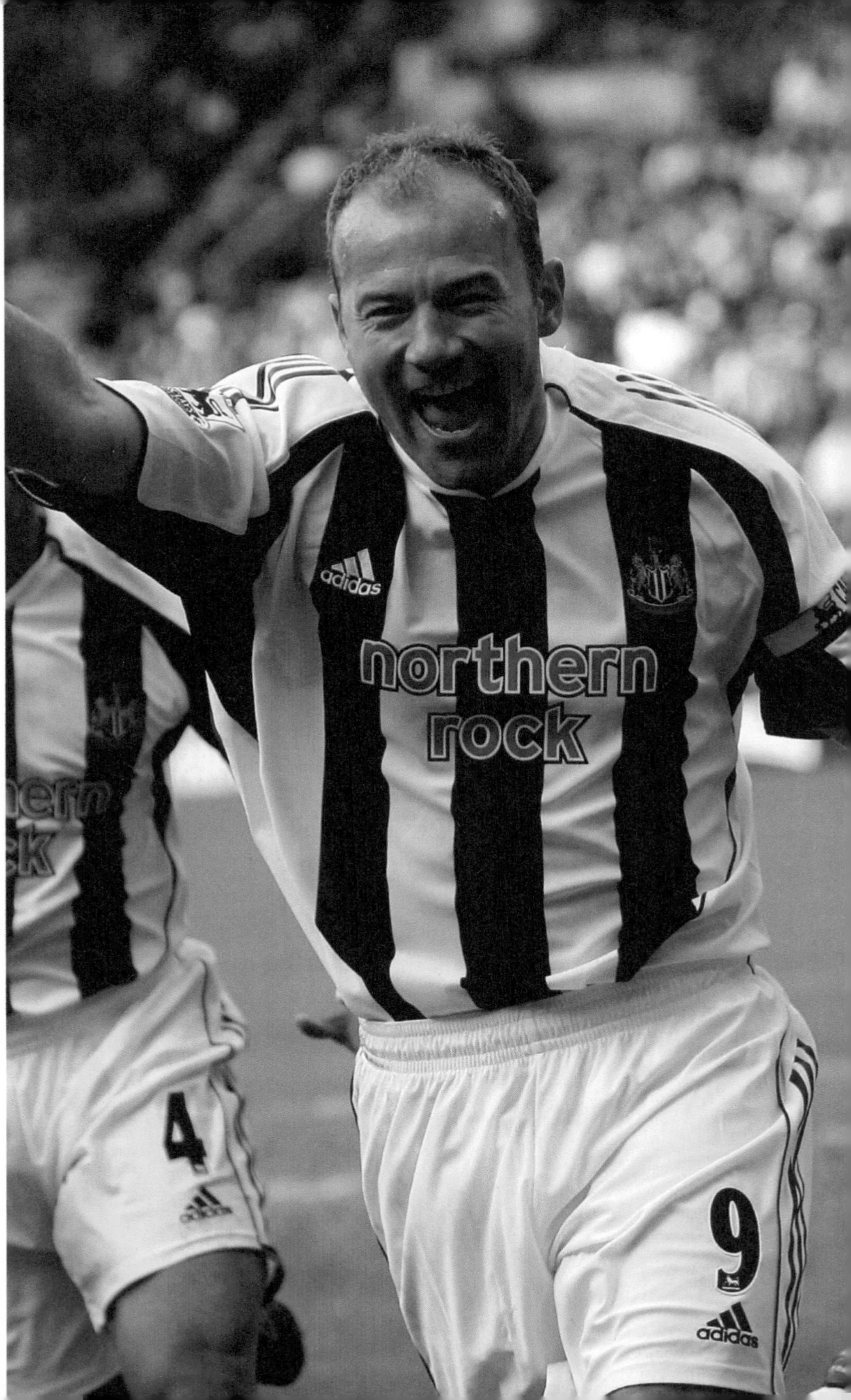

ALAN SHEARER

Alan Shearer
Striker
1996–2006

Universally heralded as one of England's greatest strikers and, at the time of writing, the Premier League's record goalscorer, Alan Shearer simply is 'Mr Newcastle'. Born and bred in the Gosforth area of the city, Shearer was a product of the famous Wallsend Boys Club before being spotted by a Southampton scout and signing a youth contract with the south coast club. Shearer made a headline-grabbing first-team debut for the Saints by bagging a hat-trick against Arsenal and went on to rack up 23 goals in 118 league matches before moving to Blackburn and repaying his then-English record fee by firing Kenny Dalglish's men to the 1995 Premier League title.

After winning the Golden Boot to help lead England to the semi-finals of Euro '96, Shearer snubbed the advances of Manchester United to join his beloved Magpies for another British record price tag of £15m. He'd go on to play in two FA Cup finals and shatter Jackie Milburn's 49-year-old record as the club's top league goalscorer. Three years after retiring in 2006, Shearer returned to Newcastle for a brief stint as manager, but couldn't save the club's Premier League status, before embarking on a successful career as a television pundit, primarily for the BBC's *Match of the Day*.

Newcastle United 2-0 Portsmouth

Premier League
Saturday, 4 February 2006
St James' Park, Newcastle
Attendance: 51,627

Newcastle	Portsmouth
Given	Kiely
Ramage	Griffin (Pamarot)
Boumsong	Primus
Bramble	O'Brien
Babayaro	Taylor
Solano (Dyer)	Routledge (Todorov)
Parker (Clark)	Davis (Diao)
Emre (Bowyer)	Mendes
N'Zogbia	O'Neil
Shearer	D'Alessandro
Ameobi	Benjani

Managers

Glenn Roeder   Harry Redknapp

Goals

N'Zogbia, Shearer

I was lucky enough to score a lot of important goals in my career, but, in terms of a buzz and a high on a football pitch, breaking Jackie Milburn's record as all-time leading scorer for my beloved Newcastle was as good as it gets. That night was also one of the only times, if not the only time, in my career that my dad ever said the words 'well done, son'.

Dad was quite a harsh taskmaster. I'm not moaning about that because that's just the way he was and how he was brought up, so I knew I'd done something special when he said that. It was just an unbelievable feeling when it happened because Jackie was my dad's hero, having sort of grown up with him.

I think part of the buzz was because the pressure had built up as I knew I was going to finish playing at the end of the season, so I had to get it in. When you put all of it together – how long that record had stood for and whose record it was – that's why it was so special.

I was actually due to retire at the end of the previous season, so didn't ever think I was going to get the record anyway. The reason I stayed on was because Graeme Souness had asked me to help him in the dressing room and then look to go into coaching if he was still manager at the end of the season. That was the main reason, but obviously the record was also in my mind, so it was a bit of a no-brainer.

I knew I wasn't as good as I had been and the longer it went on the harder it became. By the time we got to February of that campaign everyone was talking about it, while I hadn't scored for a few games, so I was going into every match thinking, *This might be the one, I might get a penalty, blah, blah, blah.*

The moment was even more special because the goal was scored at the Gallowgate End of St James' Park, where I used to stand as a kid. If you believe in fate then it was supposed to happen because my first game as a fan, watching Kevin Keegan's debut against QPR in August 1982, was in the Gallowgate End. I stood there throughout my childhood watching Newcastle, so if things were meant to happen, then it was meant to happen that day at that particular end of the stadium and the place I call home.

The goal itself came from a long punt forward and I directed a flick-on out to Shola Ameobi, who sort of flicked it back into me. It was one of the few occasions I still managed to run in behind the defence because I'd lost a lot of my pace by then.

It was just a matter of picking my spot, hitting the target and hoping for the best. The feeling that day was one that if you could bottle, then that would be it. The high I was on, the adrenaline, the atmosphere that was still going 10 or 15 minutes later was just insane. It was amazing.

Once the full-time whistle had blown and we were back in the dressing room, I received a nice reception from my team-mates and the manager – and we certainly had a good night that evening. I just went out with the guys, had a few drinks and we carried on celebrating back at my house into the early hours.

Never once when I signed for Newcastle did I think to myself, *I want to break Jackie Milburn's record*. I signed for two reasons, one because it's my club and I wanted to go back home, but also because I wanted to win things and it wasn't as if I was joining a club that wasn't challenging. Just two months before I signed in July 1996, they'd blown a 12-point lead at the top of the Premier League table.

It was a really tough decision to make because one minute I was going to Manchester United and the next I was heading to Newcastle. I'd actually found a house to buy in Manchester, it was Graeme Souness's old home, so it was really backwards and forwards what I was going to do. Then I decided I was going back home and that was it. I met Newcastle officials near Manchester Airport before flying out to the Far East with England and tried to ring Alex Ferguson, the Manchester United manager, on my way to the airport to tell him my decision because I thought it was the right thing to do. I rang him the first time and got no answer, rang him a second time and got no answer, so on the third time I left him a message, but it was no surprise he never rang me back!

I shared an England dressing room with quite a lot of Newcastle and Man United players, and during Euro '96 they all tried to convince me to join their club, which goes on all the time. I wouldn't call it 'tapping up' but friendly banter, not that I ever listened to any of them.

I had an inkling going into that tournament that I'd be on the move, but tried not to think about it because I was under enough pressure, having not scored an international goal for more than two years.

It wasn't as if I was lacking in confidence, I was the Premier League's leading scorer that season, but for England, who were only playing friendly games due to being the host country, I was hitting the post and the bar. It just wasn't happening.

I tried to keep my belief, and having Terry Venables as England manager really helped me because, as a coach and a man-manager, he was a genius. He helped by telling me before the tournament that whatever happened in the few friendly matches we had, I'd be his main striker come our first group game against Switzerland at Wembley, when thankfully I was able to get myself back on the scoresheet.

My official unveiling as a Newcastle player after the Euros is another moment that I'll never forget. It was one of those grey, miserable days, peeing down with rain and still 17,000 or 18,000 fans turned out to welcome me to the club. I was inside the stadium, so didn't see what was going on outside until I walked out at the far corner and was met by this massive sea of white and black. It was incredible.

Another of my favourite games for Newcastle was scoring on my home debut against Wimbledon. It was my dream to play at St James' Park and my dream to score there, just like I'd watched my hero Keegan do when I was an 11-year-old boy in 1982. To run out in front of my own people and find the net with a 25-yard free kick was amazing.

A lot was made of my price tag at the time as it was a record fee for a British player, but I never felt under pressure because it wasn't my money and wasn't my gamble. I just wanted to do what I was doing and nothing was going to stop that. I only felt excitement.

The first goal is always special and, whether I felt under any pressure or not, I actually was because the whole world was looking at me due to the fee. I did it in front of my mum and dad as well, which made it even sweeter.

I know I didn't manage to win a trophy, which was the main reason I went there, but I loved my ten years at Newcastle and have never, ever had any doubts about whether or not I made the right decision. If I had my time again then I'd do exactly the same thing.

The lack of silverware wasn't for the want of trying and we did reach back-to-back FA Cup finals in 1998 and 1999, but both years were difficult games, and we didn't really deserve to win either of them. We didn't turn up in the Man United one, but in the Arsenal game we hit the bar and the post and if they'd gone in at half-time 1-0 down then we'd have been on a high and it might have been a different outcome.

We'd worked our nuts off to get there and each of the semi-finals were great occasions, but Wembley is only a place for winners, not for losers, so the pain after both finals was raw.

I played under Kevin twice, once at Newcastle and then later with England. I'd met him previously so knew what he was like as a person, and also spoke to players who had played under him, so I wasn't going into it blind. I knew who and what he was.

As I've already mentioned, he was my hero and I remember he used to drive past my school on his way to training, so hundreds of us would stand outside the gates and wait for him. He was like the Pied Piper because, wherever he went, he had a trail of people following him. He was a great guy, no different to what I hoped and wanted him to be.

When you sign for a club, the manager has to play a part, but it can't be the most important thing because they might leave, and Kevin left six months after I arrived, so luckily I signed for Newcastle rather than Kevin.

He wore his heart on his sleeve and I knew how much he loved Newcastle, so I still to this day don't really understand what happened. I'm sure Kevin had his reasons, but three games earlier we had hammered Tottenham 7-1 at St James' Park and were still in with a chance of winning the league, so all us players were a bit taken aback when he went in January 1997.

Kenny Dalglish came in to replace Kevin, which I was delighted about, having worked with him at Blackburn where we won the league. I had four great years with Kenny at Ewood Park, three with him as manager and one as director of football, so I knew how he operated.

We finished second that first season, but it was tough because the following summer the board decided to sell Les Ferdinand, with whom I'd struck up a 49-goal partnership, to Tottenham and then in a pre-season game I broke my ankle, ruptured my ligaments and displaced my joint, ruling me out for seven months.

They tried to stop the deal with Les going to Spurs, but Les was disappointed, maybe rightly so, and forced it through, which left Kenny with a massive void up front, so they signed Jon Dahl Tomasson and then had to scramble to get Ian Rush in, but he was past his sell-by date. It was a really difficult time for Kenny, and he never recovered from it.

The owners must have thought it was a good time to sell Les as he was in his 30s and they were getting what looked like a big fee at the time, but it was one of those decisions that backfired and that was where it started to go wrong for Kenny.

I was fortunate enough to be part of some great strike pairings throughout my career, the SAS with Chris Sutton at Blackburn and with Teddy Sheringham for England during that unforgettable summer of '96, but my partnership with Les was right up there. Forty-nine goals tells its own story, especially as both of us missed a couple of months that season due to injury. That's just about as good as it gets, and we used to stand in the tunnel knowing we were going to beat up the two opposing central defenders, whoever they were.

Les is a great lad, and the best partnerships are the ones where you don't have to do a lot of work because it just clicks, it just happens, much like with Teddy and me for England. I don't think many people thought it would be as good as it was because Les and I were two big guys, but we both had the pace, could both finish, were both good in the air and both had a good touch, so I never had any doubt we could be a lethal combination. It was a case that if we got the service, which more often than not we did, then we were going to score.

I was lucky enough to be served by some great wide players. Nobby Solano, in particular, was unbelievable. Kenny signed him for a couple of million quid and technically he was as good as there was. He was great at moving the ball out wide and crossing first time into the penalty area, which obviously I loved.

Then there was David Ginola, who was slightly different, and we had a love–hate relationship to begin with because a big part of his game was going past players and dribbling, which was great, but there may not be the end product, which frustrated me at the start. It got better after that, and having Ginola on one side and Nobby the other was amazing. They were both great players.

We always had a great dressing room at Newcastle and the failure to win anything was nothing to do with a lack of team spirit, we just weren't quite good enough. The team spirit was amazing, we had a great craic and great camaraderie, always going out to socialise together. It was part of my job as captain to pull everyone together and create that team spirit. They had that when I arrived, so it was important we carried that on.

The record-breaking goal may not have happened at all had it not been for the appointment of Sir Bobby Robson as manager, as I was on my way out because Ruud Gullit wanted a battle with me. Ruud gambled massively when he left me and big Duncan Ferguson out of a derby game with Sunderland in August 1999. We lost and he went after that.

Ruud and I have a laugh about it now and are good friends, which is bizarre when you think about it. He just said to me, 'I was young. I was arrogant. I was Dutch!' I knew from his first day as manager that we weren't going to get on because of my personality and how big I was. He wanted to do things differently, which is fine, and you're entitled to do that as a manager, but it was just a big personality clash.

When Sir Bobby came in that changed because he got me smiling again and enjoying my football. In his first game we thrashed Sheffield Wednesday 8-0 and I got five of them, so suddenly I was back on the horse and scoring again.

Sir Bobby has this aura and personality, similar to Venables in that his massive strength was how he handled players and how he could get them to run through brick walls for him. He just had the knack of doing that. All the senior players, not just me, had been shunned by Ruud, but from day one Sir Bobby had us all back onside.

I tried my own hand at management in April 2009 and unfortunately that side of things didn't work out how I wanted, but I don't think that was any fault of my own. I was the fourth Newcastle manager in one season, so that tells its own story. I only had eight games to try to save us from relegation and, by that stage, there were huge issues and complications within the football club.

I still thought I was going to return to management and, at one stage, I really wanted to go back in, despite what happened, with us ultimately dropping down into the Championship. I loved the buzz of making decisions and standing on the touchline, which was very different to playing.

After leaving Newcastle, I met a few owners and clubs but pretty quickly decided it was not for me and focused on the punditry side of things, even though when I first started the television work I was a bit reluctant to criticise or be overly analytical as I thought I'd look pretty stupid if I then went back into management.

After a difficult decade I'm delighted I now get the chance to sit in the studio and speak so positively about the club again. Newcastle feeds off its football team and there aren't many places like it in the world where you walk around the streets and see mums and daughters, fathers and sons, and nanas and granddads all wearing black and white stripes.

It's a one-club city that's mad on its football and mad on Newcastle United – the result on a Saturday determines how the rest of the week goes for the public. It's back to being what it was when I first signed, and what it was when I first went to watch Kevin Keegan. It's all that again and more.

When I was an 11-year-old walking to the game with my dad to stand on the terrace at the Gallowgate End, if you'd told me I'd wear the Newcastle No. 9 shirt, captain the club and break the goalscoring record, I'd have never dared to believe you. I did all right!

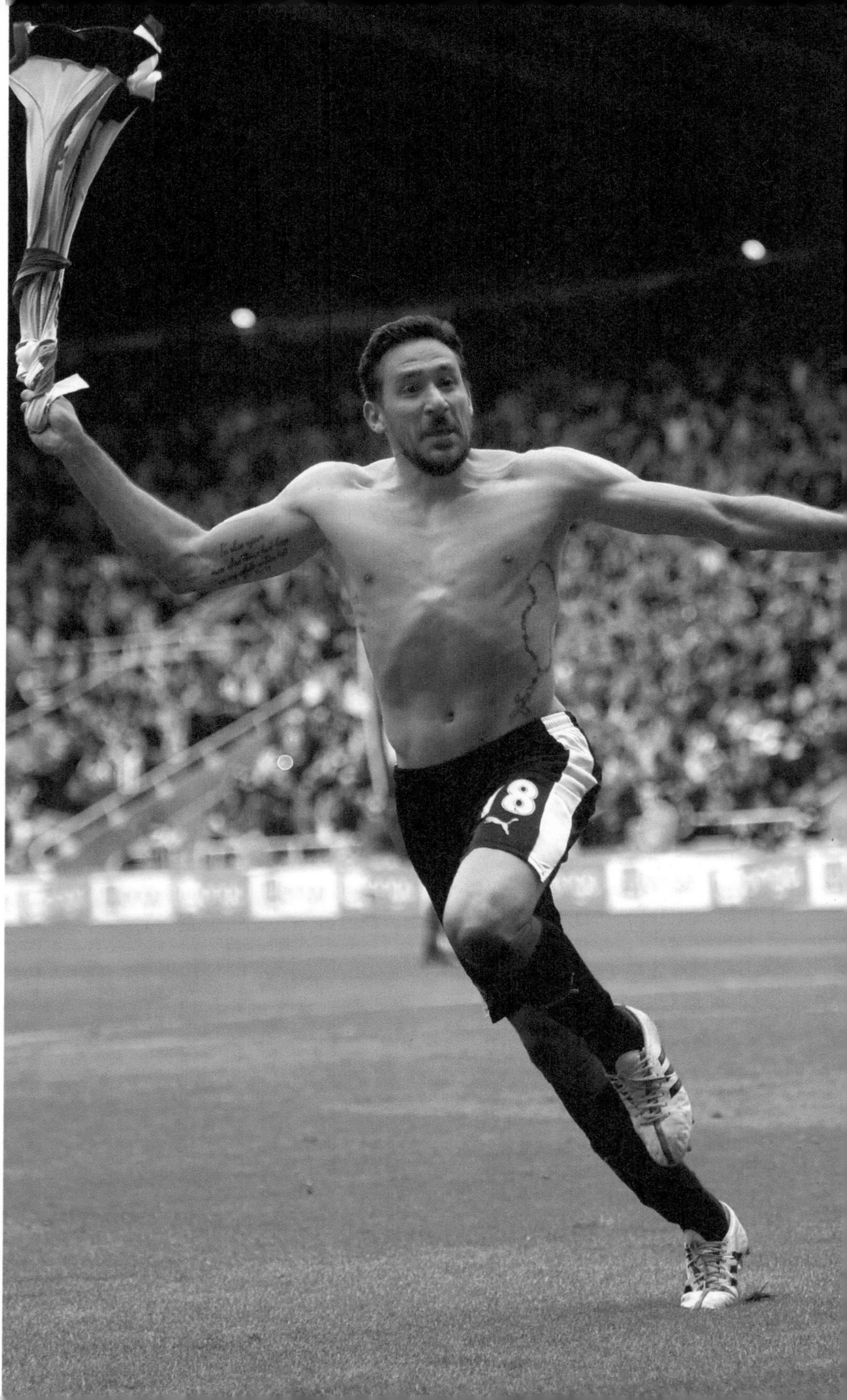

JONÁS GUTIÉRREZ

Jonás Gutiérrez
Midfielder
2008–2015

Jonás Gutiérrez's story is one that transcends football. In 2013 he was diagnosed with testicular cancer, and for the best part of the next 18 months stared the end of his career – and possibly his life – in the face. But Gutiérrez, famed for his Spider-Man goal celebration, won his battle with the deadly disease and, incredibly, worked his way back to fitness and to a spot in the Newcastle first team. His return came at the time his club needed him more than ever. He came off the bench to face Manchester United at Old Trafford, but the match for which Gutiérrez will be forever remembered came as the 2014/15 season twisted towards its thrilling climax.

In danger of being relegated, the Toon needed to get a positive result against West Ham at St James' Park, and it was the man from Buenos Aires who stepped up to write his name into Newcastle United folklore and secure Premier League survival, after overcoming the most serious of circumstances. Gutiérrez set up Moussa Sissoko for the opening goal, before finding the net himself from distance as time ticked down, to send the stadium into raptures. His celebration – cupping his ears in defiance towards the board of directors – spoke volumes.

Despite an acrimonious exit from Newcastle, which resulted in Gutiérrez successfully suing the club for disability discrimination for how he was treated following his cancer diagnosis, the Argentine still holds the Magpies close to his heart, and credits the love and support of the fans for helping him overcome his health struggles.

Newcastle United 2-0 West Ham United

Premier League
Sunday, 24 May 2015
St James' Park, Newcastle
Attendance: 52,094

Newcastle	West Ham
Krul	Adrián
Coloccini	Cresswell
Dummett	Reid
Williamson	Jenkinson
Janmaat	Burke (Tomkins)
Colback	Song
Sissoko	Nolan
Anita (Gouffran)	Kouyate (Lee)
Gutiérrez	Downing
Rivière	Valencia (Amalfitano)
Cissé	Cole

Managers

John Carver   Sam Allardyce

Goals

Sissoko, Gutiérrez

On the last day of the 2012/13 season in a game against Arsenal, I went into a tackle with Bacary Sagna, and after that I started having some pain around my groin. Over the summer the pain continued, and when I got back to the club for pre-season I talked to the Newcastle United doctor, who told me they couldn't see anything. But then the area became inflamed, so I went back to the doctor, who took me to a specialist, who did a scan and discovered I had a tumour. I remember when the doctor told me the news, I cried.

It was hard because I was in England, and although I understood the language of football, when it comes to medical issues it's harder to understand. I took the decision to go home to Argentina for treatment. I had an operation there and then two months of recovery – two months without football – before I went back to Newcastle. Then I had a situation with the manager, Alan Pardew. I was told that the club wanted to sell me! It's in the past, but even now I can't understand why they wanted to do that. It was something I didn't expect at all. I'd been playing so many years at the club, starting games, and when I got back after treatment they told me that!

However, instead of being sold, I was loaned to Norwich in January 2014, where I reunited with my former manager Chris Hughton, before he was sacked. I didn't play many games as I suffered another injury, this time to my calf.

After the season finished I had a check-up with my consultant and found out the cancer had come back, and I had to have chemotherapy. That was the worst part of it, something being put into your body that makes you feel sick all the time. I didn't have any energy. It was horrible, but I knew this was something I had to do if I was to recover. I did everything the doctor told me to, and after a very difficult few months was able to eventually go back to Newcastle United.

I started training with my team-mates and playing with the under-20s. It was a hard year for the club because they didn't have many players and there were a lot of injuries. I was feeling stronger and stronger, so with just a few games of the season to go I was called back into the first-team squad.

Coming back to play for the team was a very special feeling. I remember especially the welcome I got from the Newcastle and Liverpool fans when I was substituted on at Anfield, where we lost 2-0 in mid-April, when the crowd stood up and applauded me, but even more than that when I played at St James' Park again.

My return was against Manchester United – I came on for Ryan Taylor, one of my good friends, which made it very special, and then Fabricio Coloccini gave me the captain's armband. The welcome that the Newcastle fans gave me is something I'll never forget. It was hard to play in the beginning because I'd been out for so long! I remember going to left-back, and the first thing I did was foul a player and get a yellow card! The fans were telling the referee that he couldn't book me because I'd just come back from cancer, which made me laugh, but I deserved the card.

It was such a special feeling to be back playing for Newcastle, and I was able to play more in the following games before it came down to the last game against West Ham.

I wanted to keep playing for the club at that time, but they still wanted to sell me. However, if I had a choice about how my time at Newcastle would come to an end, then that game was it. It was like a movie.

We were in a relegation battle on the last day of the season and the stadium was packed with Geordies; you could feel the stadium shake with their noise and support. We knew it would be a tough game, but we came through it and survived. For me personally, to set up the first goal and score the second was like a dream. It was the best way to finish my time with the club, my perfect ending.

For the first goal, I set up Moussa Sissoko. I was on the left side of the field when I picked up the ball and went past a defender to cross with my left foot, and Moussa jumped above his marker to head the ball past the goalkeeper. Moussa was an excellent player, and I had a great connection with him. That was a massive goal for us, and then, with just a few minutes to go, I got the goal that I'll remember for the rest of my life.

I remember when I received the ball thinking that I could go to the corner to run the clock down – we were ahead by just one goal, needed this win and time was running out. Then something inside me said, *No, you have to shoot.* I struck the ball with my right foot and watched it deflect off a defender and roll into the corner of the net. What a feeling. It was something that was meant to happen. It was one of the best moments of my life and one of the best days of my life. It was very special, and as soon as the ball went in I knew where I had to run to celebrate.

After all the things that had happened to me, and the unfair treatment I'd had, I knew at that moment what I had to do – I cupped my hands to my ears and looked towards the owner Mike Ashley in the stands. He'd wanted to sell me, and this was my message to him.

I'll always say that I didn't deserve the treatment I received after I came back from my illness, and I don't know why it happened. But it's in the past. When I think now about my time at Newcastle I feel happy. I enjoyed it so much, and the support and the love given by the fans to me and my family is something that's priceless. I felt the love from them, and I hope they feel the love from me. For me it was my dream to play in English football, and in Newcastle my dream came true, but it was an even greater experience than I dreamed of.

A few months before I joined Newcastle in 2008, I was in talks with Portsmouth to sign for them. It was the first time an English club wanted me to join them, but my club, Real Mallorca, didn't want to sell me. It was hard for me because Portsmouth were in the Premier League at the time, and it was a good opportunity for me to go to a league that was the best in the world. I'd even gone to visit Portsmouth and to meet Harry Redknapp, which was good for me in the long term because I got to learn more about English football.

It was frustrating to not be able to leave, but that's football – sometimes your club wants to keep you, and it ended up working perfectly for me, as a few months later Newcastle came in for me. Mallorca knew I wanted to play in the Premier League, and this time they said yes.

I knew a lot about Newcastle because when I was young I'd get up on a Sunday morning and watch the games on TV. The main player I remember watching was Alan Shearer. Whenever people would talk about Newcastle, they'd talk about Shearer. He was such a legend and always scoring, so I remember him very well.

The movie *Goal!* also played a big part in me wanting to join Newcastle; in South America we really know the club because of that film. The main character, Santiago Muñez, was from Mexico and went to the North East. I guess I followed in his footsteps, but the difference is that I'm from Argentina, not Mexico.

It was incredible when they wanted me to join them and I was so happy to sign. From the moment I got off the plane I felt at home. It was love at first sight. I loved the city, the fans and the club straight away. The atmosphere was incredible – you could feel on the streets every day the passion of the people and the love they have for the club and for its players.

As soon as I got there they knew that I celebrated with the Spider-Man mask when I scored, which they liked. The celebration started when I was at Mallorca. I used to go to the cinema sometimes, on my own. One day when I left the cinema, a kid came over with his father and asked me for an autograph. The little boy said next time I score I had to do something special, so I had a think. The movie we'd been watching was *Spider-Man*, so I had the idea of getting a mask and keeping it with me, and putting it on every time I scored. Every game I had it under my underpants so I never forgot it. Unfortunately, later on, the referees told me in England that it would be a yellow card if I wore it, so I had to stop, but when I was able to do it, it was really fun and the fans loved it.

Most of the time when players sign for a club they have their surname on the back of their shirts, but not me. From the very beginning I had 'Jonás'. I love my name so I wanted to use it! When I was young it wasn't common to hear that name, so when I used to tell it to people, they'd call me any name except my name! I told them they could call me what they wanted, but when I grew up and became a professional footballer, I wanted to use it to show everyone who I was. It was very special for me to have it on my shirt.

Unfortunately, my first season didn't go to plan as we were relegated. We had a lot of managers that season. Kevin Keegan signed me, but he left after only a few games because of his problems with the owner. Then we had a series of managers: Chris Hughton, Joe Kinnear, Chris again, and then, at the end of the season, Alan Shearer. Five managers in one season is very strange, and made it a hard season for us, and we didn't get the results we needed.

Players like Fabricio Coloccini and I stayed after we went down because we wanted to get the club back to where it had to be – in the Premier League. You could see when we went down, all of the fans were crying, but they always applauded our effort. They were always behind us, and we wanted to pay them back for their support.

It was the year before the 2010 World Cup, so I spoke with the Argentina coach, Diego Maradona. I told him about the situation, that I wasn't going to be playing in the Premier League, and he said, 'Jonás, I don't care where you play, the only thing I want is that you play.' That was something that I really appreciated, because if he told me I needed to play in the Premier League then I'd be in a tough situation, because it was my dream to play in the World Cup, so speaking to him made my decision easy.

Before he became coach of the national team, I'd never met him. He means everything to Argentina, so to be with him was something incredible. He's our hero, one of the greatest of all time, and he was so good with the players. It felt like he was one of us, so to play for him at the World Cup was very special. It was a privilege for me to be in that squad with him as the coach, and with Lionel Messi on the pitch.

During my time as a professional footballer I played with, and against, some amazing players, but Messi is not from this planet. You can see what he does with the ball – the intelligence, the speed, the technique – he makes everything look easy. He tried a lot of times to win the World Cup but couldn't do it for a long time, and that was very frustrating for him, but finally football gave him the gift he deserved when he won it in 2022.

He couldn't retire without winning it, so I'm very happy for him. It was the best moment when I saw him lift the World Cup. I was in Qatar. For me I'm not fanatical if my country wins or loses; whatever the result I support my team, but the Argentina team, and particularly Messi, deserved to win it.

In 2010 Messi said some very nice things about me, saying that I was one of the best players in the Premier League, but he's a friend of mine so maybe he was just being nice. When I had my illness, he was sending me a lot of messages, which says a lot about him. He's a great human being. I really appreciate what he said about me and how good a player I was, but what was more important was how he kept in touch during my difficult times.

After being relegated we came straight back up to the Premier League. We drew 1-1 with West Brom in the first game in the Championship but then started winning and never looked back. It was great for the players' confidence and we had a lot of young players getting experience, like Andy Carroll. They showed what they could do, and experienced players like Coloccini, Alan Smith, Nicky Butt and Kevin Nolan, helped give us the perfect mix. We were really together and gave everything to be back in the Premier League.

Coloccini was a very important person for me, being from Argentina too, and we were best friends at Newcastle. I remember I'd translate for him when he arrived, because he couldn't speak English and I'd learned when I was in Argentina. We were always the first to arrive at training and would play Argentinian music in the morning. Other players would come to the changing room with their sleepy faces and say, 'Oh no, not again!' We'd always be singing together and having jokes.

I used to make jokes, but nothing too bad. I have lots of good memories with Shola Ameobi, Ryan Taylor, James Perch and

Robbie Elliott. We had a great group and were always having fun, always laughing. It was part of life to be happy, to enjoy ourselves. They'd joke with me, and I'd joke with them. We had lots of banter.

I remember once with James Perch, a ball went high in the air and he wanted to control it with his chest. I shouted, 'Time!', but then he mis-controlled it – it hit him in his face and ran away from him, and I shouted, 'No time,' in a stupid voice as he chased after it. It was just little things like this that I did with him and the other players that put a smile on my face.

Coloccini eventually became captain and was such a strong character to have in the dressing room and a leader on the pitch. We had the right mix that season to get back to the Premier League. We all knew what we had to do, and we did it.

Andy Carroll was incredible and had a great left foot. He was a nice guy and was playing in the team having grown up in Newcastle, and that's something very special. You could see the fans loved him, being at the club from the beginning. With Andy, we knew when we put the ball in the air for him, he'd get his head to it. He was a key player that season.

We got back into the Premier League and finished mid-table the following season, before finishing just outside the Champions League places in 2011/12. It's a shame we didn't make it, but if you consider how far we'd come from being in the Championship two years earlier, it was still a good achievement.

It was the end of the following season, 2012/13, that I got the injury that eventually led to the discovery of my cancer, which I was able to get through thanks to the support of my family and the fans.

I want to thank all the people who worked at the club, and the supporters, for making my time at Newcastle United so special. Geordies are very special people, and I'll never forget the way they treated me and my family.

PAPISS CISSÉ

Papiss Cissé
Striker
2012–2016

In one skilful swipe of his right boot, Papiss Demba Cissé wrote his name into Premier League folklore. The Senegalese striker scored 37 Premier League goals in 117 matches for Newcastle and was in red-hot form when he launched a first-time shot at Petr Čech's goal from an almost impossible angle. Having already beaten the Czech stopper with an audacious volley in the first half, Cissé excelled himself with his second strike of the day. Running on to a knock-down from Shola Ameobi as the clock ticked towards full time, Cissé's audacious, instinctive effort sailed into the top corner of the Chelsea net, with a stunned Čech only able to look on, helplessly.

The faces of his team-mates, opposition players and managers said it all: Cissé had scored a goal that would be remembered for a long, long time. The sensational strike won the 2011/12 Goal of the Season award, and has followed Cissé ceaselessly ever since.

For the match of his life, Newcastle's former No. 9 takes us back to that memorable spring evening in 2012, and to his relationship with another of the Newcastle XI that day – his 'brother' – the late, great Cheick Tioté.

Chelsea 0-2 Newcastle United

Premier League
Wednesday, 2 May 2012
Stamford Bridge, London
Attendance: 41,559

Chelsea	**Newcastle**
Čech	Krul
Ivanovic	Coloccini
Bosingwa	Santon
Terry	Williamson
Bertrand	Perch
Ramires	Cabaye
Mikel	Ben Arfa (Obertan)
Malouda (Drogba)	Gutiérrez
Meireles (Lampard)	Tioté (Taylor)
Torres	Cissé
Sturridge (Mata)	Ba (Ameobi)

Managers

Roberto DiMatteo   Alan Pardew

Goals

Cissé (2)

This game made my name. Afterwards, all of England knew me, because of this one goal. Despite everything I've done in my career, in England, France and Germany, this is the game everyone remembers. It's the first thing people ask me about when they meet me. Even one morning when I was training, having a friendly five-a-side game in Manchester, where I have a house. A guy I was playing with saw me and said, 'I recognise you! You scored that goal against Chelsea.' It follows me everywhere. Every day I think about it; it's like it was yesterday. It's part of me.

People ask me, 'How did you score it?' I just say that I'm a striker and that I took a shot, and it went in. I don't know how to explain it. It came from nowhere.

We were winning 1-0 at the time, and I knew Alan Pardew didn't want us to lose or draw this game: he wanted to win it. Time was nearly up. Shola Ameobi knocked the ball down after a throw-in, and in my mind all I'm thinking is, *Kick it, just kick it.* I was tired, I didn't want to lose the ball, so I couldn't do much else! But my body was in the right place, and I hit it well. I looked at it flying through the air, and it went swerving crazily to the right, and then when it went in I just thought, *Wow, what is this?* I was so, so happy, and my team-mates were so happy for me.

I always say to people who ask me about my second goal that night, to go and watch the first one! I always remember this goal as well. Davide Santon drove forward with the ball and Demba Ba and I were in the middle. I came deep, and he laid the ball back. I took a step back and the ball came to me. My feeling was, *Control the ball, then shoot.* It was one of those moments you get when you're a striker, when you have to decide what to do quickly. I took a touch with my right foot, then volleyed it into the far corner with my left, my wrong foot. People talk to me and ask me about the second goal, but strikers talk about the first goal. It was all about quick thinking and technique, a striker's goal.

The first reaction I got at the end of the game was from Didier Drogba, as I knew him very well. He asked me, 'Where did you come from, what do you eat?!' like I wasn't human. I told him I'm just normal like him, and that I eat Senegalese rice!

Alan Pardew came up to me at the end and told me how happy he was for me, and how proud he was. I had his support the whole time that I was with him. All the players had his support. When your gaffer says things like that it makes you want to play well for him. Even though my English wasn't so good then, I understood how he felt.

The next day I woke up and realised what I'd done. I had thousands of messages from all over, and people asking to interview me! From then on, every day was crazy. I was always signing shirts or having my photo taken with people, but I didn't mind that, it made me very happy. I never had the opportunity to thank all the people who supported me at that time, so I want to say thank you to the Geordie people. They were always there for me and for all of us, even in the bad moments.

Of all the teams I've played with, Newcastle is the one in my heart. This is my team. All the time I spent there, even when the situation was hard, the fans were there for me and for the team. They knew we were fighting for the club, they gave us what they could and we tried to give back to them. That's why it's still my club. I'm still black and white.

It's a crazy story of how I ended up in England. When I was at Freiburg I had two great seasons. In December 2011, Bayern Munich came to try to sign me. I'd scored 12 goals so far that season and was about to go away with Senegal to the Africa Cup of Nations. Bayern told me they wanted me straight away, to help them with the Champions League. I had to choose between Bayern Munich and my country. I had to think about what to do! I told my agent that I'd choose my country. Senegal needed me. I knew I was young, and that if it wasn't going to be Bayern, it would happen for me somewhere else.

Bayern was a massive team. They had players like Arjen Robben, Franck Ribéry, Mario Gomez and Philipp Lahm. I was scared to tell my family that I turned them down. I didn't tell them until two years later. I was worried about what they'd say, but my dad said that I should be proud of that decision: I put my country first.

The Senegal team went for a training camp a few days later, giving us time to be together before flying out to the tournament. Not long before we were due to fly out, my agent called me and told me he'd booked me a flight to Newcastle, where I was going to sign. As soon as I knew I was going to a club in England I was so happy. I wanted to play there.

I had a friend, Ibrahima Sonko, who had played as a centre-back for Stoke City and Senegal, and always talked about England. I had a feeling that I had to play there. This was in my mind when my agent called me. I wanted the challenge of going to England, somewhere where they didn't know me. I wanted to make my name and prove myself to everybody.

I went and saw the Senegal coach and told him I had to leave to go and sign for Newcastle, but I'd have to leave that day, that moment, and I'd come back the next day for the tournament. He told me it wasn't possible, with the times of the flights. Eventually he told me to go, to do what I had to do and to come back when I was signed.

I tried to see Demba Ba, but I didn't have time. I told the coach to tell Demba I was going to sign for Newcastle. When I arrived in Newcastle, I got to the club and they took me to the hospital for my medical. I signed my contract, and said I have to go back home to play for Senegal. The feeling I had was that everything was good. They did everything they could for me to get me home. They got me a flight to Senegal and I was back at the hotel in time to leave with the team the next day.

Nobody knew where I'd been. I told them I'd been to see family! The only person I told apart from Demba was the goalkeeper Khadim N'Diaye, who was my best friend in the national team and my room-mate. When I saw Demba the next morning I told him my news. He said to me, 'Well done, bro.' He was very happy that he'd have a team-mate from the national team with him in Newcastle.

When we got to the AFCON tournament, I was very frustrated – they didn't play me. I was top scorer in qualifying with six goals in nine games. I sat on the bench until the last game, when we were out. I said to my friend, Khadim, that all the goals I was supposed to score for my country, I'd score for Newcastle. I don't know why I said that, but then when I signed, I was right.

When I arrived in Newcastle I knew about the cold, wind and rain, but it was cold in Germany, too. The only thing I had to adjust to was the rain, but I adapted quite quickly. Soon I was dressing like a Geordie boy, wearing a T-shirt when it was so cold! My team-mates would look at me like I was crazy, and ask me what I was doing, but I was fine.

On my first day, I met Alan Pardew in his office, and he told me how he wanted to play, how he wanted to use me. He said I'd be on the bench for my first game and that I should watch and understand how we play, and if I was ready I could start to get some minutes. Then he asked me which squad number I wanted. I told him I always play wearing the No. 9. He turned behind him, to a member of his coaching staff, and said: 'He wants the number nine.' He turned back, and said: 'You know what? If you're a man, you'll wear the number nine shirt. But if you're going to wear the shirt, and be scared, then it's better that you don't take it. Because this number is for a big man. I'm going to show you.'

Then he pulled down a projector screen from the ceiling, turned the light off and pressed play on a video. Wham: I'm seeing Alan Shearer. My god. He was shooting from everywhere. Goal. Goal. Goal. I'm thinking, *Who is this guy?* He said, 'This is Alan Shearer. Do you still want the number nine shirt?' I knew what he was trying to tell me: the guy who has this number *has* to be a big player. The truth is, from that moment, I wanted it more. I wanted to do something, something like he'd done.

I was on the bench for my first game, against Aston Villa. I don't think even the fans were accepting of me having the shirt. I think I'm lucky because my English wasn't so good then, and if I'd understood what some fans were saying then, maybe I'd have felt more pressure, and having that number would have been more on my mind.

I knew I had to bring my A-game and keep my standards high, even in training. Luckily, it started very well for me. I came on as a substitute against Villa for my debut and scored a great volley to win the game, then the goals kept coming. I scored 13 in 14 games, which made me very happy.

One thing people remember about my time at Newcastle was what happened with Wonga. I don't mind talking about it because I did nothing wrong. It all started with me and Demba. The manager came in and told us the club was going to change the sponsor to Wonga. I had no idea who they were. Demba explained to me about them being a loan company, and said that we'd have to find out if our religion, Islam, would let us wear the shirts.

Demba left to go to Chelsea and I was alone. I asked the club to help find me an Imam to tell me if I could wear the shirt. I couldn't train because even the training top had Wonga on it. All the time I wasn't playing and training was because I was looking for an Imam – I even went to Manchester to find one, but I couldn't. Everything in the newspaper was a mess and even in my country they were killing me. The club was good to me though, they gave me a personal trainer to help keep me fit while this was all going on.

Eventually we found one, and he told there wasn't a problem with me playing in the Wonga shirt, because it was my job. As soon as he said this, that was it. I went to the club and said I could come back, and they said yes, and we had a friendly game the next day in Scotland. I went up there, and all the fans in Scotland were calling me 'Wonga'. It made me laugh. That company, like the goal against Chelsea, follows me everywhere now.

I played with some incredible players at Newcastle. We called Hatem Ben Arfa 'the phenomenon'. Honestly, in all my career I never played with a footballer like him. Technically, running with the ball, shooting, he had everything, but I don't know what was going on with him. We'd say to him, 'Where are you, bro?', when he wouldn't be involved so much in games. I'd say everything Messi can do, Hatem can do. I saw him training every day and he could do everything. I was so happy to have him in my team.

Sadio Mané, my team-mate from Senegal, is up there too. I knew him before he came to England because we lived near to each other in our home country. He was like my little brother, and we speak all the time. I'm proud of him for everything he has achieved. He has worked so hard and deserves to be winning league titles and the Champions League. He came from a village in Senegal and went on to be one of the greatest players in the world. One time I saw him on Instagram wearing a black and white shirt, and I messaged him saying, 'Bro, this shirt looks good on you! You have to go to Newcastle!' We didn't really speak about it, but black and white did suit him.

Fabricio Coloccini was incredible. Sometimes I speak to defenders now and ask why they're not more relaxed. They think they have to give the ball quickly, but I say, 'No, look at Coloccini!' He was so cool and calm, defenders have to be like him. He was so quiet, and the way he hit the ball was so clean. Next to him was Steven Taylor – he was crazy. He never gave the ball short, he was always hitting long for the strikers and running up the pitch with a style that said *I'm the man!* He was so funny, you always laughed with him. I never saw him angry in all the years I was at the club.

Then there was Fabricio's compatriot, Jonás Gutiérrez, who was our big man. The way he came back to football after his cancer was amazing, and I was so happy he could come back. We were sad for him, and wanted him to get back on the pitch. When he scored the goal against West Ham to keep us in the Premier League, that was amazing for him but also for us. We were so happy for him, because he's such a great guy.

Yohan Cabaye was like a magician, we knew he could find us with passes wherever we were. Demba Ba, in front of goal, he was so accurate. I'd watch him in training and think, *What the heck?!* – he never missed. He had power, accuracy, could jump and had good decision-making. He had more swagger than anybody else I played with. We were a good pair with a good connection, but he had more than me. In front of the goal he was unreal.

For me, that was my dream team. But there was one person in the dressing room who became like a brother to me – Cheick Tioté. He was the rock in this team. He gave energy to everybody. When I saw him behind us, I knew it would be okay. He'd say: 'If you lose the ball, don't worry, I am going to take it back and I am going to give it back to you.' He never complained – he was always willing to go and get the ball. He made us feel good. He was my man. A very good friend and brother. We spent every day together.

Even when I was playing in China we'd talk all the time – he was playing there too. Our cities were about one hour away from each other on the train. One Ramadan I had some time off, so I decided to go and see him in Beijing. I called him and told him I was going to see him. When I got there, we spent hours that night speaking and laughing. I told him I'd booked a hotel and he was mad at me – he wanted me to stay with him! I apologised and said that I'd come to see him the next week, when I had three days off, and would stay at his house. But this never happened.

The next week I was going to a restaurant with my driver and two friends. My driver got a message, and after he read it he wasn't driving the same. He got another message and I saw his hand start to shake. He told me to look at my phone, and pulled over to the side of the road. He showed me a picture from a game, with Cheick lying down on the pitch. I thought it was some sort of sick joke.

He showed me a news story written in Chinese and explained it all to me, and I told him, 'No, this cannot happen.' Then suddenly my phone started ringing and it was my club, who asked me to come back. I asked them what had happened, and they told me my friend had passed away. In my mind this was impossible, I was supposed to see him tomorrow. One of my friends started crying, and then I did too. I never cried before like that in my life. For weeks afterwards I still couldn't accept it, I'd wake up in the night not believing it had happened.

He was such a good man. I have only recently been able to start talking about him and not lose my voice or start to cry. Now I accept it happened, but it still makes me very sad.

When I eventually left Newcastle in 2016, I didn't want to go. It was another decision I had to make quickly when the offer came from China. I spoke to Rafa Benitez – he encouraged me to think about it, and to make a decision that was right for me. When the team went down, I felt like we'd maybe done our job and needed to let a new group come in and build a new team.

I don't regret my decision to leave because I see where the club is now and it makes me happy. To get to the Champions League for the first time in so long in 2023 was amazing. It's where they deserve to be. I haven't been back since I left but I hope to come back soon to the 'big house' to watch the boys in black and white, to go back to being a Geordie man and to support my team.

LES FERDINAND

Les Ferdinand
Striker
1995–1997

Les Ferdinand signed for Kevin Keegan's Newcastle in 1995 and was one of the infamous 'Entertainers' that went on to enthral fans up and down the country with delicious displays of attacking football. He arrived with an impressive scoring record from Queens Park Rangers and, during a surprisingly short spell with the club, racked up a mammoth 50 goals in just 84 appearances for the famous black-and-white. He formed a formidable strike partnership with Alan Shearer and, along with Faustino Asprilla, David Ginola and Peter Beardsley, was a key part of an attack that struck fear into the heart of defences in the early years of the Premiership, as it was then called.

Despite never winning a trophy with the Magpies, Ferdinand helped conjure up magical moments and memories that will live long in the minds of every fan and he cemented his place in Newcastle United folklore – he's still affectionately referred to as 'Sir Les' on Tyneside. The match of Ferdinand's life was against their main rivals during Keegan's era – Manchester United, under the indomitable Alex Ferguson. Having lost out on the title to United the previous year – despite having had a 12-point lead over the Red Devils at one stage – and been thumped 4-0 in the Charity Shield by the same team a couple of months earlier, the Toon welcomed their nemesis to St James' Park in October 1996, seeking payback. Keegan's team were on a six-match winning run and gained some semblance of revenge as they demolished their visitors with an unforgettable display and a performance perfectly capped off with an iconic chip from a certain Belgian centre-back ...

Newcastle United 5-0 Manchester United

Premier League
Sunday, 20 October 1996
St James' Park, Newcastle
Attendance: 36,579

Newcastle	Manchester United
Srníček	Schmeichel
Beresford	Pallister
Albert	Irwin
Peacock	Johnsen (McClair)
Watson (Barton)	May
Lee (Clark)	Neville
Batty	Poborský (Scholes)
Ginola	Butt
Beardsley	Beckham
Ferdinand	Cantona
Shearer	Solskjaer (Cruyff)

Managers

Kevin Keegan   Alex Ferguson

Goals

Peacock, Ginola,
Ferdinand, Shearer,
Albert

It was my second season playing with Philippe Albert and I'd got to know how he operated. As soon as I saw him get the ball 35 yards out and start to surge forward, I knew he wasn't looking to pass. I thought he was going to unleash a rasping shot like I'd seen him do a lot in training, so the last thing I expected was him to show the ability and vision to spot the great Peter Schmeichel off his line and chip the ball over him like that. What a goal and what a day to score it!

This game meant so much to us. Previous matches were definitely on our minds that afternoon and we were still sore that we somehow lost 1-0 to Manchester United at home the previous season, when we threw the kitchen sink at them but the ball just wouldn't go in. The scars of them pipping us to the league title then embarrassing us in the Charity Shield at the beginning of the season were still raw and I'll always remember Kevin Keegan's team talk. Propped up against the wall of the changing room, he just said one thing: 'You owe those people out there.' To a man, we all looked around the changing room and knew we owed the fans not just a performance but a result. We'd given them the performance the season before, but lost. We were on top for 75 per cent of that game and looking like we were going to win it. Schmeichel was in the form of his life and some of our finishing was poor, so this time around we had to be more clinical.

We started so well, getting the first goal after only 12 minutes. We had a corner, and I knew myself and Darren Peacock were always the ones they aimed for from set plays. Darren went first and managed to get a flick-on and it crept over the line. I know with goals like that, when it looks like it might have gone in, players will celebrate like it definitely has, even though you're not sure. However, I was certain it had gone over the line so wheeled round and celebrated straight away – and sure enough it was given. I'll always remember the commentator Andy Gray saying that the linesman took a risk there, but the right risk because it was a legitimate goal!

That helped us to relax because we'd started on fire, just like the year before, but getting that opening goal gave us the momentum we needed and we just carried on from how we started, with David Ginola scoring a fantastic second goal. David picked up the ball on the left side of the box, cut in and whipped one into the net with his right boot with a great strike.

From then we controlled the game, and I got my goal after about an hour. It was a great ball from the right from Alan Shearer. You're taught as a centre-forward to head the ball back the way it comes to give yourself the best opportunity of scoring, so that's exactly what I did. I managed to get up above the defender David May and head it back the way it had come. Sometimes you head a ball and think to yourself, *I know this is going in*, and this was one of those times. It came off the bar and bounced over the line to put us 3-0 up and we were in total command. We kept pressing and just never stopped.

We were relentless on the day, we just kept going and going. Sometimes you can go two or three ahead and become a bit complacent, but what I enjoyed about that Newcastle side more than anything was we never really did that. To capture the league, a team needs to win a game 1-0, an ugly win. We were never able to do that and maybe that cost us our chances of league titles, as we put our foot on the throttle and kept it there. That's what we did that day against Man United, but this time it worked out well.

Another attack ended up with Peter Beardsley having a shot and Schmeichel made a save, and it dropped to me. I'm thinking, *I've got my second here*, but he pulled off another unbelievable stop! Fortunately, Alan was there to knock the rebound in. That looked like that was it, 4-0 – I'd scored, Alan had scored – we were in dreamland, then Philippe stepped up with that cheeky chip that put the icing and the candles on the cake for us.

We were known as 'The Entertainers', and everyone always remembers us, but at the end of the day we didn't win anything, and there's not a day that I don't wake up and think about how we didn't win the Premier League. We were right there with one hand on the trophy and it just slipped out of our grasp. We were 12 points clear and when we lost our first three points we thought we'd get that lead back with a game in hand, like it was just going to happen. But we were tactically naive and just weren't able to go and get those scrappy wins that we needed.

The decision to join Newcastle United in 1995 was an easy one to make. I was courted by a few different clubs and met with a couple of them before Kevin Keegan came down to see me at a hotel on the outskirts of London, and I spent five minutes with him and that was it. I'd played at St James' Park before for QPR, where we beat them 2-1, and I remember walking off the pitch and up to the changing room and saying to the boys, 'Can you imagine playing in front of these week in, week out?' Newcastle fans have got it, Liverpool fans have got it – if you go there as an away team and are seen as an underdog and you perform well and win, they clap you off the pitch. It happened to me at Anfield when I was at QPR, and it happened to me at St James' Park on that day, and that stuck with me. Once I'd spoken to Keegan that was it, I was going to Newcastle.

When I left QPR, I knew I was coming to a really good team. We'd played Newcastle on a number of occasions and Keegan had added to that squad, so I knew I was going to be playing with a top group of players. At times, we'd be at the training ground on a Friday for a Saturday game, or Tuesday before a Wednesday game, the ball would be absolutely zipping around and I used to think to myself, *Wow, whoever plays against us tomorrow is in trouble.* That's how confident I felt in my team-mates. It was the demands that Kevin Keegan put on us in training. There was no messing around. We didn't train for long, that was one of his things, but you'd always train at max tempo. What you saw on a matchday was us replicating what we did on any other weekday.

Faustino Asprilla was a great signing that year. Normally foreign players that come into an English club want to adapt and try to learn the language as quickly as possible, but Asprilla was the first one who came in and didn't give a damn about learning the language, but the lads accepted it. He was brilliant, a great character and a great player. I know people talk about him getting the blame for us not winning the title that first year he arrived, in February 1996, but that couldn't be further from the truth. If anything, he added to our squad rather than taking anything away. We had Shearer, obviously, who's the best striker I've ever played with, and players like Rob Lee, one of those who I didn't realise how good he was until I played with him, and Peter Beardsley, who was just brilliant.

I remember when we signed Alan, a year after I'd joined. We were about to go abroad for a pre-season tour, and Kevin Keegan pulled me over at the airport and said, 'Listen, I haven't told anybody else, but ... we're going to sign Alan Shearer today. I want you to know first and foremost that everybody is going to suggest that you're on your way out because we're signing him, and other people in the country think you two can't play together. But I'm of the firm belief that you two can. I'm not bringing you together to prove anybody wrong, I just think this is the right move for Newcastle United.'

I said, 'Okay,' then went to walk away, and he pulled me back. He said, 'One other thing. He's asked for the number nine shirt.' So I said, 'What did you tell him?' And he replied, 'I said I'd ask Les.' He told me Alan had worn the No. 9 shirt all his life, at Southampton and Blackburn, but I had too! He said he'd also be speaking to Peter Beardsley because Alan wanted the penalties too. At the end of it, I said to him the mere fact he came to me as a manager and asked me meant he wanted him to have the No. 9 shirt. I was thinking you're the manager, if you want him to have that shirt, you let him have it.

Another part of me was thinking, *I've never stood on the Gallowgate or at the Leazes End and supported, hero-worshipped, the fella wearing the No. 9*. Alan did all of that. I knew what it meant to him, so I wasn't going to throw my toys out of the pram. I brought all of those things into my mind and gave him the shirt.

After Keegan left in January 1997, Kenny Dalglish came in and I thought he was going to be an ideal replacement. Kevin had told me the year before that the club needed to raise £6 million and been offered that kind of money for me, but he'd told them there was no way in this world he was selling me. When Kenny came in that problem still existed – the club needed to find a way to raise money, and clubs started to bid. I spoke to Kenny and he said to me that clubs were bidding. He didn't want me to go, but Newcastle couldn't see how they were going to raise the £6 million they needed. I just asked him to keep me informed.

Come pre-season in 1997 I was returning from a hernia operation that I'd had in the summer, so I was back early doing my rehab. We were lined up to play in the Umbro Tournament, a pre-season tournament being held at Goodison Park. As we were leaving to go to Everton on the Friday, I received a call on the Thursday at the hotel I was staying at to say Tottenham had made a bid and the club had accepted it. I asked what that meant and was told I had to go down for a medical the next day. I said I'd go down over the weekend and do the medical on the Monday and was told, 'No, they want you to come down tomorrow and do the medical.'

I went to the training ground the next morning to say goodbye to everyone because I wasn't sure I'd be back. I picked up my boots and went into Kenny's office. He just said to me, 'I really hope you fail the medical.' It was really strange. My agent told me at the time that he'd told one of the Newcastle board members how I didn't want to leave, and the board member turned round and said, 'You don't always get what you want in life,' and I thought to myself, *I've just played two years for this football club, given my best, scored 50 goals in 84 games and that's the response you've given.* I was so disappointed with that, I have to be honest.

I drove down to London, which took forever, then across to Mile End and had my medical, but wasn't due to see the Tottenham chairman Alan Sugar until a couple of days later, on the Sunday. On the Saturday night, Alan Shearer broke his ankle in the Umbro Tournament and I subsequently got a call from my agent saying Newcastle wanted me to come back. They'd give me this and that, and I'd return as a hero. But all that kept ringing in my head was what the board member had said. And I thought, *I'm going to use that on you: you don't always get what you want in life*. That was it, and that was the end of it. I made a decision based on pride rather than what was the best thing for my career at the time.

When I look back, two things really stand out in my career. We've seen lots of players go back to former clubs and, no matter how well they do, they always get booed. When I went back to QPR with Newcastle, having been at QPR for eight and a half years, I wondered what reception I'd get. At the final whistle, I'd scored and we'd won. All the Newcastle fans were singing my name, so I went and celebrated with them, then all the QPR fans started chanting my name so I went over and celebrated with them too. The whole stadium was singing my name. Afterwards, all the players were telling me how amazing it was they'd done that for me.

Then once I'd left Newcastle, I went back to St James' Park with Spurs and exactly the same thing happened. As soon as the final whistle was blown, to a man they all stood up and sang my name. Whereas I was able to go to all four corners of the ground at QPR, I couldn't do it that day. I got so choked up because I couldn't believe after just two years with the club I was getting that kind of reception. It was the first and last time in my footballing life I'd felt like that.

When I'm with friends now and a Geordie comes up to me and they start talking about my time at the club, when they leave I say to my friends, 'Jesus, I was only there for two years.' And they're so surprised. Most people know me as a Newcastle player more than anything else. I was at QPR for eight and a half years, I was at Tottenham for five and a half years, but that's who I'm remembered for! It's a really nice feeling because what that tells me is that I gave my all. Wherever I've gone in my career that's all I've tried to do. To be appreciated in the way they appreciate me, even though I didn't win anything during my time with the club … it's very special.

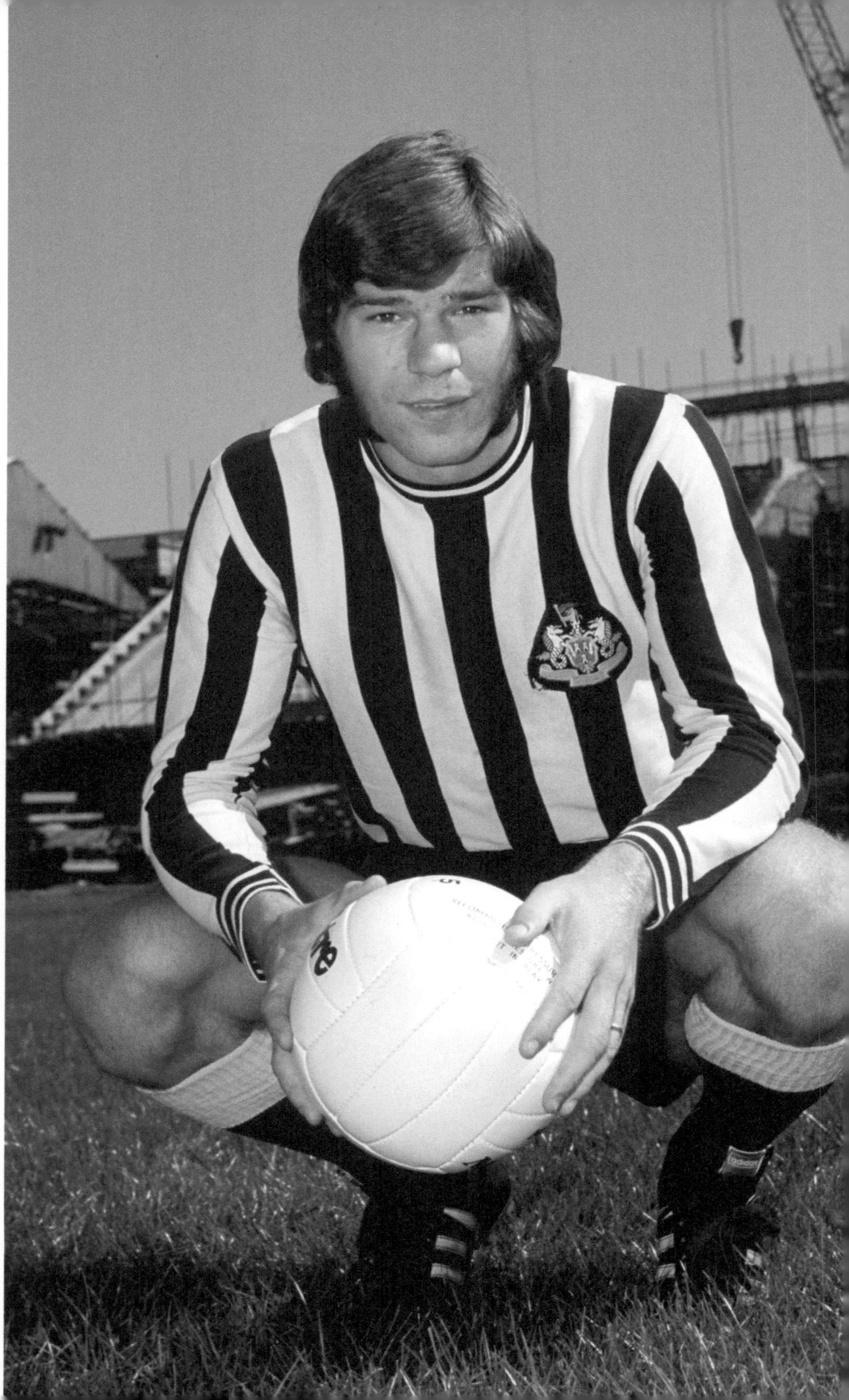

MALCOLM MACDONALD

Malcolm Macdonald
Striker
1971–1976

Malcolm Macdonald earned himself legendary status at Newcastle United thanks to an almost unmatched capacity to find the back of the net. With electric pace, bear-like strength and a sledgehammer of a left foot, Macdonald terrorised defences during five seasons on Tyneside, topping the club's scoring charts for four campaigns in a row.

The Londoner was signed by Joe Harvey as he looked to revamp his team in 1971, linking up well with fellow forwards John Tudor and Alan Gowling, and talented midfielder Terry Hibbitt. After several successful years, Macdonald was sold to Division One rivals Arsenal by new manager Gordon Lee.

Macdonald's career in black and white got off to a flyer on his home debut, when a superb hat-trick against a Liverpool starring the likes of Kevin Keegan, Ray Clemence and John Toshack earned the Magpies their first win of the season. The match also stands out as the day Macdonald earned the nickname with which he shall forever be associated: on 21 August 1971 Supermac was born ...

Newcastle United 3-2 Liverpool

First Division
Saturday, 21 August 1971
St James' Park, Newcastle
Attendance: 39,736

Newcastle	Liverpool
McFaul	Clemence
Craig	Lawler
Clark	Smith
Gibb	Lloyd
Burton	Hughes
Moncur	Lindsay
Dyson	Callaghan
Tudor	Heighway
Macdonald (Cassidy)	Thompson
Young	Keegan
Hibbitt	Toshack

Managers

Joe Harvey   Bill Shankly

Goals

Macdonald (3)   Hughes, Keegan

I first met Bobby Robson when I was an eight-year-old boy in 1958. For my eighth birthday I got an autograph book. I was living in Finlay Street in Fulham, which leads down towards Craven Cottage, and it would take me about 40 seconds to get to the ground to watch games. All the players used to arrive by bus for training, and there was only one player who had a car – that was future England captain Johnny Haynes, who drove a dented old Ford Popular.

I'd stand out by the bus stop and wait for players to come off the bus and sign my book. One day, Bobby got off the bus and I asked if I could have his autograph. 'Course you can, son,' he said. He took my book off me, handed me his kitbag, which weighed a ton, and went walking off towards the ground, with me running after him as quickly as I could. He started asking me a whole load of questions. He asked me if I played, and I told him I was in my primary school team. He asked me what position I played, and I said it depended on where I was needed. 'Ah, you're one of the better players then,' he said. He asked what foot I kicked with, and I told him I preferred my left, and he stopped, looked around and said, 'So you're a rare one.' He then proceeded to give me a lesson on what a left foot does for a football team, how it changes the game, and it was absolutely fascinating. I didn't need to get a word in, I just got this amazing lesson about the value of being left-footed. To this day I remember it made me feel really special. We got to the gate of Craven Cottage and we stopped, he signed my book, gave it back to me, took his kitbag, said, 'See ya, son,' and off he went into the stadium.

Ten years later he was appointed Fulham manager. I'd been playing for Tonbridge for about 15 months and just been away for an under-19s tour with Crystal Palace, who were interested in signing me. I hadn't made any decision about what I was going to do. My manager at Tonbridge, Harry Haslam, told me not to rush into anything as there was a lot of interest in me. He told me Bobby wanted to sign me for Fulham, my boyhood club, so there was no contest for me. He made an appointment for me to see Bobby at 9am the next day.

When I arrived, I walked up the steps at the side of Craven Cottage and told the receptionist that the manager was expecting me. She directed me down the corridor, so I went down it and knocked on the door. There was a 'come in!', so I went in and stood inside the door. Bobby Robson was reading and he didn't look up at me for about six minutes, leaving me standing there feeling like a prat. I later found out that he did that to everybody when there was a contract to be discussed, as a bit of a power play!

Eventually he looked over the top of the paper and suddenly really took an interest. He stared at me and then pointed. He said, 'I know you, you're that little squirt that used to assault all the players for autographs as they got off the bus! I remember you, once you followed me all the way from the bus stop down to the gate and you never shut up once!' He told me the terms and that there was no room for negotiation, so I signed.

Back then I was a full-back. When I was 14, the sports master at my school came to me and told me he was going to nominate me for the London Grammar Schools side, and asked what position I wanted to be put down as. I had to think quickly. I was a late bloomer physically, lacking inches, weight and muscle power. I thought, *Where can I get away with that?* I was going to be playing against 18-year-olds that were six-foot plus. I thought carefully and said left-back; you can get away with being smaller there. I got through the trials and went on to become a left-back. From there it stuck. I was eventually spotted by Barnet, then went to Tonbridge and then on to Fulham.

We had a terrible start to my first season at Fulham and ended up ravaged by injuries. The reserve-team forwards were being called up to go into the first team and were getting crocked as well. It literally was a case of the coach in the reserves' dressing room saying, 'We've got no forwards now, does anybody want to play up front?' I stuck my hand up and said I would, so I was put up front with the reserves, and then they had another injury in the first team. Bobby Robson came and told me I was going to be in with the first team and would be in the side on Saturday.

The previous season we were relegated from the First Division and, after a horrendous start, we were now bottom of the Second Division. We lost in my first game, which meant in the next match the team could hit an embarrassing record of 1,000 minutes without a goal. It was Crystal Palace at home – and I scored. You'd have thought this would bring a tumultuous reaction from the players because I'd saved them from reaching the embarrassing milestone. My strike partner Frank Large came running over, but every single other player turned their backs on me. There was a clique of senior players, led by Johnny Haynes, who wanted to preserve their power within the club. Because I was a younger player who had recently signed, they just didn't want to know. I scored in the next four games and got the same reaction from the other players. I was treated like an outsider. They wouldn't even really pass to me. Then, after the sixth game, Bobby Robson was sacked, Johnny Haynes took over and I was dropped. It was beyond common sense.

At the end of the season I managed to get myself an interview with the chairman. I told him I couldn't afford to live on what I was earning, and if he wasn't going to give me enough money to enable me to live, the next time I was on the training ground I was going to go and right-hand Johnny Haynes. He said, 'Where would you like to go, son?' and that was the end of it. He phoned Luton and agreed a fee. Alec Stock, who was Luton manager, came and put a contract in front of me and doubled my money. They were in the Third Division at the time.

When I'm asked who made the biggest impression on me, I always say it was Alec Stock. I learned something hugely important from him – before my first game, we were sat around in the changing room and he told me he expected 30 goals from me in 46 games. Who scores 30 in 46?! It turns out I got 29 that season. What I learned was: you've always got to set yourself a target in life; never make it easy; set it as high as you can. If you set yourself an average target you'll be average.

At the end of the season we earned promotion to the Second Division, where we had 42 instead of 46 games. We were on course for promotion again, but cocked it up over Easter. Towards the end of the season, Alec Stock approached me on a day training at the ground and told me that, with promotion out of the window, Luton would need to sell their best asset – me. He informed me Manchester United, Chelsea and Newcastle United were interested, and all I had to do was keep scoring until the end of the season, which I did.

We got to the last game against Cardiff, which we won 3-0 with me scoring all three goals, and a few days later I met Alec Stock, who told me he'd done a deal with Newcastle. I had the choice of going elsewhere, but Newcastle had recently won the Fairs Cup; Manchester United were a struggling side with a lot of old players, and I didn't fancy that. Being a Fulham boy, there was no way I was going to sign for Chelsea.

I went down to the Midland Hotel where the team was, and bumped into the Newcastle manager, Joe Harvey. I put my hand out and introduced myself, and he said, 'So you're the little bastard who's just cost Newcastle United an extra £30,000. We had the deal arranged at Easter that we would pay £155,000 for you, and you score a hat-trick in your last game and your manager has been here this morning and put the fee up ten grand a goal!'

They ended up having to pay £185,000 for me and Alec was one of the rare managers who had in his contract that he'd receive 5 per cent of all transfer money he brought in, so he made an extra £1,500 on top of what he was already making.

On the Monday I went up to Newcastle, and Alec organised it with the club sponsor that I could go in a Rolls-Royce. A huge gaggle of press was awaiting my arrival. I flew through the medical – I'd never missed a game through injury – and then did a press conference and at the end spoke to the journalists one to one. I was speaking to one reporter, when suddenly there was this hush that came over the room. I looked around and there was a fella who appeared, smart but casually dressed, and he walked across to me, and said, 'Malcolm, I'm very pleased to meet you. Welcome to the North East, welcome to Tyneside, and welcome to Newcastle United. You are going to love it here. More importantly, the fans are going to love you.'

Then he added, 'Oh, and by the way, my name is Jackie Milburn.' He told me that as I'd signed, I should get myself moved up as soon as possible. He said, 'How about a bit of house-hunting?' and we arranged to meet in the St James' Park car park that Friday at 10am.

He proceeded to chauffeur me around in his car. We left the ground and went round Fenham, across the Town Moor, through Gosforth and down to Jesmond, then turned on to the Coast Road and drove all the way down to North Shields, Tynemouth, Cullercoats, Whitley Bay, up through Seaton Sluice and Blyth. I saw a road sign that said 'Ashington' and realised that was his birthplace.

As we were on the way there, all of a sudden his arm flashed out in front of my face, he pointed out of the passenger window and said, 'Well, you soft southerner, what is that?' He was pointing to a coal mine, and to a big structure with a wheel on the top. I told him I thought it was called a pit wheel, and he said, 'Ah, so you're not such a daft southerner after all. But that's not any old pit wheel. That's the wheel that sent me a mile underground. That's where I was working, but football was good to me. Newcastle United was good to me. They got me out of the mine, and what a life I've had since.'

He continued, 'But my relatives and my friends are still a mile underground. They come out of the pits on a Friday, they get themselves cleaned off and on a Saturday they head into Newcastle, have a couple of pints and then get themselves to St James' Park, where they will create such an incredible atmosphere for you. So don't let them down. You have got to keep scoring and scoring and scoring and they will love you for it.'

This was just after the end of the 1970/71 season, so it wasn't until a few months later that I had my home debut against Liverpool.

Bob Moncur, the skipper of the side, had just had a book published and I agreed to go along with a few of the players to Waterstones to do a signing session. We were signing solid for about two and a half hours before we called time. We went to an Italian restaurant for a bowl of pasta, and then walked up to the ground. I was walking among thousands of fans with their black-and-white scarves, which was just incredible.

We'd had a poor start in the opening two games and hadn't scored – losing at Crystal Palace and drawing 0-0 at Tottenham – before the game with Liverpool. Going down the tunnel I could hear this noise, which just built and built into a crescendo as I walked out on to the pitch for the first time. It was a real cauldron of an atmosphere, which was something I wasn't at all used to – at Tonbridge we were lucky if we got 1,500 people in. Fulham were having a nightmare so got low crowds and Luton were restricted size-wise, and here we were in St James' Park, which was absolutely packed.

It wasn't just me making my debut, but also Terry Hibbitt. Terry was absolutely brilliant that day.

Most players get really tense before a game, whereas I went the other way. I could go and have a lie down on one of the physio beds before kick-off because I was so relaxed, and that probably helped that day.

Liverpool's Emlyn Hughes was the first to score with an absolute rocket from outside the box, and my first goal came a few minutes later from the penalty spot. A fella called David Young was in the side, who only played a few games before he left and went to Sunderland. He got forward and into the penalty area and was taken down by Kevin Keegan. I stepped up and smashed the ball right into the top corner from the spot. Liverpool then won a penalty, but Willie McFaul pulled off a fantastic save from Tommy Smith, who was playing in midfield with Hughes.

For my second goal, which gave us the lead, Terry Hibbitt made a run through the inside-left channel, and I came off Larry Lloyd. Hibbitt played a pass that enticed Lloyd to go for the ball, I nipped in front, went round him and smacked it into the far top corner. A strange thing happened then. I wheeled away and all of my team-mates came up to congratulate me, but as the celebrations stopped and I started to come back for the restart the cheers stopped and turned to song. And everybody was singing the same thing. The hit musical at the time was *Jesus Christ Superstar* in London, and it was the title song from that, but the crowd had changed the words. It was: 'Supermac, superstar, how many goals have you scored so far?' That was ringing all around the ground, and I was just thinking, *Who handed the song sheets out?!*, because everyone seemed to know the words! That was my nickname born, and it stuck with me for the rest of my career.

In the second half I netted my third, and again Terry Hibbitt was involved. He took the ball and just started running with it. Liverpool kept backing off, and he got to about 20 yards from the edge of their box and knocked the ball to John Tudor, who doesn't get credit for the things he did on the pitch. The ball came to him, and instead of controlling it he lifted it over the defender's outstretched leg and dropped it in my path. I came on to it and whacked it into the corner for my hat-trick. Kevin Keegan got a consolation a few minutes later, but it wasn't enough to stop us getting the win.

Not long after bagging my third, I learned a great lesson: Ray Clemence took great exception to anyone scoring a hat-trick against him. The number of times since I've sat in a lounge in the England squad and Ray would be across the lounge, just staring at me. I never confronted him about this, because I didn't want to give him the satisfaction! Towards the end of the game he duffed a goal kick, which was so unlike him as he was such a fine striker of the ball. I tried to control it, but it went up in the air off my shin, and I started sprinting. The ball was coming down and I realised Ray Clemence was sprinting straight at me. I looked at him and thought, *I can't wait for this to get down on the ground.* I went up and lifted it over him. I came down and watched as the ball landed on the roof of the net, and that's when Ray Clemence hit me with six studs and knocked my front teeth out.

I was semi-conscious, trying desperately to remain awake as I was taken off. As I got to the sideline I blacked out, and was taken up to the treatment room, where I was out cold until way after the end of the game. I came to and was lying on the physio bed, which is where, before a game, I'd have a kip for ten minutes. Frank Clark came in, stood at the foot of the bed, and I said, 'Hey Frank, I've just had the most unbelievable dream. We won the game and I scored a hat-trick.' He said, 'Bonny lad, you did score a hat-trick!'

When I look back, I had an incredible few years on Tyneside. While I was there I was part of history as I witnessed probably the most famous FA Cup goal ever as we were beaten 2-1 at non-league Hereford in February 1972. I was about a yard away from Ronnie Radford when he hit that rocket, which flew in from about 40 yards. We'd gone down to Hereford originally with an overnight bag and ended up staying down there for about three weeks, waiting for the pitch to be deemed ready. The weather had been so bad and the pitch was just horrendous. It was covered in straw to be kept in a reasonable state. They were trying to play the FA Cup game on the day the pitch became even remotely playable. It was so bizarre.

We were staying in Worcester, just up the road from Hereford, and there was a Cecil Gee shop nearby. We originally went in there for underpants, then we needed shirts and all sorts. We were travelling from Worcester to Newcastle, playing a game, then travelling back. Eventually the pitch was deemed playable, but it was still absolutely horrendous. It was an absolute bog in places, but then elsewhere it was rock-hard with ice.

When Ronnie Radford scored that iconic goal, I was trying to get back to tackle him. I was right behind him as he hit it, and under my breath saying to Willie McFaul the goalkeeper, 'Don't even bother going for that.' It was one of those perfect strikes of a ball. Quite unbelievable.

The person who benefited most from that goal was actually the late, great John Motson, who died in February 2023. He was something like commentator number five for the BBC, and got all the rubbish jobs. They sent him to this because it was a third-round replay being played on the same day as the other games in the fourth round. The BBC probably thought it was going to be a two-to-three-minute highlight, but they ended up showing almost all the game, and John made his name on that and became number one commentator within weeks.

I scored 138 goals in 256 games during my five years on Tyneside, just short of 30 a season, which is pretty good going. It was an incredible time for me. It becomes a very personal thing scoring goals up here, and I'm sure Alan Shearer wouldn't disagree. If you score goals for Newcastle everybody is your best friend, and it's all done in such a respectful manner. There's nowhere else in the country where you get that kind of response. People used to come up and say to me, 'Thank you.' What does a footballer do that deserves thanks? It was just that I was scoring goals and the fans live and breathe goals, so they live and breathe the goalscorers: Hughie Gallacher, Jackie Milburn, myself and Alan Shearer.

My time at the club came to an end when Gordon Lee came in. I used to hate taking days off – you can't take days off from goalscoring. I'd literally think about it all the time. I'd be walking down the street and pick a shop window, imagine it was the goal and the people walking along were the defenders, and think about how I could get a shot into that net.

I received permission from Newcastle to go abroad to play during the summer, so I went to South Africa and turned out for Lusitano in Johannesburg in the summer of 1975. We'd train in the evenings, so I was having a lie down in the hotel before training one day and I got a phone call from John Gibson, a reporter from the *Evening Chronicle*. He let me know that Newcastle had appointed a new manager, and gave me three guesses to work out who it was. I guessed Bobby Robson, he said no. I guessed Brian Clough, again no. I said please don't tell me it's Jackie Charlton, I don't think I could cope with that. He said, 'No, it's Gordon Lee.' I said, 'Gordon who?! Never heard of him.'

The next day's *Evening Chronicle* back page had one of its biggest-ever headlines: 'Gordon Who? says Supermac'.

I came back about five days before pre-season training and decided to introduce myself to the new manager. I knocked on his door, went in and said, 'Mr Lee, I'm Malcolm Macdonald, I've come in to introduce myself.' His first words were, 'Tell me about Terry Hibbitt, I hear he's a troublemaker.' He had Terry marked, and he left in ugly fashion.

One day Gordon came and stood in front of me, before a ball was kicked, and said, 'I've just signed the man who is going to score more goals than you.' I replied, 'No you haven't, because he doesn't exist.' He'd recruited Alan Gowling, and played him up front and me in midfield! I finished up pipping him by one goal overall.

Funnily enough, before the 2023 League Cup Final against Manchester United, I received a postcard from Alan, who's living in Tenerife, and it reminded me of another game, when we played together against Manchester City in the League Cup Final in 1976 at Wembley. He thanked me for the ball I played for him to knock in, which was our equaliser that day, but unfortunately we lost 2-1.

You always want to respect your boss, but I couldn't respect Gordon, and that led to me leaving. In 1976, Arsenal agreed a fee with Newcastle and I went down to London, and nothing happened for a week. Eventually Terry Neill, their manager, took me to see Arsenal's chairman Denis Hill-Wood, who lived on the Surrey–Hampshire border. We got there, went through his house and out into his back garden, which was the size of the Oval cricket ground. Dennis was sitting at a table in the middle; walking over to him we felt like two opening batsmen going out!

He told me Arsenal had offered £275,000, which Newcastle accepted, but then reneged on the deal and asked for more money. Then they offered £300,000 and the same thing happened. He asked me what I'd do if I didn't sign for Arsenal and I told him I'd definitely be leaving, and that I might go abroad, possibly to Belgium.

His answer to that was to wave his hand, and his butler walked out with a telephone on a 200-yard-long cable! Denis Hill-Wood dialled a number from memory, and it was the Newcastle chairman Lord Westwood's house. He made a final offer of £333,000, confirmed Newcastle wouldn't be changing their mind, and the deal was done. He waved his hand again and the butler came out with a tray holding three of the biggest glasses of gin and tonic I'd ever seen, like pudding bowls. And that was that. It was the right time to leave Newcastle for me, but I had a fantastic few years there and got to play for England during my time on Tyneside, but that didn't work out the way I wanted. Alf Ramsey originally brought me in and was absolutely terrific, a great footballing man and a great footballers' man. But he was sacked, which I thought was absolutely scandalous. He'd got rid of the old guard, and we went to Portugal to play against a fantastic Portugal team. We absolutely murdered them, hit the woodwork and their keeper had the game of his life, and we drew 0-0.

It wasn't long after that the FA sacked Alf. They gave the job to Don Revie, and he and I had never really got on. I guessed he didn't like me very much because I was forever scoring goals against Leeds. We often played them later in the season, and one year – 1972 – they were pressing for the league and needed one point to win the First Division. We played them on the Tuesday and they played Wolves on the Thursday. We beat them 1-0, and I scored, and then they were beaten 2-0 by Wolves, which meant Brian Clough's Derby County won the title instead.

Don Revie didn't pick me for his first three games, and they went badly. There was a great clamour in the media to call upon me as I was the league's leading goalscorer, so he brought me into the squad. I turned up at the hotel for the first game, against the world champions West Germany, and he said, 'I don't want you here. You've been foisted on me by the press. If you don't score on Wednesday I'll never pick you again.'

We played the game and Colin Bell got the opener, and then Alan Ball knocked the ball over to the far post and I nodded it in. After the game, Revie went round and shook everyone's hand from the team, except mine, and walked out of the dressing room.

The next game was against Cyprus in April 1975, where I scored a record five goals, and after that I never played again at Wembley for England. It left a bad taste, but then in football you're forever dealing with personalities, and personalities will sometimes clash – you just have to live with it.

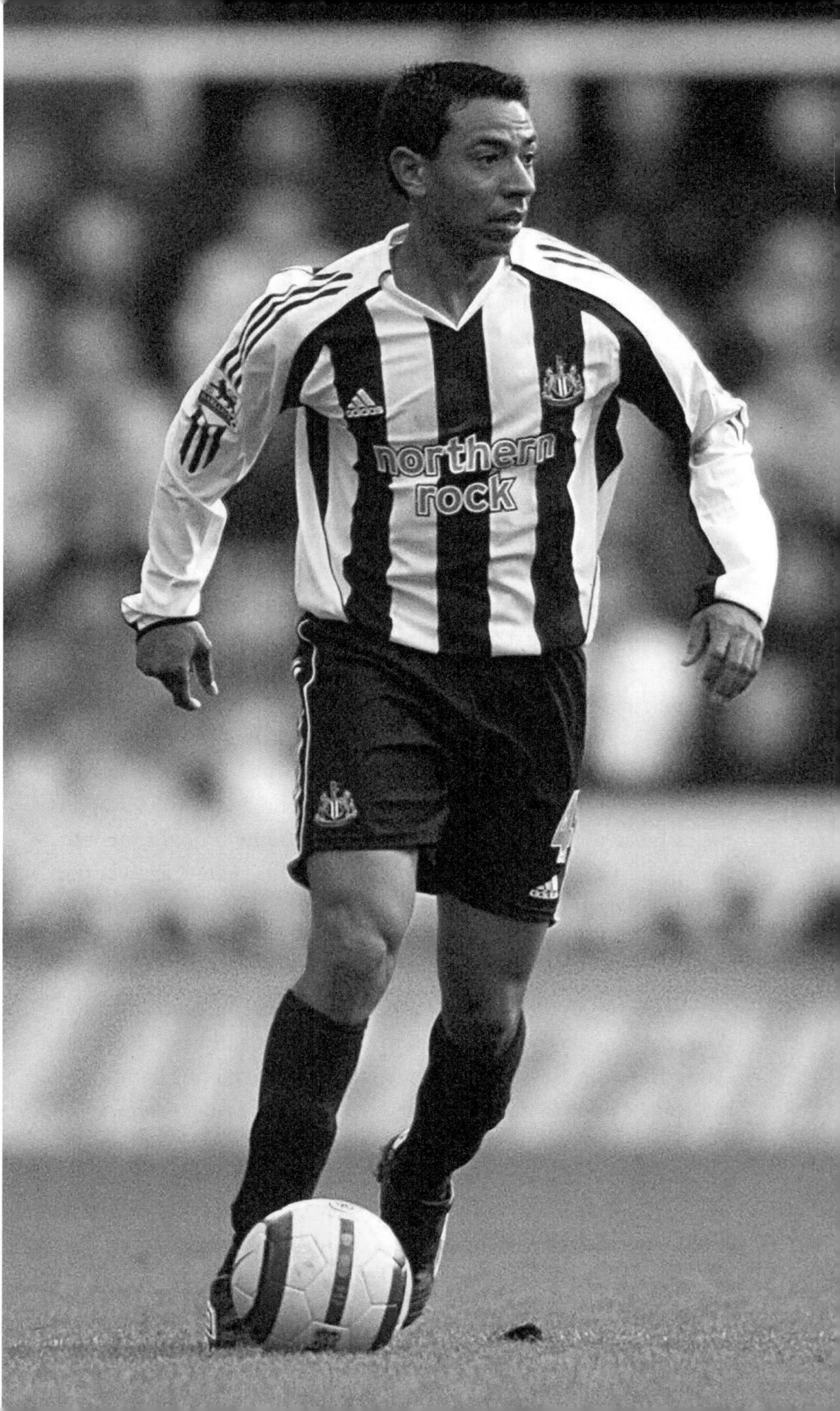

NOLBERTO SOLANO

Nolberto Solano
Winger
1998–2004 and 2005–2007

Nolberto Solano, affectionately known as 'Nobby', became the first Peruvian to play in the Premier League when he joined Newcastle from Argentinian giants Boca Juniors in the World Cup summer of 1998. The trumpet-playing wing wizard soon had the Toon Army dancing to his tune thanks to his cultured crossing ability, set-piece prowess and eye for a shot. In two spells at the club, Solano racked up an impressive 48 goals in more than 250 appearances and countless assists for the likes of Alan Shearer, who describes his much-loved former team-mate as 'underestimated'.

The self-proclaimed 'adopted Geordie' also turned out for Aston Villa, Hull City, Leicester City and even League One Hartlepool United, but is most revered at St James' Park, partly for his role in Newcastle reaching the 1999 FA Cup Final, another first for his beloved homeland.

Leeds United 3-4 Newcastle United

Premier League
Saturday, 22 December 2001
Elland Road, Leeds
Attendance: 40,287

Leeds	Newcastle
Martyn	Given
Kelly	Hughes
Mills	O'Brien
Ferdinand	Dabizas (Distin)
Harte	Elliott
Johnson	Solano
Batty	Dyer
Bowyer	Speed
Kewell (Blake)	Robert (Bernard)
Viduka	Bellamy (LuaLua)
Fowler	Shearer

Managers

David O'Leary	Bobby Robson

Goals

Bowyer, Viduka, Harte	Bellamy, Elliott, Shearer, Solano

I was playing for Boca Juniors when the opportunity to join Newcastle United landed in my lap and how glad I am it did. My agent at the time asked me if I'd be interested in moving to England. It was a little bit strange back then for South Americans to come to the Premier League and was more common for them to go to Spain or Italy as it was easier to adapt.

At first the rumour was that Arsenal were interested in me and I told my agent that I was ready to go to play in Europe as that was my dream. Then he said to me that Newcastle was a greater possibility than Arsenal. I knew a little bit about Newcastle because they'd started to become quite famous in South America as they were playing regularly on television and had Faustino Asprilla, who had scored in the Champions League against Barcelona.

Kenny Dalglish was the manager who signed me, and I was very grateful to him for giving me the chance to make history as the first Peruvian to play in the Premier League. I was very proud of that and over the moon with the facilities and quality of the players that I was training with every day. I was very happy to make the move.

Everything was very new, like driving on the wrong side of the road and I couldn't believe how green and how cold England was, especially in Newcastle where it was wet and windy most of the time, but I managed to adapt quite quickly to the climate as it's also cold in Argentina during the winter months.

I'd never experienced the clocks changing before so that was a bit of a shock, seeing how dark it got so early. The clocks thing confused me a lot because we'd be in the pub and it was so dark that I couldn't work out if it was 4.30 in the afternoon or 4.30 in the morning. Also, I couldn't speak any English at the time so imagine how hard I found it to understand Terry McDermott and Kenny Dalglish, a Scouser and a Scotsman!

I didn't have a translator or anyone to help me learn the language, so it pushed me to watch television with the subtitles on and teach myself. It was difficult at the beginning because it's frustrating when you're trying to express yourself and want people to know who you are as a person. As a footballer you can show it on the pitch, but I've always been a very sociable guy.

I've also always liked music and different generations of music. I used to play the trumpet at school, so when I moved to England and was bored after training I decided to take it up again. I knew my neighbour played the flute, so I knocked on their door and asked if they knew anyone who did trumpet lessons.

I've always loved salsa music and knew a guy from Ecuador and another from Cuba, and between us we formed a band and started to play in local bars. Damien Duff and Kieron Dyer would come and watch us. Whenever I was injured and had to go into the training ground for physio I'd take my trumpet and my sheets to read the music and play.

Before training Bobby Robson used to like to gather everyone together beside the pitch and explain what we were going to do in the session, so one day, before anyone knew I could play, I hid in a tree and started to blow the trumpet just as he began talking. He didn't know who it was and shouted, 'You think you're f**king funny? Show your face here.' He laughed when he found out it was me.

Playing in England was very different to what I had been used to in Argentina. The passion in Argentina is absolutely crazy, especially among the fans behind the goals playing their drums and I always felt a lot of pressure in that environment, turning out for one of their bigger clubs. Coming to Newcastle felt like playing football in paradise because the fans sit down, and it's all much more professional.

It also impressed me how much the football team meant to the people of Newcastle, with 52,000 crammed inside St James' Park for every home game. It was all about going to the pub and then the football and then back to the pub again!

I was also quite surprised how every night in Newcastle was so lively. You could go out Monday, Tuesday, any night of the week. It was crazy because in South America you have to wait until the Friday or the Saturday night to go out and enjoy yourselves.

As players we always had a good time when we were winning games, especially at Christmas where we'd have fancy dress nights and things like that. It was very good fun. When I arrived, Warren Barton used to be in charge of organising the team nights out and he was a very good man. After Warren left the club, we had to share it around a bit more but there was always someone there to arrange a night out and to take the money out of your wallet for the kitty.

Duncan Ferguson was a heavyweight drinker. I'd normally drink beer, although I couldn't believe how quickly some of my new team-mates could down a pint. Duncan would be on the vodka or gin, anything he could get his hands on, but we were careful and sensible about when and where we went because we had to look after ourselves and it was dependent on how the team were doing. Alan Shearer always used to say that in bad moments it wasn't the time to show your face or be partying.

'Big Dunc' was a lovely guy until he got on to the pitch. If you were friends with him, no problem, but don't get him upset! Steve Howey was another brilliant person to be around.

A few months into my first season we reached the FA Cup Final and up until we started to progress through each round I never realised just how important that competition was to the fans. To win the Premier League was obviously the pinnacle but lifting the FA Cup was also important, especially to Newcastle, who hadn't won anything for many years.

The truth is we didn't play that well in the final and clashed with probably the best Manchester United team ever as they were winning everything at the time. Looking back now I believe Ruud Gullit should have prepared for the match in a different way because the build-up to Wembley felt like we were playing a normal game and not a big final, and that didn't work for us.

Unfortunately, two or three months after I arrived, Kenny was sacked and then I had to deal with Ruud Gullit and then Bobby Robson. At the time I don't think Ruud had enough experience to be a man-manager. It was a tough time for him because he had to deal with older players like John Barnes, Stuart Pearce and Rob Lee, all of whom had been at the club a long time. He didn't manage that well and fell out with Alan Shearer. He left Alan and Duncan Ferguson on the bench for a derby against Sunderland, which is always an extra special match, and that killed him. We lost 2-1 but I suspect that whatever the result Ruud knew after putting Shearer on the bench he was on his way out of the club. It takes a crazy manager to leave the city's favourite player out of the team in a game of that magnitude.

Ruud was a good coach and very good at setting the team up, but he wasn't strong enough at managing people, that's why when Bobby arrived he found it very easy to bring everybody together and we started to be a little bit more successful.

When Bobby came in to replace Ruud I knew a little bit about him; I knew he was one of the most important British coaches of the time and about his history at Barcelona working with the great Ronaldo when he was a young lad in the Netherlands. The reputation and compliments were there, and he was born in Durham so was also a bit of a local legend.

The first time I was introduced to him he told me about the Newcastle fans and North East people, about how much they love football and that we needed to give everything for them. We had a great time with him, winning many games and qualifying for the Champions League. It was amazing.

The game I've chosen as the match of my Magpies life was a really important one in terms of finishing in the top four and it was even more incredible because we had to come from 3-1 down to beat Leeds 4-3 at Elland Road, which is never easy.

We took the lead through a goal from Craig Bellamy, who we used to call 'the Bulldog' because he was small, but would come and bite you. He was a winner and in training would always give everything. He and Kieron Dyer had great pace, which as a winger makes it easy when you have players of the quality of Craig and Alan up front. Craig was a grumpy boy and always moaning but was a great lad.

It was a very strange match and I remember talking to Gary Speed on the pitch and we both felt we were playing well as a team, but it felt like every time Leeds got a chance they scored, with their goals coming from Lee Bowyer, Mark Viduka, who was a top striker at the time, and Ian Harte.

Even trailing by two goals with half an hour to go we had confidence we could come back. Rob Elliott, who didn't score many, got us back to 3-2 before Alan equalised with a penalty and I was fortunate enough to score the winner, the all-important seventh goal of a crazy afternoon.

Bellamy went in for a tackle with Eirik Bakke, and Kieron won the ball, so straight away I sprinted in behind Harte, who luckily was not very fast as I wasn't either, on to the through ball. I waited for the keeper to come out and commit, but he stayed in the goal, so I just hit it into the net. I knew how important the goal could be but still remained quite calm as I celebrated with the fans, but in the dressing room after the game everybody was very pleased and very happy with what we'd just done.

The win meant we were actually top of the league heading into Christmas and, of course, we were all wishing and dreaming we could win the title, but we never looked further ahead than the next game because there was still a lot of the season to go and we knew teams like Manchester United, Arsenal and Chelsea would be chasing us. Of course, we looked at the table and said, 'Come on guys, we need to push and carry on and need to be consistent,' but everybody knows the Premier League isn't easy and it's only really once you get to April that it starts to become clear where you are and where you can go.

Leeds ended up finishing five points behind us, which is another reason why the result was so defining for us, because we knew we had to beat them to put a gap between the two teams. They were a very strong team at the time and had just signed Rio Ferdinand and Robbie Fowler as well as having Viduka, Bowyer and Harry Kewell.

Newcastle had qualified for the Champions League a few years earlier under Kevin Keegan and it meant a lot to the fans to get back there. It was the same for the players because you dream of playing in that competition against some of the best teams in the world.

Because we finished fourth, we had to play a two-legged play-off against FK Željezničar in Sarajevo to reach the group stages, and going to Bosnia was a little bit crazy because they hadn't long come out of war, and I remember we had an escort from the army from the airport to the hotel and to the stadium itself.

There were two group stages that season and we lost our first three games before beating Juventus and Dynamo Kiev at home and then winning 3-2 at Feyenoord to progress to what many people christened the 'group of death'. It was a really tough group with Barcelona and Inter Milan, who were both very experienced European teams, and the German side Bayer Leverkusen, who had reached the final the previous season. We were close to reaching the knockout stages after a 3-1 win over Leverkusen at St James' Park and an incredible 2-2 draw with Inter at the San Siro but lost 2-0 to Barcelona at home and went out. It was an amazing experience to be a part of and we as players and the fans enjoyed every minute of it.

That season we went one better than the previous year and finished third in the Premier League behind Manchester United and Arsenal, and ahead of Chelsea, but we missed out on a return to the group stages after being knocked out on penalties by Partizan Belgrade in a qualifier.

After the Belgrade game things turned a bit strange for me as Bobby started to leave me out of the team. He told me not to worry and that we had a lot of games to play, so I just needed to be patient. I said, 'Okay,' but I remember we played Middlesbrough away and I wasn't even on the bench and he put me in the stand. For me that was the moment I decided that I didn't want to fight with somebody I respect, so I went to the chairman and told him that if I got the opportunity in January, please let me go because I can't stay here as Bobby obviously doesn't fancy me anymore.

I was only 28 and wanted to play football, so when the opportunity came from David O'Leary to go to Aston Villa, I accepted it straight away. I very much enjoyed my time there, scored goals and the Villa fans voted me Player of the Year, but even when I was playing for Villa, in my head I was always still engaged to Newcastle and maintained my relationships with Alan Shearer, Shay Given, Stevey Harper, Shola Ameobi and Kieron Dyer.

Alan was always texting me asking me to go back, and then he messaged me to say Graeme Souness wanted me to return. I was quite lucky because it was difficult for Villa to let me go and then, as I was travelling to Newcastle from Birmingham and was only an hour away, I had a call from Rafael Benitez's agent to say he wanted me at Liverpool. I was shocked and very flattered but had already given my word to Newcastle. Maybe if they'd let me know earlier I'd have had a big decision to make but I always liked it at Newcastle and had my heart set on going back. Liverpool went on to win the Champions League that year, but if we could read the future, then everything would be perfect!

I was pleased to come back to the club, but it wasn't the right time as Souness had already fallen out with several senior players. So once again, within three or four months of my arrival, the manager was replaced and on this occasion it was Glenn Roeder who took over. Maybe I was a bad luck charm, but Glenn was a lovely guy, and I had a very good relationship with him. He was a nice human being.

I know why Alan Shearer was so keen to get me back, because I was basically his bitch! Every time I got the ball, he'd scream at me to cross it in for him, and I'd say, 'My friend, let me have it for one minute!' In all seriousness, we had a great relationship and linked together so well because I knew his game and knew that he wanted the ball played into the box quickly. He was a goal machine and that's why he has the club scoring record. I was always pleased to assist him and make goals for him to win games. We had a good connection, and it was the same with Laurent Robert from the opposite wing with a wonderful left foot, we both supplied him with a lot of chances.

Now the game has changed a lot and I don't think Alan would be very happy as a modern No. 9 because the ball doesn't go forward as quickly and spends a lot of time going back and forward between the lines. There's not much direct football.

After Glenn left, Sam Allardyce arrived with about 16 backroom staff! I did one pre-season with 'Big Sam' and went to see him and asked if I'd be part of his plans. He said, 'Nobby, I cannot promise you anything because I want to bring in some younger players.' He didn't give me any sign that I could compete for a place in his team, and when a manager gives the impression that he's not convinced by you, it's time to move on. I moved to West Ham, and Craig Bellamy and Kieron Dyer were already there, so it was like a mini-Newcastle reunion for me.

Sam wanted to come in and change everything straight away, and unfortunately for him it didn't work out and he was sacked. I think he was quite arrogant and set in his ways and even brought speakers to the training ground to start coaching using a microphone. Everybody knew he had a very specific style of football and it worked successfully for him at Bolton to stop them getting relegated, but it didn't work if you wanted to fight to be in the top four. For me it was another experience and I hold nothing against him. Newcastle is still very much my second home.

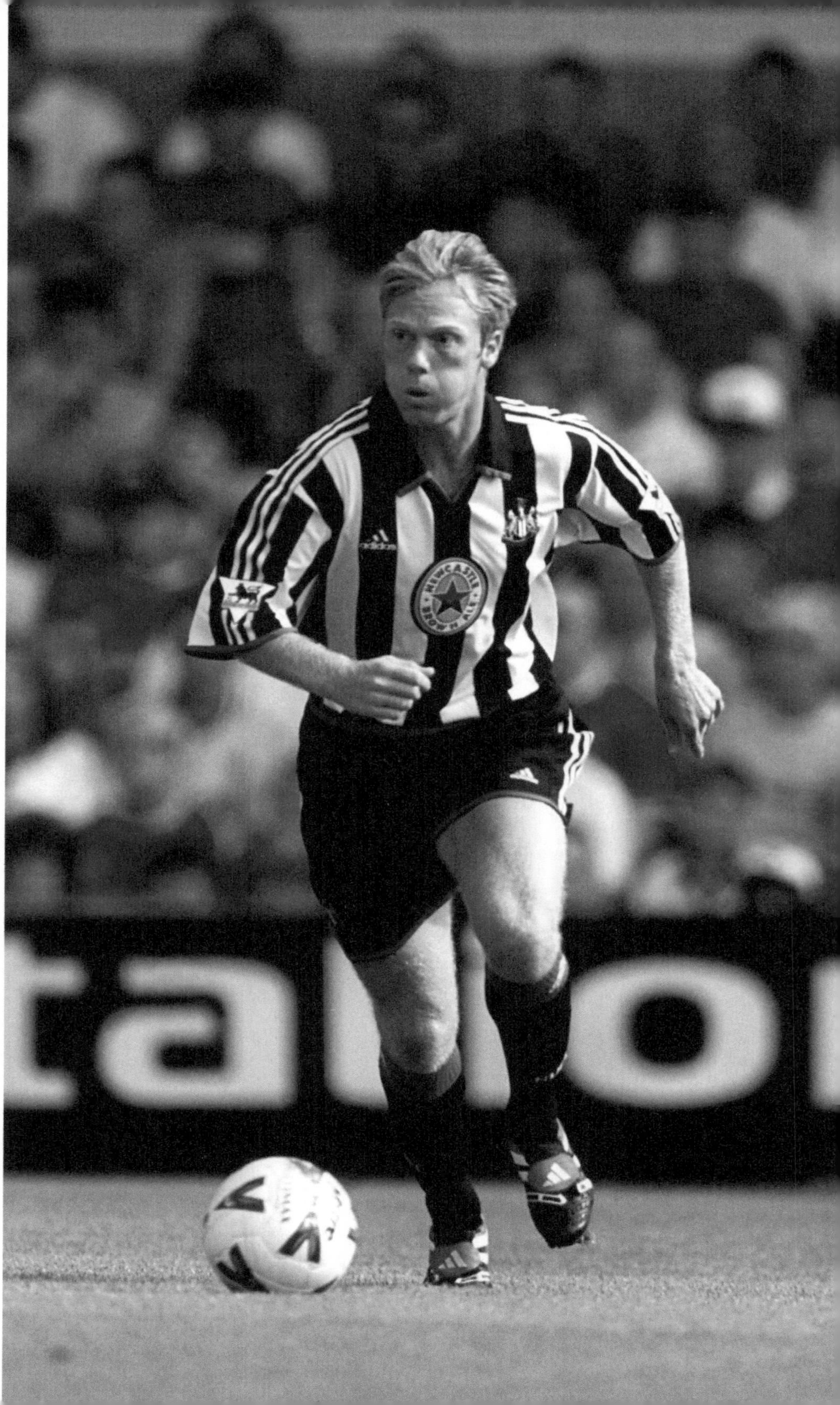

WARREN BARTON

Warren Barton
Defender
1995–2002

Warren Barton began his league career at Maidstone United, splitting his time between football and a day job working in the mailroom of a London accounting firm. He impressed on the pitch, and was snapped up by Wimbledon, who paid £300,000 for the dynamic right-back, at the time a record fee paid for a Fourth Division player. After five years with the Crazy Gang, Barton left the capital in 1995 to make the long trip up the A1 to the North East, where he joined Kevin Keegan's Newcastle United for £4m, becoming the most expensive defender in English football. He went on to make 213 appearances for the Magpies before leaving, reluctantly, to make the switch to Derby County, as then-manager Bobby Robson sought to bring through younger players.

Barton looks back on his Magpies career fondly and, although a Londoner, considers Newcastle 'his club'. For the match of his life, the now US-based Barton takes us back to the last day of the 1996/97 season, where a spot in the Champions League was at stake.

Newcastle United 5-0 Nottingham Forest

Premier League
Sunday, 11 May 1997
St James' Park, Newcastle
Attendance: 36,554

Newcastle	Nottingham Forest
Srníček	Fettis
Barton	Cooper
Beresford	Lyttle
Peacock	Chettle
Albert (Gillespie)	Phillips
Elliott	Woan
Batty (Beardsley)	Bart-Williams (Allen)
Watson	O'Neil (Saunders)
Asprilla (Clark)	Gemmill
Ferdinand	Thomas-Moore
Shearer	Campbell

Managers

Kenny Dalglish   Dave Bassett

Goals

Asprilla, Ferdinand (2),
Shearer, Elliott

In the early 90s I was at Wimbledon and in Terry Venables' England squad preparing for Euro 96, and there was speculation linking me with a lot of clubs, such as Celtic, Manchester City, Everton, Arsenal, Newcastle and Sheffield Wednesday. Wimbledon at the time was like a conveyor belt of players being sold, and it looked like I was to be the next one to go.

I'd actually spoken to David Dein at Arsenal and he said they wanted to sign me, but were in between managers and waiting for someone new to come in. That somebody turned out to be Arsène Wenger. Not long after, I received a phone call from my agent informing me of interest from Blackburn Rovers under Kenny Dalglish, only for it to be called off by Wimbledon as I was travelling there on the M25. It was then that Newcastle made their move and Kevin Keegan came to London for a meeting with me and my agent, where it was all virtually agreed there and then. I was sitting down when Kevin walked in with his assistant Terry McDermott, tapped me on the shoulder and said, 'Come and join a big club.' Five minutes later it was nearly all done – it was never about money, but the opportunity.

Although born in Islington and being an Arsenal fan, Kevin Keegan saying what he did and actually making the effort to come all the way down, was a huge thing for me. I remember playing against Newcastle in January 1995, months before I signed. I was doing a cool-down afterwards with a team-mate and looked around me and said to him, 'Imagine playing for this lot.' It was a cold Wednesday night and the stadium was packed, the atmosphere was fantastic. It was at the back of my mind and then everything aligned. I'd played non-league and twice been told I was too small, so to then go and represent England three times and play for Newcastle was a dream come true.

I became a Newcastle player in June 1995 and, shortly afterwards, Les Ferdinand and Shaka Hislop also signed, before David Ginola arrived a few days later. It was such an exciting time, and that summer was seen as the final piece of the puzzle to get us over the line and try to win the Premier League, but unfortunately it just didn't happen.

I'd say the reason for 95 per cent of that group of players joining Newcastle was largely down to Kevin Keegan's presence – and the squad was filled with good people. On one of my first days at the club, I was having breakfast with Les Ferdinand at the hotel and Kevin called, asking me to take our new signing David Ginola to the training ground. All of a sudden a silhouette of this gentleman appeared. I could make out a beaded necklace and white shirt, hair back and glasses, and even Les uttered, 'Wow, who's that?' David was like a god gliding through the restaurant in which we were eating our bacon and eggs. He had his coffee and cigarette and possessed an aura about him.

What we had at the club was a great nucleus of players like Steve Watson, Steve Howey, Lee Clark, Robbie Elliott, Peter Beardsley and Rob Lee. They took us under their wing and made us feel incredibly welcome as soon as we arrived. We had a lot of fun and banter and, even though the training was at a high level and competitive, we did it with a smile on our face – and that was down to Kevin. He'd get a food truck in for the fans who had come in to watch training and he and Terry McDermott would be there with a cup of tea and a sausage sandwich, overseeing us train, with the fans all nearby taking pictures. We'd have hundreds of people turn up at the training ground, watching us train in the cold, snow and rain, regardless of the weather, which was a new experience for me. It used to take us about 25 to 30 minutes to get from our cars into the changing room because we knew our responsibility to sign autographs and take pictures with people. That was a pretty big part of what that era was all about and why we're so fondly remembered, because we always endeared ourselves to the public and the fans – we were part of them and they were part of us, win, lose or draw.

We all got on well and every so often would go out on a Monday night with all the players there, even Pavel Srníček and Shaka Hislop – two goalkeepers fighting tooth and nail for the same spot yet best friends. We didn't have many players with experience of winning a major trophy. Peter Beardsley was the only one after capturing the league with Liverpool but when David Batty arrived that number doubled, having won the Premier League with Blackburn and the old First Division with Leeds United. Tino Asprilla came in and was a great character who probably spoke four words of English, but communicated and got on really well with everybody, especially Alan Shearer. You'd never put those two together, yet they had a great rapport with each other.

There were so many characters but Kevin held it all together as he knew how to be with everyone, like with David Ginola, he'd always talk to him in English with a French accent! I think Kevin was a bit in awe of him, how tall and good-looking he was. If it was someone's birthday or they'd had a kid, there would be flowers and a gift for them. He knew what buttons to press, but if we wanted to get something to him we'd speak to Terry McDermott, who was a bit of a buffer between the manager and players. We knew if we told him anything, within two minutes it would reach Kevin's ears, and he might switch something up.

You look at the great English teams like Arsenal when they had that famous back four, and Manchester United when they had Beckham, Scholes, Giggs, etc., they possessed a special bond – and we had that too. All the personalities were different but as a squad we all got on, and that was a big part of us getting so close to pulling off the Premier League title.

That first season in 1995/96 has gone down in history. People still talk about that team – The Entertainers – even though we didn't win anything. It's often said that nobody remembers who comes second, but that side will always be remembered.

I'll never forget my debut against Coventry on the opening day. Les and I were staying in a hotel the previous night and the fire alarm went off at 2am, leaving us standing in the hotel car park in our pyjamas! A few hours later we were off to St James' Park together and all along the road were black-and-white flags everywhere, families walking along with their black-and-white shirts. There was such an amazing atmosphere at the game, and excitement. We got off to a flying start, triumphing 3-0 through goals from Rob Lee, Beardsley and Les, then embarking on a run of four straight league wins, with a great team spirit.

The excitement was something else and we were performing so well. David Ginola was doing things I've never seen before, taking on top Premier League defenders like Lee Dixon and Gary Neville and embarrassing them. In March 1996 we topped the Premier League and hosted Manchester United – and Peter Schmeichel probably had one of his best-ever matches as a goalkeeper; we just couldn't score. That 1-0 loss put a seed of doubt in our mind. By that stage, Kevin Keegan had started changing personnel, such as bringing in Tino Asprilla and ousting Keith Gillespie, moving things around a little bit, and we lost momentum. I remember me, Peter Beardsley and Les Ferdinand speaking in the changing room after one loss, trying to work out how we could fix it. We agreed the manager wasn't going to change the way he played, so we needed to win it his way – never defensive, we wouldn't try to see games out – it was his way.

But it started to slip through our fingers and was devastating to finish second at the end, not just for us as players but for the fans and for the city. I think that's where we felt we let everybody down. I've spoken to lots of lads from the team since then and we feel the same, we wish we could have just done it for them, for the public in particular, and for Kevin Keegan.

The following season we were determined to go again, and when Alan Shearer signed we felt we were back in business. However, it was déjà vu when we came second once more, albeit a bit more transitional that season, especially with the manager changing from Kevin Keegan to Kenny Dalglish mid-season. Still, come the last game of the campaign, we had plenty to play for, with qualification for the Champions League if we beat Nottingham Forest and other results went our way. And boy, did we beat them!

I was in more of a midfield position that day, which is where Kenny wanted me when he tried to buy me at Blackburn. He liked me to play with my energy and enthusiasm for the game, to try to make things happen, and fortunately I was able to perform like that on that day.

We had a couple of chances early on and then I set up the first of our five goals. I won the ball in midfield, played a one-two and then slid it through for Tino, who got us up and running after 20 minutes with a lovely finish.

For the second I won the ball in midfield and started a flowing counter-attack. Asprilla was the provider this time as he slipped the ball through for Les Ferdinand, who stuck it home for his 20th goal that season.

I was involved again for the third goal, picking the ball up on my favoured right-hand side, and I just saw Les running through like a steam train. I played it through for him and he smashed the ball straight through their goalkeeper.

Robbie Elliott then had an opportunity but shanked it. Luckily, the ball ricocheted through to Al, who did what he does best and headed home, so we had all three strikers on the scoresheet. Robbie then got a goal himself to finish the game off nicely, smashing it in with a first-time shot from about 25 yards.

When the full-time whistle blew we knew we'd made it through to the Champions League, but then it began trickling through that Sunderland and Middlesbrough – two of our big local rivals – had both been relegated, so you can imagine the excitement around the ground as we reached the Champions League and that lot down the road all got relegated. It was a sweet sound as we were doing the lap of honour – party time at St James' Park. It was an exciting time for us all going around the ground – if we'd won 5-0 but not qualified it would have been tough to take, but that excitement to get what the fans wanted, competing at the top level, was what it was about. That game seemed as though everything was falling into place and we were playing with that freedom again. I felt in the zone as a player.

I was lucky, playing so many games for such a fantastic club, and was involved in some great matches – that night against Barcelona and some of the games against Arsenal I really enjoyed, but this one sticks in my mind because it got us into the Champions League, and that's what we all wanted as a group. If we couldn't be winning something then we wanted to be playing at the highest level and, at the time, only two teams qualified from England. Once you started to get the third- and fourth-placed teams getting in there, that did take away a little bit of the glory, but even now it's still the highest level for a player.

Of course we'd have loved to have won the league, but at that time Manchester United were head and shoulders above everyone else, so reaching the Champions League was a good consolation, and we knew we had a chance if we got through the qualifying rounds.

In 1997/98 we had a really tough time, with David Ginola and Les Ferdinand having left, while Alan Shearer did his ankle against Ajax and we were really struggling. When you lose three big players that was always going to happen. We went into the Champions League trying to do the best we could, but Jon Dahl Tomasson got injured, Tino got injured, although we've always got that great night against Barcelona. Getting that performance against Forest and getting that win had put us in that bracket to be up there with the elite teams.

When Kevin left in January 1997, the club brought in Kenny Dalglish, who had been successful with Blackburn and was another playing legend, so you could sort of cover the cracks at the club, but then it didn't really work out with him – the fans weren't too happy with the way we played and the decision to sell Les Ferdinand to bring in a full-back. When he left, Ruud Gullit arrived in August 1998, wanting to play his 'sexy football' and, as a player, you try to prove yourself yet again. Ruud was excellent in terms of football – he got us to the FA Cup Final and back into Europe – but his man-management was very, very difficult. He left Alan Shearer out of the team against Sunderland in August 1999 and didn't even tell him! I went into his office with Gary Speed and told him that if you're going to leave Al out then you have to speak to him, and he didn't. Gullit resigned days after losing 2-1.

Then Sir Bobby Robson came in and it was like a transition to how it was with Kevin Keegan all those years before. He understood the club and the fans and, as a package, is the best manager I've ever had. Within 13 months he had us back in the Champions League, competing in Europe and returned smiles to the faces of the fans. I look at Eddie Howe now and he reminds me of Kevin and Sir Bobby. What really did it for me was when Eddie turned up at work at 6am on his first day, was there until 11 o'clock at night, and there was a fan waiting outside. He could have made out he was asleep, or on his phone, but he stopped to sign his autograph and have a quick chat with the guy and then drove off. That's the type of thing Bobby would have done and tells me that Eddie Howe understands what it means to be a manager of this football club, how fortunate he is and the responsibility he has to the public.

Sometimes that can suffocate you. Kenny was a very private person. The Geordies wanted to know about him, but Kenny wasn't like that and preferred to be his own person. He didn't want to be in the middle of it and, although he was great with the public, you have to embrace it, and we've had players that found that difficult. Alan got injured and Jon Dahl Tomasson came in for him one game. He had a chance against Sheffield Wednesday, but missed it and never got over that, not because the public were on his back but because they demanded more, and it's the same with managers.

Because Eddie gets what the public want, they'll stick with him and support him if he's trying to do the right thing. If he's doing something they don't like, they'll let him know. Sam Allardyce had it, Graeme Souness had it, fans want you to do it a certain way and that's in their DNA, in their blood. You can't merely accept it, but have to also embrace it. When Bobby came in after Ruud, when things were flat, the first thing he did was to engage with the fans, he was one of their own. He'd speak about his times as a kid going into St James' Park, so supporters could relate to that and understand what he was going through. He was honest with them, and that provided the momentum to get back into the Champions League. He was able to do that with very limited resources, building the club back up again with players like Kevin Gallacher, Jermaine Jenas and Lauren Robert alongside players such as Craig Bellamy, Shay Given, Kieron Dyer, Gary Speed and, of course, Alan Shearer, and that was down to Bobby knowing what the public wanted. They'd had Chris Waddle, Gazza, Peter Beardsley, and he tried to give the fans the same sort of exciting players, and that's what Eddie wants now, to go out trying to be on the front foot and winning games.

The public have worked hard Monday to Friday to be able to support you, so, as a player, you need to go out there and try to win rather than playing not to get beat. I think the owners were surprised by the fans' reaction when they came in after 14 years of Mike Ashley and realised they must serve them properly by getting in the sorts of players we saw in that first January transfer window – like Dan Burn, Bruno Guimarães and Kieran Trippier.

If they can keep doing this and attracting top players, they'll be up there and winning things before you know it.

SHAY GIVEN

Shay Given
Goalkeeper
1997–2009

A son of county Donegal on Ireland's picturesque west coast, Shay Given's incredible goalkeeping talent was first spotted by Celtic as a 14-year-old schoolboy. Following his release by the Scottish giants aged 19 without playing a single match, Given was snapped up by Kenny Dalglish as understudy to Tim Flowers during Blackburn's surprise 1995 Premier League title-winning campaign. He had a successful loan spell at Newcastle's bitter rivals Sunderland before following Dalglish to St James' Park in a £1.5m deal in 1997.

The 6ft 1in stopper, famed for his incredible agility and rapid reflex reactions, quickly made the No. 1 jersey his own and would go on to play more than 400 times, including the 1998 FA Cup Final defeat to Arsenal. When he left for Manchester City after becoming disillusioned with Mike Ashley's running of the club 12 years after his arrival, Given was just 34 matches away from becoming Newcastle's record appearance holder and has subsequently been voted by Toon fans in to their best-ever XI.

Given made amends for his Newcastle Wembley heartache by winning the FA Cup with City in 2011. He's also the second-most-capped Republic of Ireland international and helped his country reach the last 16 of the 2002 World Cup. After spells at Aston Villa, Middlesbrough (on loan) and Stoke, Given retired in 2017, widely regarded as one of the greatest goalkeepers to have graced the Premier League.

Newcastle United 3-2 Barcelona

Champions League, group stage
Wednesday, 17 September 1997
St James' Park, Newcastle
Attendance: 36,600

Newcastle	Barcelona
Given	Hesp
Barton	Barjuán
Albert	Nadal
Watson	Reiziger
Beresford	Figo
Gillespie	Enrique
Batty	De la Peña
Lee	Celades
Barnes (Ketsbaia)	Anderson (Dugarry)
Asprilla	Rivaldo
Tomasson (Peacock)	Amunike (Ćirić)

Managers

Kenny Dalglish	Louis van Gaal

Goals

Asprilla (3)	Enrique, Figo

I was really young when I joined Newcastle. This was my first season at the club and my first taste of Champions League football. It was a big story when the draw was made and we pulled out Barcelona, one of the heavyweights of Europe. There was a sense of 'wow, here we go. We have arrived.'

There was a lot of excitement about them coming to St James' Park in the weeks leading up to the game and a lot of the noises coming out of Barcelona were that we'd be one of their easier games in the group. They strutted into Newcastle and thought they were just going to turn up and show us what the Champions League is all about. They had some heavyweight names on the team sheet like Luís Figo, Luis Enrique, who went on to manage them, and Rivaldo – players of real calibre. I don't know where we got the reports from, but we heard there was a swagger coming into town. It was like they believed because we were Newcastle and hadn't played in Europe before, they'd sort us out, so we used that as motivation, but still knew we had to be at our best to beat them.

It was a crazy night when everything just came together, and the atmosphere was the best I ever experienced in any club game. You couldn't hear a thing inside the stadium, which made it hard for me when I was screaming at my centre-backs. The record books say there were 37,000 fans there but it felt like there were 137,000, and standing in the tunnel before kick-off we were hit with a wall of noise.

It was special even just coming out to warm up and kicking a few balls up in the air because you knew it was a massive occasion, a night-time game at a packed stadium under the floodlights. Even thinking about it now makes the hairs on the back of my neck stand up because St James' is just a special place to play whenever it's rocking and bouncing like that. All these years later the Newcastle fans still ask each other, 'Where were you when we beat Barcelona?' It was one of those special, historic nights.

Tino Asprilla got a lot of the headlines because he scored a hat-trick but Keith Gillespie was like a man possessed and had probably his best-ever game in a black-and-white shirt. The Barcelona full-back couldn't get near him.

I shared digs with Keith at Manchester United when I was 15 and on trial there. Would you believe he took me to the bookmakers? I didn't even know what one was. A lot of players have their vices and Keith's gambling problem has been well documented but, for many of them, crossing the white line was like a freedom, and once the referee blew his whistle they could forget about it for 90 minutes.

The first goal was a penalty and then Tino scored two almost identical headers, one in each half, with Keith flying down the right wing and putting in perfect crosses for him. Tino seemed to have extra time to hang in the air before powering the ball home. They were both brilliant headers.

Tino was a mad character and a bit out there. Maybe different is the best way to describe him. His English wasn't great but every time he saw me, he would say, 'Hey Given, Bastardo!' I'd reply, 'Your English is getting good,' but then I'd just see his big teeth start laughing at me. He was so laid back, even with some of his performances and that could look like he wasn't bothered, but he just played with a relaxed vibe. As he proved that night, when he was on song he was a top player and that's why he was brought to the club.

He loved the Newcastle nightlife and was no stranger to the Quayside. He used to take an interpreter around with him, so his English was okay on a night out. He had a few parties and rented a few properties that didn't end up in the best state after he'd finished with them.

As a group of players and team-mates we'd socialise together a lot and that helped us on the pitch because there was a real togetherness. Tino was a big part of that. Sometimes the fans would even join us. There was no social media or camera phones so we'd enjoy the craic with the supporters.

We had some big characters in that team, including the Georgian international Temuri Ketsbaia, who was responsible for one of the craziest celebrations the Premier League has ever witnessed. I also happened to be on the bench that day and Temuri was sitting next to me, seething about not being in the starting line-up. He'd played well in the previous game, so he was even raging when he came on as a substitute. He scored the winning goal, and it was just a mental explosion. I think some of the players had to plead with the crowd to give his top back because he threw it into the stand and the game was still going on. He even tried to get his boots off but had tied them too tight. Temuri was a good guy and just passionate about not playing. His reaction was a relief at scoring but also a message to the manager: 'I f***ing should have started!'

Back to the Barcelona game and I had no chance of stopping the Enrique header to get them back in the match. Then I made a mistake in the 89th minute by dropping a cross before Warren Barton shanked a clearance straight to Luís Figo to make it 3-2, which makes it sound like a closer encounter than it was. It was a nervy final few minutes and we were all buzzing to hear the final whistle because they had a lot of pressure and created some chances as well.

It's all a bit of a blur, but I remember having some important saves to make. However, I've watched the highlight packages from the game and those things only ever seem to show the goals rather than any saves from a goalkeeper. There's loads of footage out there of goals being scored against me, like Dennis Bergkamp's famous solo strike and Wayne Rooney's volley into the top corner. My kids watch them and think I was always picking the ball out of the net, but I tell them I did make a save once in 1997 from Rivaldo.

If Barcelona were heavyweights of European football, then we were novices and didn't end up doing very well in the group. A few years later we drew 2-2 in the famous San Siro against Inter Milan in front of a jam-packed away end. I know it's getting a bit creaky now and there's talk of knocking it down and building a new ground, but that's one of the best stadiums I ever played in. That was another special night in the Champions League for Newcastle because Inter were flying at the time, so it was a big result to go there and get a draw. As players we all had to be at our maximum to get a result in these games because these guys had been around the block a few times.

I was only 21 when I joined Newcastle, having worked with Kenny Dalglish at Blackburn. Kenny was brilliant for my career in general and put a lot of faith in me by giving me the No. 1 jersey in the Premier League and Champions League. He'd say stuff like, 'You are my man,' and 'I haven't brought you here just to make up the numbers.' Stuff like that would really get into your head. He'd add a bit of banter to it as well in his cheeky Glaswegian accent and that would make you feel more relaxed before a big game, but at the same time would remind you how good you were. He always managed to get the balance right.

As I've already mentioned, I had a trial at Man United and they actually offered me a contract, but I turned them down in favour of a move to Celtic. I was a big Celtic fan growing up and United had Peter Schmeichel just coming into his prime, whereas Celtic had Packie Bonner, who was 34, so my dad and I felt that was a quicker route to playing first-team football. I met Sir Alex Ferguson at the 2023 League Cup Final some 30 years later, and he's like an elephant who never forgets. He said to me, 'I still cannot believe you turned me down to go to Celtic.'

I left Celtic at 18 and had to go back to Ireland and stay at home for a month or two because I didn't have a club before Blackburn offered me a contract. If you'd have said then when I was back in Donegal that three years later I'd be rocking out at St James' Park in the Champions League with the No. 1 jersey on my back, people would have looked at me and gone, 'Yeah, good one mate,' because that was just a dream.

My brothers and sisters are all quite academic and all went to university but had it not worked out as a footballer I don't think I'd have gone down that route. I was the sporty one in the family and at school I played all sorts of sport: basketball, Gaelic football, volleyball and, obviously, football. The teachers used to have a pop at me and say that I only attended to play sport.

My family used to run a driving range so I'd probably have got involved in that and stayed in the north-west of Ireland and not seen much of the world, but even when I left Celtic I still believed I had a talent and saw that as just a small sideways step before I could move on. I had real faith in my own ability.

The same season we beat Barcelona we reached the first of our back-to-back FA Cup finals, although the memories of the two semi-finals are probably better than the finals themselves. We played both semis at Old Trafford and beat Sheffield United and Tottenham, respectively.

Man United fans will be mad with me but I've never witnessed an atmosphere like that at Old Trafford. It felt like the stands were actually moving, it was mental. Obviously winning those games helps because Wembley isn't a great place for losers, but the vibe inside the stadium in the changing room after the games and going back to Newcastle was very special.

We used to have a few beers on the bus and would even stop on the way home for fish and chips, which seems mad now with all the sports science and teams having their own chefs to even contemplate refuelling with fast food.

People say we were poor in both finals and we probably were, but in the 1998 game against Arsenal we had a couple of big chances at 1-0 down. Alan Shearer and Nikos Dabizas came close to scoring and had one of those gone in and we'd got it back to 1-1, it's amazing what a difference that would have made to the mindset of both sets of players. It would also have given our fans a massive lift. Maybe it's just me trying to convince myself but I feel it would have given us momentum and belief.

I'd worked with Alan as a young keeper at Blackburn and that was good for me personally because he always did finishing practice after training, which I'd be involved in. That helped with my confidence levels because I felt that if I could save shots off him then I could make saves against anybody come a Saturday afternoon. He was one of the best in the business and his record backs him up. He had a few bad injuries at Newcastle and we always missed him when he didn't play because with him leading us out we always had a chance of winning games. Even opposition players would glance over and see we had one of the best strikers in world football, so that gave us an extra boost.

I worked with eight managers in my time at Newcastle and Ruud Gullit was probably the big one that I didn't see eye to eye with because he dropped me for the second FA Cup Final, in 1999 against Manchester United. I played in every round up to the final and Ruud didn't even tell me himself, and instead left it to the goalkeeping coach, Terry Gennoe. The message I got was that Ruud felt my kicking was poor in the previous game and therefore I wasn't going to play, but that should have come straight from the manager, so I felt sorry for Terry having to do it.

I don't think I ever had a conversation with Gullit, as it was only a couple of days, maybe even as late as the day before the final. It was tough because Steve Harper was a good friend of mine and he was playing in the final. I was devastated but at the same time I had to put a bit of an acting face on for him because he was always there supporting me, and it wasn't his decision. I was f***ing raging.

We had a good goalkeepers' union at that time. Pavel Srníček, who sadly passed away while out running a few years ago, was a brilliant guy who used to wear a T-shirt saying 'Pavel is a Geordie' because the fans loved him so much. Shaka Hislop was a great guy as well, a funny, laid-back sort of character. One of his favourite tongue-in-cheek sayings was, 'What is the point in me trying to save the ball when there is a perfectly good net behind me to stop it?'

In terms of the other managers I played under, Bobby Robson was pretty special, one of the guys who, being from the area, got the club and knew what it meant to play for Newcastle. He was always quick to tell us how privileged we were to get the chance to pull on that shirt. He'd tell us Newcastle was a working-class city and that the fans worshipped us, so it was up to us to repay them on the pitch. Man-management was one of his biggest strengths.

It was a really difficult decision to leave Newcastle because I was only 30 or 40 games away from becoming the club's record all-time appearance-holder. Some of the Newcastle fans will say I did the right thing because it was shambolic at the club at the time. We were selling all our best players or losing them on free transfers and it was literally going down all the time.

When Man City came in for me they were a club investing heavily in the team going the other way and from a young age I've always believed you only get once chance in life and one career. We didn't win a trophy at Newcastle because collectively as a group and as individuals we weren't good enough to do so.

It was a crossroads because I could have stayed at Newcastle for the rest of my career and I thought I'd do that, and then you think about all the other goalkeepers City could have signed with the money they had behind them. For them to come and say they wanted me was a big thing. If it was the ownership Newcastle have now I'd never have left, but we'd just been battered by Liverpool in that famous game at St James' Park when they could have scored ten. At the end of that match I felt like the club was floating along rudderless with no direction from the top.

I didn't have an agent but I had a solicitor, Michael Kennedy, who used to look after a few of the Republic of Ireland lads. I spoke to Mike Ashley and the managing director Derek Lambias in the office and they were saying they wanted me to stay and become a pillar of the football club. It sounded good, but I don't like talking about finances, so Michael said, 'Okay, let's see what you have to offer, but Shay does not want to be part of this conversation.' I went out to the car park and within about 60 seconds Michael came back out to me and said I wouldn't be staying. He said what they were offering was embarrassing and that riled me a lot.

That was the final nail in the coffin, and the worst thing about my departure was that by the time it got to deadline day the club said if I didn't put in a transfer request they wouldn't let me go. I was looking at the clock in a hotel in Manchester and knew if I didn't sign the transfer request, and therefore void the clause, the move was off. The bigger picture was that I had a clause in my contract entitling me to 10 per cent of the fee, which was £6m; £600,000 was a lot of money to anybody but Ashley was adamant that if I didn't sign the transfer request I wouldn't be going.

Basically, after 12 years of service, without a testimonial, that was the way Mike Ashley forced me to leave the club, and the next day in the media the message was that after I put in a transfer request they had no chance of keeping me, when in fact it was because he wanted the money. I was hung out to dry and never got to thank the fans or anything like that. That was the bit that stuck with me, and it wasn't the supporters' fault or the manager's fault. It was only one person's fault and that was Mike Ashley.

Some of the fans were angry that I left but they bought me for £1.5m and sold me for quadruple that. It was a bit of a s**t ending but I believe the true Newcastle fans appreciate what I did for the club. I gave them the best years of my career and know how special the Toon Army are. I look forward to seeing them back in the Champions League and back competing for Premier League titles.

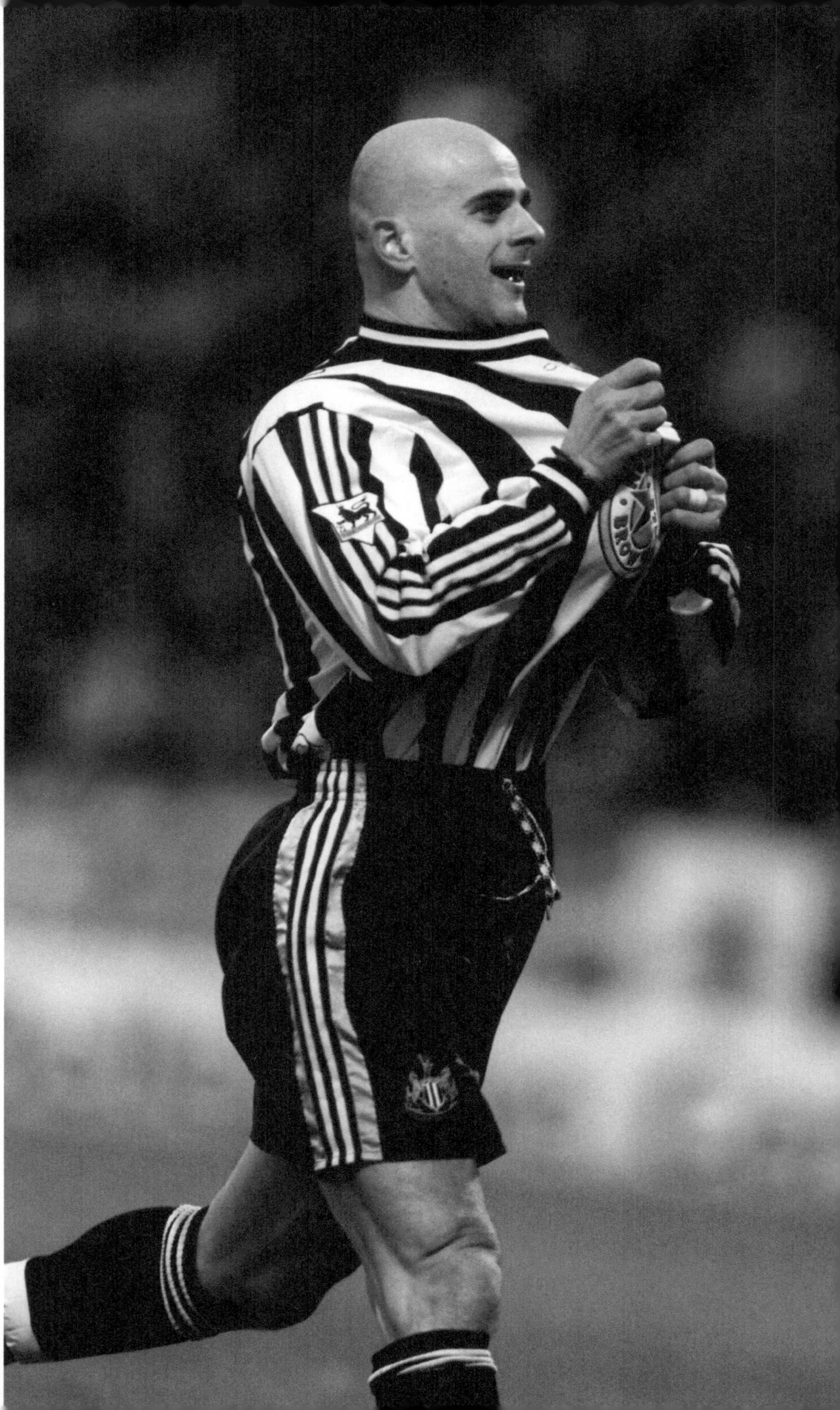

TEMURI KETSBAIA

Temuri Ketsbaia
Forward
1997–2000

Georgia is more famous for exporting wine than Premier League footballers, but the Eastern European outpost can claim to be the birthplace of one of Newcastle's ultimate cult heroes: Temuri Ketsbaia. That cult status was earned not so much because of the goals he scored, but more due to *that* iconic shirtless celebration.

The Georgian Geordie, as he's affectionately known by fans, was signed on a free transfer in the summer of 1997 after running down his contract at Greek club AEK Athens. Ketsbaia instantly endeared himself to the Toon Army by scoring an extra-time winner against Croatia Zagreb to fire the Magpies into the Champions League for the first time ever. He also helped the club reach successive FA Cup finals in 1998 and 1999 before being sold to Wolves in 2000. He later moved north of the border for a brief spell at Dundee before pursuing a coaching career, including spells in charge of the Georgia and Cyprus national teams.

Newcastle United 4-1 Everton

FA Cup quarter-final
Sunday, 7 March 1999
St James' Park, Newcastle
Attendance: 36,584

Newcastle	**Everton**
Given	Myhre
Barton	O'Kane
Howey	Materazzi
Dabizas	Weir
Domi	Watson
Lee	Unsworth
Marić (Georgiadis)	Barmby
Hamann	Hutchison
Solano	Grant
Shearer	Cadamarteri (Oster)
Ketsbaia	Jeffers (Bakayoko)

Managers

Ruud Gullit	Walter Smith

Goals

Ketsbaia (2), Georgiadis, Shearer	Unsworth

Whenever people think about my time as a Newcastle player they always remember the iconic celebration, the sight of me wearing no top and crazily kicking the advertising boards after coming off the substitutes' bench to score against Bolton. But that's not what I want my legacy to be as I did many better things than this for this great football club. It wasn't a pleasant situation and was the wrong time for me to score a goal because I was so angry and disappointed that I wasn't getting many chances to play. I just loved football and the Premier League is the best and most passionate league in the world, so to sit on the bench at a full stadium when you want to be on the pitch is hard to accept. The celebration was just my way of expressing that disappointment, but it was not nice for the fans, my team-mates and people around me to see the way I reacted.

I much prefer talking about the match against Everton because I believe it was the best game I ever played in a Newcastle shirt. That it took us into an FA Cup semi-final makes it even more special. I won a few man-of-the-match awards in my time at the club but on this day it all just came together and I was able to produce my best performance.

We were playing against a very big team in Everton, who themselves had been FA Cup winners just three years earlier, so to score two goals and set up the fourth for my good friend and team-mate Alan Shearer was an incredible feeling.

The pitch wasn't in a great condition because of the heavy rain in the lead-up to kick-off, so it wasn't easy to play good football. Perhaps that's why when I picked up the ball on the halfway line I just decided to run towards goal and take a shot from outside the penalty area, which I was delighted to see fly into the net.

David Unsworth equalised for Everton early in the second half with a trademark left-foot shot before our Greek midfielder, Georgios Georgiadis, put us back in front. Georgios then set me up to make it 3-1 with only 17 minutes left and we knew at that point the game was virtually over. Alan made absolutely sure with a really powerfully hit shot from my unselfish pass.

Some people have told me I should have gone for goal myself to complete my hat-trick, but Alan was in a better position, and I always tried to look to make chances for him because he was such a phenomenal striker, and I knew that he almost never missed. It was better for me to pass the ball.

Even though I'd been playing in Greece, everybody there watched the Premier League, so I knew all about Alan. I was lucky I had the chance to play with some exceptionally good players at Newcastle and he was right at the top of that list. Alan was very serious but also a genuinely nice person on and off the pitch, so we had a good connection. He was unbelievable, always an example for everybody, and wanted very much to win a trophy for Newcastle, but unfortunately it didn't happen.

We went on to beat Tottenham in the semi-final and not for the first time Alan was our hero, scoring twice in extra time after a 0-0 draw in 90 minutes. That prompted a big celebration and the atmosphere in the dressing room was fantastic. Getting to the final was a great achievement for me and for the club, especially as we managed to do it two seasons in a row.

Sadly, we lost both finals, but when you look at the teams we played they were better than we were. Arsenal won the Premier League and the FA Cup and Manchester United were league champions as well and would go on to be crowned champions of Europe a few days after beating us.

I didn't sleep very well the night before either final because I was constantly just thinking about the game the next day and was really nervous. Nikos Dabizas was my room-mate, and we only had the television to take our minds off things. We knew they'd be difficult games, but it's a shame we couldn't get the results we were hoping for and deliver silverware for our wonderful supporters.

When I signed, I knew all about the team but didn't know how passionate the fans were. When I saw and felt it for the first time, it was unbelievable. I never saw supporters like Newcastle United ones at any other club I played for. It was amazing to play in front of them, especially at home.

The atmosphere at the old Wembley Stadium, where I was lucky enough to play three times – in two finals and one semi-final – and lost all three, was phenomenal, with black-and-white jerseys everywhere we looked. When we came back to Newcastle after each final there were thousands of people on the streets to cheer us home, even though we didn't have the cup in our hands. That was really amazing. Just imagine the celebrations if we'd won!

I think I played better against Manchester United than Arsenal, and hit the post in the last minute of that game. It would have been very emotional to become the first Georgian to score in an FA Cup final, but it wasn't meant to be. We had chances against Arsenal as well, but maybe our best opportunity of winning the cup was in 2000 when we lost against Chelsea in extra time in the semi-final. That year, if we'd got to the final, we'd have played against Aston Villa.

We were obviously a very good cup side, which was strange in some ways because we weren't doing particularly well in the league during that period. Maybe that helped because the fact we were in mid-table meant we could give more attention to the cup matches. We had some good draws en route to Wembley as well, which always helps.

I managed to win two cups in Greece with AEK Athens, but nobody was happy because we didn't win the league championship. It was a bit of a surprise to me how important the cup was for fans in England.

When I signed for Newcastle, I had better opportunities to get more money than they were willing to pay me. I had offers from Greece and also from Germany, but Newcastle was my number one choice, and when I first heard they were interested in me I just forgot any other teams or any other opportunities I had. I wanted to come and play in the Premier League, so it was a big opportunity for me, and I didn't have to take a lot of time to make my decision and accept their contract offer. I just grabbed the opportunity.

Georgi Kinkladze was my team-mate in the Georgian national team and was already playing in the Premier League for Manchester City. We knew each other very well and were good friends. Georgi was a young player when he went to England, and I'd say he didn't play even to 50 per cent of his ability, because if he was more professional or more driven, he'd have done much better than he did. He told me there was a huge difference between the Premier League and the Greek League and said it was very tough, with a lot more running and fighting on the field. I faced all the same difficulties when I got to Newcastle.

I started very well and scored the goal against Croatia Zagreb that secured qualification for the Champions League, which instantly earned me the respect of the fans. I can't say I scored a lot for Newcastle; in fact, I got more assists than goals. I remember I scored a great goal against Southampton when I dribbled past three players and then scored with my left foot, and another of my favourite goals was in the 1-1 draw at home to Tottenham.

I'd love to say I was a big-game player, but I just loved football and always had a great connection with the supporters because I always tried extremely hard to do my best for the team and they appreciated that.

I played under three different managers: Kenny Daglish who signed me, Ruud Gullit and Bobby Robson. They were all hugely different characters, but I count myself lucky to have been given the chance to work under them all. I'd say Kenny was my favourite and I owe him a lot because he was the one who gave me the opportunity of my life. It wasn't easy to bring a player from Greece to the Premier League.

I enjoyed playing under Gullit but always felt like I had to prove to him I was good enough to be in the team, because when he arrived I wasn't playing regularly. I got my opportunity in a game against Southampton, scored twice and played very well but still found myself in and out of the team. I liked Ruud, he was a good coach, but unfortunately he had problems connecting with some players, especially Alan, and that situation didn't go his way and that was the main reason he left the club.

I also had a good relationship with all my team-mates and we used to socialise a lot together as friends. Five months after my arrival Nikos Dabizas joined the club and we knew each other very well from our time in Greece. Our families were close so that made it easy for me to adapt. Nikos and I were together almost every day and I was also close to Nobby Solano and Shay Given.

I'd have loved to have stayed longer than I did because when I moved on I still had two years left on my contract, but things were starting to go badly for me. When I knew that I wouldn't get the chance to play, I had to go somewhere else. I wasn't willing just to sit on the bench or in the stands and pick up my wages.

My future was made very clear to me at the start of pre-season when we took 25 players on a tour to the USA, and I wasn't one of them. I knew after that I had no chance to play. I never spoke to Bobby Robson much about the reasons why, I just told him I wished to leave and then I signed for Wolverhampton Wanderers. To be honest, the way it ended hurt me a lot because I wanted to stay and see out my contract, and if I'd had more opportunities to play, maybe I'd have done more good things for the club.

I had a wonderful time there and I always look back on it as a very special moment in my career. My family and I loved Newcastle, we loved the city and all the people around it. My daughter is studying at Newcastle University, so I get to visit a lot and always get recognised by Newcastle fans, even when I'm travelling in London, which is lovely. I'm embarking on my own coaching career now and I'd love one day to come back as manager.

I'm delighted at the time of writing that the club are doing so well under their new ownership. Like many people, it was a pleasant surprise for me to see how quickly they got themselves into contention for the top four and playing once again in cup finals at Wembley. Of course, having money to buy good players helps, but the way the managerial staff got the team playing was unbelievable. Long may it continue.

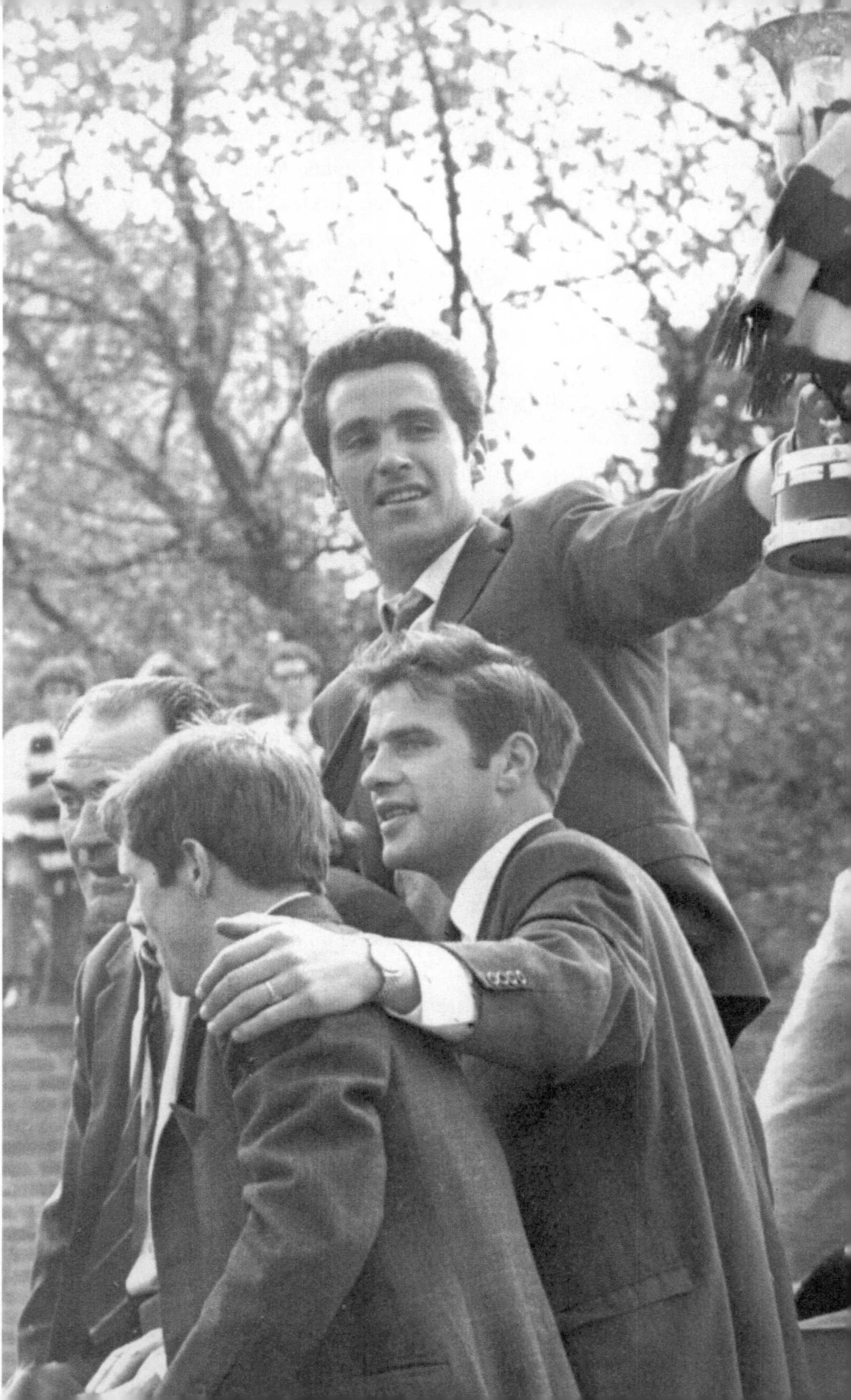

Bob Moncur
Defender
1962–1974

Not many centre-backs can boast of scoring three goals in the final of a European tournament, but Bob Moncur can. Newcastle United had luck to thank for qualifying for the 1969 Fairs Cup, a competition featuring a 'one city, one team' regulation, which ruled out many of the teams that finished above them in the First Division in 1967/68. Having ended the season in a mediocre tenth place, most would have written off Newcastle's chances of advancing far in the competition, let alone winning it. The national newspapers gave them no chance, but Joe Harvey's team defied the odds to conquer Europe, beating some of the continent's top teams along the way.

The foundation of Newcastle's success that year was an iconic, stubborn defence, with Moncur its beating heart. Having performed his job with aplomb during the preceding rounds, the Scotsman hit new heights in the two-legged final against Hungary's Újpest Dózsa. His goals and leadership steered the team to victory, and to European glory. At the time of writing the trophy remains the club's last major piece of silverware.

Moncur, who believes he'd have probably signed for Manchester United instead of Newcastle if not for the absence of Matt Busby during his trial at Old Trafford, still lives close to St James' Park and is rightfully revered as a hero by the Toon faithful.

Newcastle United 3-0 Újpest Dózsa

Fairs Cup Final, first leg
Thursday, 29 May 1969
St James' Park
Attendance: 60,000

Newcastle	Újpest Dózsa
McFaul	Szenmihályi
Craig	Noskó
Clark	Káposzta
Gibb	A. Dunai
Burton	Solymosi
Moncur	Göröcs
Scott	Bánkuti
Robson	Zámbó
Davies	Fazekas
Arentoft	E. Dunai
Sinclair (Foggon)	Bene

Managers

Joe Harvey   Lajos Baróti

Goals

Moncur (2), Scott

Newcastle fans often think I was left-footed because I scored three goals in the Fairs Cup Final, and they were all with my left foot, but it was actually my wrong foot. When I first came down to Newcastle in 1960, David Craig and I used to do a bit of practice after training. There was the outline of a goal painted on the gym wall, and he and I used to go and play a bit of a squash game with our feet. Our thinking was that as professional footballers we should be able to kick with both feet. David and I used to have to hit the ball first time within the goal, back and forth to each other, only using our wrong foot. We'd be doing that for hours and hours, and we ended up both being two-footed players.

To this day, I ask kids, 'What foot do you kick with?' and when they say left or right I say, 'Wrong answer. Next time I ask you, you should be saying both feet.' As a professional player, your feet are the tools of your trade and you should be able to use both of them, I don't care what anybody says.

When I was 15, I was on trial at Manchester United for about six weeks, before I moved to Newcastle United, but they didn't want me. Sir Matt Busby was still recovering from the 1958 Munich air crash, and I think if he'd been around they'd have signed me, but they said no. I had great delight going back the next year with the club I signed for, Newcastle United, and knocking them out of the FA Youth Cup!

Sir Matt was back at the club then, and when he saw me play in that game he said, 'I have just seen the next captain of Scotland.' He was proved right some years later. Who knows how different things might have been for me if he'd been there during those initial six weeks?

After Manchester United I went to a few different clubs like Wolves, Preston North End and some others, but I didn't fancy any of them. When I came down to Newcastle, I just loved the place, and it had the advantage of being close to home, which was Kirkliston, near Edinburgh, where my parents were. I look back now and think at 15 that was a massive step for me. That's also when I met one of the people who became a very close friend –

David Craig, who ended up at right-back and is one of the longest-serving players the club has ever had. We lived near each other in digs and remained the best of pals long after we'd both retired.

When I first came to Newcastle I was a defender, but was played inside-left and scored five goals in one game during my trial, so that's where I was kept, including in the FA Youth Cup Final in 1962. Eventually I was moved back, which was a good thing for me as I don't think I'd have made it as a forward, as I just wasn't quick enough.

My professional debut in 1963 was away at Luton, but it took me a while to establish myself. The year we got promotion in 1965 I only played 11 games. The club had three stalwarts in Stan Anderson, John McGrath and Jim Iley, and whenever any of those three were injured, I could play in any of their positions. It wasn't until the following season of 1965/66 that I started to get into the side and make my mark.

Come 1969 we had two factions in the team – the golfers and the guys into horse racing, but come matchday we were all together. We all got on great and that's what won us the Fairs Cup. I look back now and can say that was the best team I ever played in. There were no prima donnas, no one absolutely outstanding, just a bunch of very good pros and players. Pop Robson was a great goalscorer, Wyn Davies terrified Europe with what he could do in the air, and at the back we were very, very tight, with Frank Clark and myself, and a back four that played together for about four or five years.

We were lucky to get into the competition because we finished tenth in the First Division in 1967/68. The point of the cup originally was to promote business between cities, and you could only have one team from one city, so because of this we managed to qualify. I was actually on holiday in Marbella when I got a phone call from the journalist John Gibson saying we were in Europe. I joked, 'I know John, I'm in Marbella!' He told me the rules and I couldn't believe it. I always say to people that we went in the back door, but came out of the front door.

We took each game as it came, and looked at it as a bit of a jolly. We'd play, say, Arsenal on the Saturday then be flying out to Europe afterwards. We were playing the games with no pressure, just going out and enjoying ourselves.

We played a series of huge clubs to get to the final. We had to play Feyenoord first, who were massive, and beat them 4-2 on aggregate, and then Sporting Lisbon, who were also a great side. We won that 2-1 after two legs, Pop Robson getting the winner at St James' Park. After beating Real Zaragoza on away goals in the third round, we came up against Vitória Setúbal in the quarter-final, and we beat them 5-1 at home before going to Portugal. They tried every trick in the book to upset us – they had motorbikes going round the track, flares going up, all sorts of things to try to disrupt us. It was a disgrace in terms of sportsmanship.

The semi-final against Glasgow Rangers was huge. We had five Scotsmen in our team, and I was the only one who had never played in Scotland. For the first leg we went to Ibrox and played in front of 75,000, which was the biggest crowd in Europe at that time. Because I'd left home when I was 15, I had no experience of what Ibrox would be like; I thought we'd beat them. The Scots lads in our team, you could see on the bus on the way up that they were nervous, because as a Scotsman playing at Ibrox you were used to getting stuffed! But I knew we were better.

We drew 0-0 there then beat them 2-0 at our place, a game that attracted interest for all the wrong reasons. All the Rangers fans were in the Gallowgate End, on the terraces, having had a lot to drink. We scored and they started to throw bottles on to the pitch, but they weren't going the full distance so the bottles were hitting their supporters at the front! The fans spilled on to the pitch to defend themselves, and it was labelled an invasion and a riot at the time, but I still to this day think, in fairness to some of the Rangers supporters, they just wanted to get out of danger.

Because of the trouble the players were taken off at 2-0 and we were off for a little while, and the Rangers board offered to concede defeat there and then, but we had to go back on because the rules stated that 90 minutes had to be played.

I went up to the boardroom after the game and the Rangers chairman was visibly shaking from what he'd seen. I felt sorry for Rangers and the board, because it was just caused by a few idiots. The next morning I went down to see where they'd been, and the number of bottles and cans in the stand was unbelievable – you couldn't see any of the terrace!

Come the final against Újpest Dózsa, I felt the pressure a little bit, because they were quoted by Don Revie, whose Leeds side had been knocked out by them, as the best football club he'd ever seen, and they had nine Hungary internationals, and Hungary in those days was a very strong nation.

We got to half-time in the first leg at home and it was 0-0, then in the second half we scored three goals – I got my two and Jimmy Scott got a great goal. Before I scored, Wyn Davies broke his jaw when he went up for a header and headed my head! He was the king in the air but I got in the way. He wasn't happy with me after the game.

For the first goal I was up for a free kick and the keeper saved a header from Wyn, but the ball came back to me and I was in the right place to bury it. My second goal was a bit more fortunate, I was on the halfway line when a clearance came straight to me. I didn't control it well and it bobbled in front of me. I thought I'd better go and get it. I then started to advance and saw Jimmy Scott, so gave it to him. For some reason I kept going, and Jimmy gave it me back. I knocked it inside again and somehow it came back to me. By that time I was on the edge of the box, and I thought to myself, *S**t, what am I going to do now?* I was panicking then, so just decided to hit it. It wasn't the best shot in the world but was so accurate it went beyond their keeper right into the corner. Afterwards Frank Clark, who hardly ever scored, was telling me how lucky I was it had gone in. He was jealous because he'd never scored a goal at that point.

Jimmy Scott got the third, running through and tipping it over the advancing keeper, which made it 3-0 at half-time in the tie, with the second leg to come in Hungary.

I always pride myself on following through on what I say, and I'd told a guy who ran a local dog track that I'd go and help out with a presentation at the Mayfair Ballroom, which used to be on the site where The Gate is now in the city centre. I said I'd be there weeks before, way before we knew we'd be in the final. After the game I left St James' Park, and all the press boys were after me, but I told them I had a prior engagement. I walked to the Mayfair and into the building not long after the game had finished, so soon that the people there didn't know the score! They asked me the score. I shouted back, 'We won 3-0.' They asked who scored and I just pointed at myself and shouted, 'Two!' I was always proud of myself that I kept my appointment, in spite of what happened that night.

We were thinking that 3-0 was a good start after the first leg, bearing in mind we were solid at the back, so we weren't too fazed about going to play at their place. But then in the first half of the second leg we got absolutely battered, and were 2-0 down at half-time. We came off and Joe Harvey did his famous team talk where he said, 'All you've got to do is score a goal. If you score a goal, they'll collapse like a pack of f**king cards.' We hadn't been over the halfway line, boss, how were we going to score a goal?

So it happens I got the goal we needed right after the break. I went up for a corner, which I always did. Jackie Sinclair took it, Wyn Davies went to head it and missed it badly. It went back out to Jackie, who whipped it back to me and I got one back with a first-time shot. I knew when I hit it that it was a goal. That goal killed them.

When we were invited over for the 50th anniversary of that game, we were on stage with some of the Hungarian players. They were asked about the game and they said they thought they'd beat us. At 3-0 down, they thought they were good enough to come back in the second leg, but the goal I got stuffed them because of away goals counting double.

On the day even I was confused. I remember running back after we scored our third goal over there and asking Frank Clark how many they had to get to beat us, and he told me not to worry, we had enough, and so it proved.

At the final whistle we started running around the pitch, celebrating, and credit to the Hungarian supporters, who stayed and clapped us. We were running around the track with the cup and I felt someone jump on to my back. I shrugged them off and started shouting at them, turned round and it was my wife Camille, who had run on the pitch! I owed her an apology for that.

Back at the hotel afterwards we had a presentation and I was called up as the captain. They gave me a tray with about 20 miniature Fairs Cups on it, instead of a medal, and I had to walk back slowly to the table, trying to balance them all on the tray, and start dishing them out to the lads. It's a lovely little trophy but mine is now a bit battered because my kids thought it would be a good idea to use it as a goalpost in the living room when they were knocking a ball around!

At the celebration party afterwards the chairman Lord Westwood came up to me and said, 'I'd like you to make sure we get some champagne for the boys ... but not the French stuff ... the local stuff.' He wanted to save a few bob. It was a great night and we were out until about 4am but had to fly back the next morning.

The plane was quiet because we were all hung-over. Joe Harvey came up to me on the flight and told me he wanted me to get off with the trophy first. I thought I'd look like a bit of a prat, but he told me to do as I was told, so I did it. When the door opened at Newcastle Airport the whole place was covered with masses of people. It was like when you step off a plane in a warm country and you're hit with the heat, that was the feeling I got from the sight of the fans and the noise they made.

We had to get on to a bus to parade the trophy into the city, but it couldn't be a double-decker because we had to go under quite a low bridge on the way back to the stadium. We had a single-decker bus instead, so they pulled the sunroof back and stuck in a long, office-style wooden table, which we could stand on and have our heads out of the top.

We went through Woolsington, and I was holding the cup up high in the air, celebrating, when we went under the bridge and it hit an electric wire that was dangling under it, and huge sparks flew out, so there was a big black mark on the cup afterwards. If the table hadn't been there to break the flow of the electricity I could have been electrocuted!

We headed on towards the city centre, and there were just thousands of people out to see us – people took days off and brought their kids, it was incredible. We spent a couple of hours going around the stadium, with Joe Harvey leading us in a sing-song. It was a great homecoming.

However, even after we won it, I didn't realise just how big a thing that was for Newcastle United, and that lasted until I became a fan. I went to the first game in the Premiership in 1992 against Tottenham Hotspur. I was sat in St James' Park, and saw the fans and how happy they were to be back in the top flight and I had tears in my eyes. Then I realised what it meant to the fans all those years ago.

A few years after the Fairs Cup Final we had a chance for silverware again, in the FA Cup Final against Liverpool in 1974. The team didn't play to its potential on the day – I couldn't believe it was 0-0 at half-time, and 3-0 at full time flattered us. I knew it was probably going to be my last game for the club, and so it proved.

Not long afterwards I made the move down the road to Sunderland. How that came about was that Bob Stokoe, their manager at the time, was a player for Newcastle when I was a youngster at the club. I knew him as a friend back then, I used to play golf with him. Bob had tried to get me a few years earlier, but by the time we got to the cup final I'd made my mind up to leave. I felt, as skipper of the team, there were too many other people who thought they knew better than I did. There were two cliques in the team, and I didn't want any of that. I rang Bob after the cup final and told him it was time for me to leave and asked would he still want to sign me, so we did a deal.

I actually signed live on TV, which was unheard of at the time. I was on the World Cup 1974 panel, along with Brian Clough,

Malcolm Allison, Derek Dougan, Pat Crerand and Jack Charlton. I'd done the deal before I left for London and had said I'd officially sign when I came back. While I was there I had dinner one night with the commentator Brian Moore, and I told him I'd be going back after the World Cup to sign for Sunderland. He almost choked on his food! He couldn't believe it. The next thing I knew, the ITV managing director, John Bromley, told me I'd be doing a signing live on TV. I look back and think what a scoop that was for them.

At that time Cloughie was at Brighton (he'd tried to get me for Derby a few years earlier) and he offered me all sorts to sign for Brighton instead of Sunderland – a house, a car, cash and more, telling me Sunderland were s**t.

Brian Clough and Bob Stokoe hated each other. Brian did his knee ligaments against Bury playing for Sunderland at Roker Park years earlier when he went over the keeper in a challenge. He was lying on the ground in agony. Stokoe, who was playing for Bury, came over and said, 'Get up you soft s**t!' Cloughie never forgot that, because that injury finished his playing career. So when I'm there about to sign for Stokoe, Cloughie pulled every trick in the book to upset the move.

Bob came down with my wife Camille from Newcastle on the train, and Cloughie was there to meet them at the station. He got hold of Camille and took her off, and then bombarded her with all the same stuff he'd been throwing at me, while I chatted with Bob.

I got to the stage where I was questioning it myself, such was Cloughie's insistence. He had me rattled, but one of the reasons I didn't want to go to Brighton was we were settled where we were, with the kids at school, so I could just travel to Sunderland from where we were living. Brighton just wasn't right for me. And it's just as well I didn't take him up on his offer because he left Brighton after about three weeks.

I signed on TV – the first player to do it – and I was quite happy to be in London because to the fans up here leaving Newcastle to go to Sunderland was criminal, so being in London I knew nobody would be able to lynch me! I got stick but it wasn't nasty. I'd served Newcastle well for over a decade and had been a good player for them. I was actually peed off with the Newcastle board that they wouldn't let me leave on a free, but they charged Sunderland £30,000 to buy me. I could have probably got some of that as a nest-egg, they could have given me a testimonial perhaps, but it didn't happen.

I never regretted the move but there were some bumps in the road. Bobby Kerr had picked up the FA Cup for Sunderland in 1973, just a year earlier, and Bob Stokoe made me captain without telling me or him, announcing it to the press before he'd spoken to us. I thought, *Jesus Christ, you don't think it's hard enough me coming? I'm getting stick from the Newcastle fans for leaving for Sunderland, and the Sunderland fans are going to be up in arms about me replacing their FA Cup-winning skipper as captain!*

After two successful seasons there I was headhunted by Carlisle United to become player-manager in 1976, and that's where I brought Peter Beardsley into the game.

I had two lads over in Newcastle scouting local clubs. One of them called me up and told me there was one lad playing for Wallsend Boys Club that I had to get. I knew they were good judges, so I went over and watched him play, and thought he could be good for Carlisle. Newcastle couldn't make their mind up about him, so I organised a friendly game up near Newcastle Airport and sorted the deal out after the game, at The Diamond pub in Ponteland, but I had to get the deal past the Carlisle United board first.

Peter had just turned 18 so would have to sign as a professional and would cost the club £25 a week. Carlisle had a budget for 18 professionals, which we already had on the books, so the chairman at the time told me I'd have to get rid of one to bring in Peter, which I didn't want to do. I went to a board meeting to plead my case to the nine directors. I gave them all the spiel about how good he was, and they had the vote, and they voted in favour of signing him.

The meeting dragged on before another of the directors piped up: 'It's about this boy from Wallsend who the manager wants to sign. I would like to ask the manager a question: Where is this boy going to live?' I thought to myself, *Oh no, I hadn't thought about that.* It was another £25 they'd have to dish out a week for lodgings, and the whole meeting erupted. They had another vote, and they were about to shoot it down when I had a brainwave. I said, 'Mr Chairman, I have the answer. He can come and live with me.'

I got home from the meeting, got through the door, and Camille asked me how it went. I said it went fine, but, by the way, you've got a lodger. Peter ended up living with us for about eight months until he got proper digs.

He left for Vancouver Whitecaps around the time I went and managed my boyhood club, Hearts, which was one of the worst mistakes I made, but that's another story. I told Peter not to go to Vancouver, because I knew there were a lot of big clubs that were looking at him. Anyway, he went, and eventually he came back, and I had a hand in that too. Willie McFaul, who played at Newcastle with me, including in the Fairs Cup Final, was assistant to Arthur Cox at the club then. I told Willie he should get himself to Vancouver and bring him back. Eventually they listened and he came to Newcastle, which was the right place for him. The rest is history. He's one of the finest players I've ever seen play for the club, but if he hadn't come to Carlisle, he might never have become the player that he did.

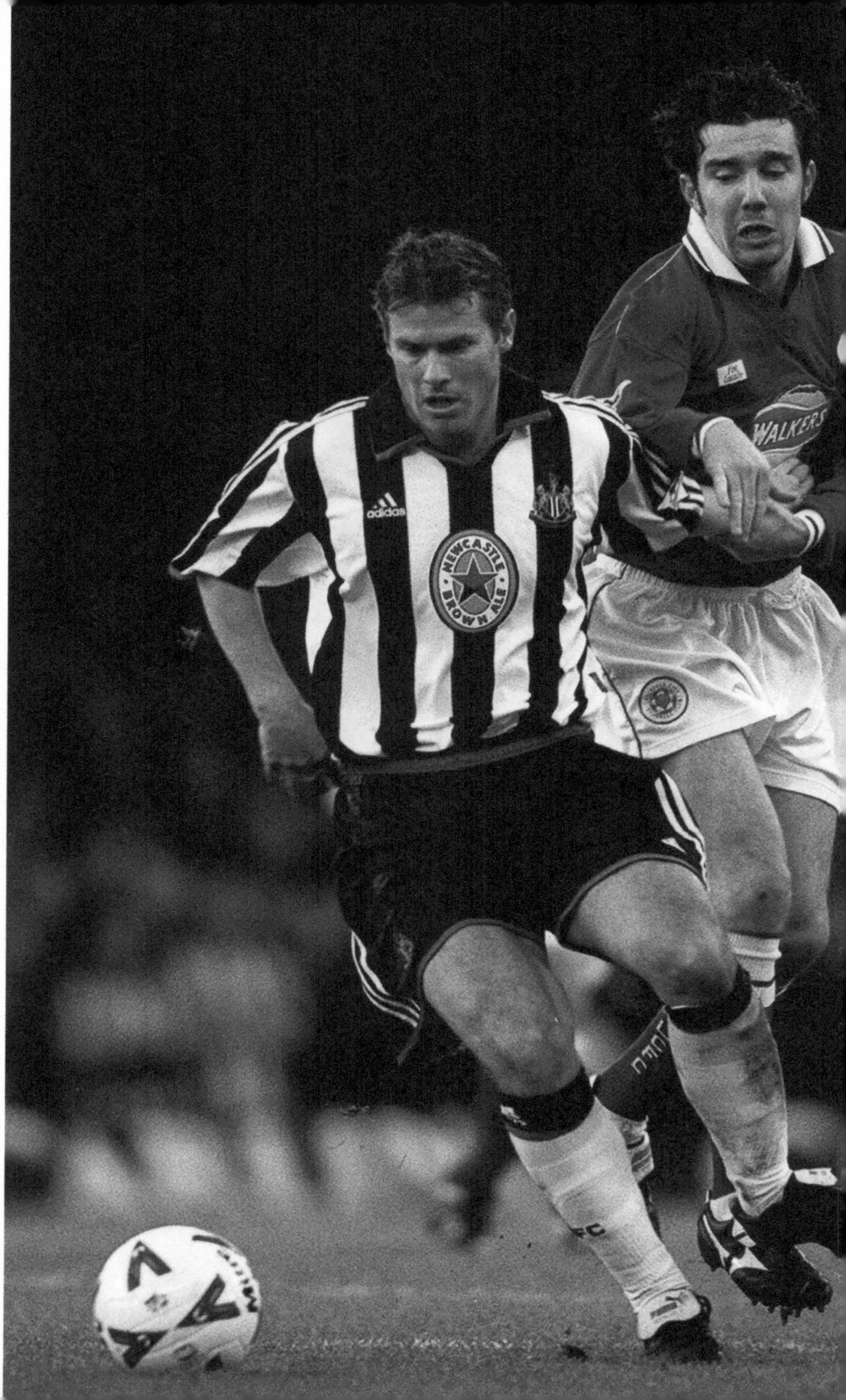

ROB LEE

Rob Lee
Midfielder
1992–2002

Londoner Rob Lee spent ten years on Tyneside, starting life with Newcastle in the old First Division and helping gain promotion to the Premier League in his first season. He went on to become an integral part of Kevin Keegan's 'Entertainers', helping his side to back-to-back second-place Premier League finishes, and earning two FA Cup runners-up medals in 1998 and 1999.

Lee was frozen out by Ruud Gullit, but after the Dutchman was sacked in 1999 was able to play for another three years at St James' Park, before leaving, having racked up more than 300 appearances.

For the match of Lee's life, he recalls the UEFA Cup first round tie against Royal Antwerp, in Belgium, the club's first foray into Europe in the best part of two decades. The dynamic midfielder scored an unprecedented hat-trick of headers to ensure Newcastle's return to continental competition began with a bang.

Royal Antwerp 0-5 Newcastle United

UEFA Cup, first round, first leg
Tuesday, 13 September 1994
Bosuil Stadion, Derne, Belgium
Attendance: 19,700

Royal Antwerp	Newcastle
Svilar	Srníček
Vangompel	Hottiger
Broeckaert	Beresford
Kulcsar	Venison
Smidts	Fox
Emmerechts	Albert
Kiekens	Lee
Porte	Beardsley (Watson)
Severeyns	Cole (Jeffrey)
Zohar (Ferreira)	Peacock
Godfroid	Sellars

Managers

Urbain Haesaert — Kevin Keegan

Goals

Lee (3), Sellars, Watson

The one thing that swung my decision to join Newcastle was Kevin Keegan. I absolutely idolised him as a boy. I had a poster of him on my bedroom wall and had to pinch myself when he asked me to come and play for him.

I was coming to the end of my contract at Charlton Athletic and had made my mind up that I wanted to try something different. I'd been at Charlton for eight years and had an agreement with the manager Alan Curbishley that I could go. I spoke to Middlesbrough first, they were in the Premiership, but decided I didn't really want to go north! I was a Londoner through and through, so turned them down. Then, all of a sudden, I had a phone call from Kevin Keegan, saying, 'Come up north and sign for Newcastle.' To have my hero ring me up and tell me I'm a good player – I just couldn't turn down the opportunity to play for him. He also told me that Newcastle was closer to London than Middlesbrough, in a bid to convince me, which I believed.

He said that I was on a little tug-boat, and Newcastle United was going to be a huge ocean liner. He said, 'Make sure you're on board here, because we are going places.' He was right. I signed, and after only a week or two of training, still playing in the second tier, he told me that I'd play for England one day. Of course, he was right again. To hear him say that to me was a massive boost. There were other players at Charlton who had more ability than me, but sometimes you just need to get the right club and manager at the right time and that's what happened for me, and that's what turned me into an international and Premier League player.

I still see Alan Curbishley now and we have a laugh and a joke about him selling me. At the time I think Charlton were top of the First Division and Newcastle were second, and we went on to win the league. He tells me now he learned when he sold me that you should never sell your best players to your rivals!

Kevin was great with me. He knew I was London through and through so he allowed me time to go home and see the family and helped me adjust, then after a couple of years I was hardly going back at all, I loved it up there.

A couple of things really made me feel at home. I was playing for a manager in Kevin, and an assistant in Terry McDermott, that I idolised. We had some great players that were a little bit older than me but that I'd been watching for years, like Barry Venison, Paul Bracewell and Kevin Sheedy, so I was enjoying myself on the pitch and off the pitch. I found people so friendly. I'm still friends with the people I lived next door to when I first moved up there. I was made to feel very welcome from the word go, not just from the club but the fans and the ordinary man on the street. I've always said that if you go up there it's like a goldfish bowl, it's one city, one team, but if you play your heart out for them, they'll love you forever, and I go back there now and they still do, so I must have done something right.

That first season I played every game in midfield, and I could see we had a very, very good team and we won the first 11 games, which propelled us onwards, and we didn't really look back. But at that moment I couldn't have known how far we'd go, and how quickly we'd get there. It was a juggernaut. No sooner had we got promotion to the Premiership than Kevin Keegan was telling Alex Ferguson we were coming after his title! I think all other managers and teams coming up would be thinking if they finish mid-table it's a good season, but Kevin wasn't like that. The minute we got in there he was saying, 'We are going to win this,' and that rubbed off on all the players.

When we got back into the top flight, expectations were there straight away, but we got beaten in our first couple of games before we went to Old Trafford, where everyone was expecting us to lose to Manchester United, and we got a point, Andy Cole scoring his first Premiership goal for us in a 1-1 draw. From that moment it was like a light bulb had switched on. We knew we could play in this league and come the end of the season we'd got ourselves to third place, which for a recently promoted team was a massive achievement. I can't remember another team coming up and finishing so high, and I'm not sure we'll see it again.

We started the 1994/95 season on fire, our best start to any top-flight season, winning five games in a row and then we played our first game in Europe in 17 years – away to Royal Antwerp. We had no real experience in the squad of playing in Europe – even Peter Beardsley had missed out when he was at Liverpool because of the ban on English sides. Terry McDermott and Kevin had both won the European Cup, but the players had next to no experience of it.

Nothing changed in the build-up to the game. Kevin picked his side – we always had the same shape – and we treated it like any other match. The only difference is we flew to it rather than going on the coach. As a side we were in our own bubble, and it's only once you retire that you realise what was happening outside of that. I've looked back and seen Newcastle fans taking over Antwerp and spoken to fans about what happened when I scored, but at the time you don't realise what's happening around the game you're playing in.

From the start we just attacked, as usual. We had Ruel Fox on one side, Scott Sellars on the other, and then we had Peter Beardsley, who had just come back from a fractured cheekbone, and, of course, Andy Cole. I was playing in midfield next to Barry Venison, who suited my style of play perfectly as I could just bomb forward and score goals.

You see midfield players now looking to get on the ball and play the perfect pass, and I barely did that! I got the ball, gave it to someone else and got in the box and got on the end of things. I look back at most of my goals and they're all very similar. That kind of midfielder is a dying art now – Frank Lampard and Steven Gerrard were the last ones to do it. With the academies it's all about getting and keeping the ball. There aren't many midfielders playing now who bomb forward and score goals.

I was in the form of my life leading up to that game, playing with confidence and scoring for fun. I thought I'd score every game, so I thought I'd get a goal that game, but not a hat-trick, certainly not of headers! I know those goals so well. The first came so quickly, within a minute. John Beresford got the ball on the left and whipped in a cross, which I chucked myself at and met it with a diving header. I wasn't bad with my head for someone not particularly tall, and I had a good leap.

I didn't have to wait long for the second one either, and I started and finished the move. I gave the ball to Foxey, who charged up the right and crossed it, and I got in front of Andy Cole to score a second. We were two up within ten minutes.

For my hat-trick goal I actually mis-controlled it, the opposing player got a tackle in and the ball ricocheted out to Marc Hottiger. I actually should have passed to him in the first place, but I was on such a high that I started going off on my own. When Marc got it, he took a couple of touches, I got myself in the box and it just came to me on my head again. I didn't know at that point that I'd scored three with my head. I knew I'd scored a hat-trick, but until a team-mate came up to me afterwards and pointed out they were all headers, I hadn't noticed.

We got five goals that day and we were saying afterwards that we couldn't believe Andy Cole hadn't got one. At that point he was scoring almost every game, so to score five without him finding the net was strange. He was involved in the goal between my second and third as he laid it off for Scott Sellars to score. Scott was usually the guy who would be setting up me or Coley, he was a fantastic player.

Steve Watson came on towards the end and scored a great individual goal to finish it off as he had been doing all season really. But the unsung hero of that day was our goalkeeper, Pavel Srníček. If I hadn't got a hat-trick I think he'd have been man of the match. What a fantastic keeper, and man, he was. But that was Newcastle, even when we battered teams we gave them chances.

I was at the club for ten years, five of those with Kevin, and he always bought better and better players and it was up to you to keep up. Any players that we bought that couldn't keep up were shipped out, so it was up to you to keep up with the new signings, whether that's Les Ferdinand, David Batty or Tino Asprilla, you had to maintain a high level or you were gone. That was something that I adjusted to well. When better players came in, I played better.

Kevin had the vision and was pulling everyone in the same direction – the owner, the manager, the players and the fans. We were letting in three or four thousand people just to watch us train! I'm not sure how that would go now because it's very secretive, but Kevin was never like that. He didn't mind people coming in. He liked it and made us sign all of the autographs, even if it took us a couple of hours.

Kevin had made Peter Beardsley captain, and when he was injured I'd step in and take the armband. When Kenny Dalglish arrived, he told me he wanted me to be his captain, and it was one of the biggest honours of my career. Not many people get the honour to be skipper of a club like Newcastle United.

One of my most memorable moments was captaining the club in the FA Cup Final in 1998, which we lost 2-0 to Arsenal. When I was little, playing for my school team, I dreamed of captaining a side in the FA Cup Final at Wembley and here I was doing it in real life. I'd grown up in the same area as Tony Adams, who was six months younger than me, and he was always the star for his Sunday League team. He lived next door to my mum and dad, so it was strange that the first time I captained my club in a cup final it was with him leading out the opposition. I grew up with former Everton and West Ham striker Tony Cottee as well, and his team used to beat my team 10-0, and he would score eight!

Newcastle always seemed to get bad luck. We were playing against an Arsenal side that were arguably the best team in Europe at the time, and they did the double that year to prove it. We'd lost Kevin Keegan halfway through the season and Kenny had come in and done a good job, but we were on a poor run of form going into that game. Saying that, we were quite lucky to get there in the first place after lowly Stevenage had forced us to a replay in our third round match.

Then for the FA Cup Final the following year, in the 1998/99 season, which we lost 2-0 to Manchester United, we came up against a team that was chasing the treble. We never got an easy ride. By that time Ruud Gullit was at the club and had stripped me of the captaincy and didn't even want to play me. He was playing me in the cup games because he had nobody else to go on the right-hand side of midfield. It was the first time I'd had that with a manager. I got on with all managers I'd played with, but not with him. I was captain when he came in after Kenny, but we just didn't see eye to eye.

It was a strange situation in that final: I knew that if we won the cup, which I was desperate to do, I'd probably have been gone, because Ruud would have been in a very strong position and he didn't want me there. I'm playing thinking if we win this game it will probably be my last outing for Newcastle. As it was, we lost the final and started the 1999 season poorly and Ruud was gone within a few games, which meant I got to have another couple of years at the club.

I turned up to pre-season training and didn't have a shirt number. Ruud took the No. 7, which I'd had the whole time I'd been at the club, away from me. There was me, Stuart Pearce and John Barnes all turning up and being told to train with the youth team, or to not come in at all. He didn't tell me himself that he'd taken the shirt, he got Steve Clarke to tell me the bad news, which he often did. I think I got caught up in the bad blood between Ruud and Alan Shearer. Al wasn't getting a game either – Ruud brought Duncan Ferguson in to replace him, but didn't realise there was no way in hell the club would sell him. Freddie Shepherd made that quite clear; there was no way he was selling Alan. I was a good friend of Alan's so maybe I got in the middle of that a little bit, or maybe he just didn't fancy me as a player. Even if that's the case, I don't think that after what I'd done for the club that I deserved to have my shirt taken away from me.

Bobby Robson came in after Ruud left, and he was a great guy. He had what he called his 'blue chip brigade' of me, Warren Barton, Gary Speed and Shay Given, senior players that he wanted in the team. He got Alan back in and in his first game we beat Sheffield Wednesday 8-0. He was like Kevin, getting people laughing and joking, pulling in the right direction again.

He almost got us to the FA Cup Final again in 2000, but again we fell just short, when we were beaten 2-1 by Chelsea in the semi-final. That should have been the final. They had such a good team, with players like Marcel Desailly, Gus Poyet and Dennis Wise, so it would have been a showpiece final. We felt whoever would win that game would win the cup – we thought that, and I think Chelsea thought that too, and so it proved to be as they beat Villa 1-0 at Wembley.

We hadn't played well in the last two finals but in that game, which was under Bobby Robson, we played very well. Bar Gus Poyet and his two great goals, we'd have won, and I think we deserved to win, but you don't always get what you deserve in football. I got a header to equalise in that game, which wasn't much consolation if I'm honest. At the time of writing I'm the last Newcastle player to score at Wembley, but would, of course, rather not have that record.

Looking back, going to Newcastle was the best decision I ever made, on and off the pitch. I loved it up there, I loved the people, and football-wise it put me on a different level. I went from being a winger at Charlton in the old First Division to 18 months later playing for my country in central midfield. Representing your country was the dream for players back then, but I'm not sure it is now. For youngsters these days it's more about the money. Although we were well paid then, I think players now go into the game to become wealthy, whereas my aim was to play for England, to play at Wembley, to play in an FA Cup Final, and I was lucky enough to be able to do all of those things.

Kevin always said that football was entertainment. Go and entertain them. And that's what we did. I look back to when I was a kid, and if there was one way I'd have wanted to play football it would have been that way. I loved it. Rarely did we speak about the opposition, it was always what we could do.

The 'Entertainers' team is part of history. People will say we didn't win anything, and we didn't, but we played the way we wanted to play. I genuinely wouldn't have swapped my five years under Kevin, playing the way we played, for a Premiership winners' medal playing long-ball football. I had such a good time, I enjoyed every single game; even when I was injured or knackered, I wanted to play.

I enjoyed it so much, but it goes so quickly. I'm grateful to be able to look back at so many wonderful years at Newcastle United. The fans are amazing. They've been starved of success for so long and I'm just so hopeful that can be put right soon.

FABRICIO COLOCCINI

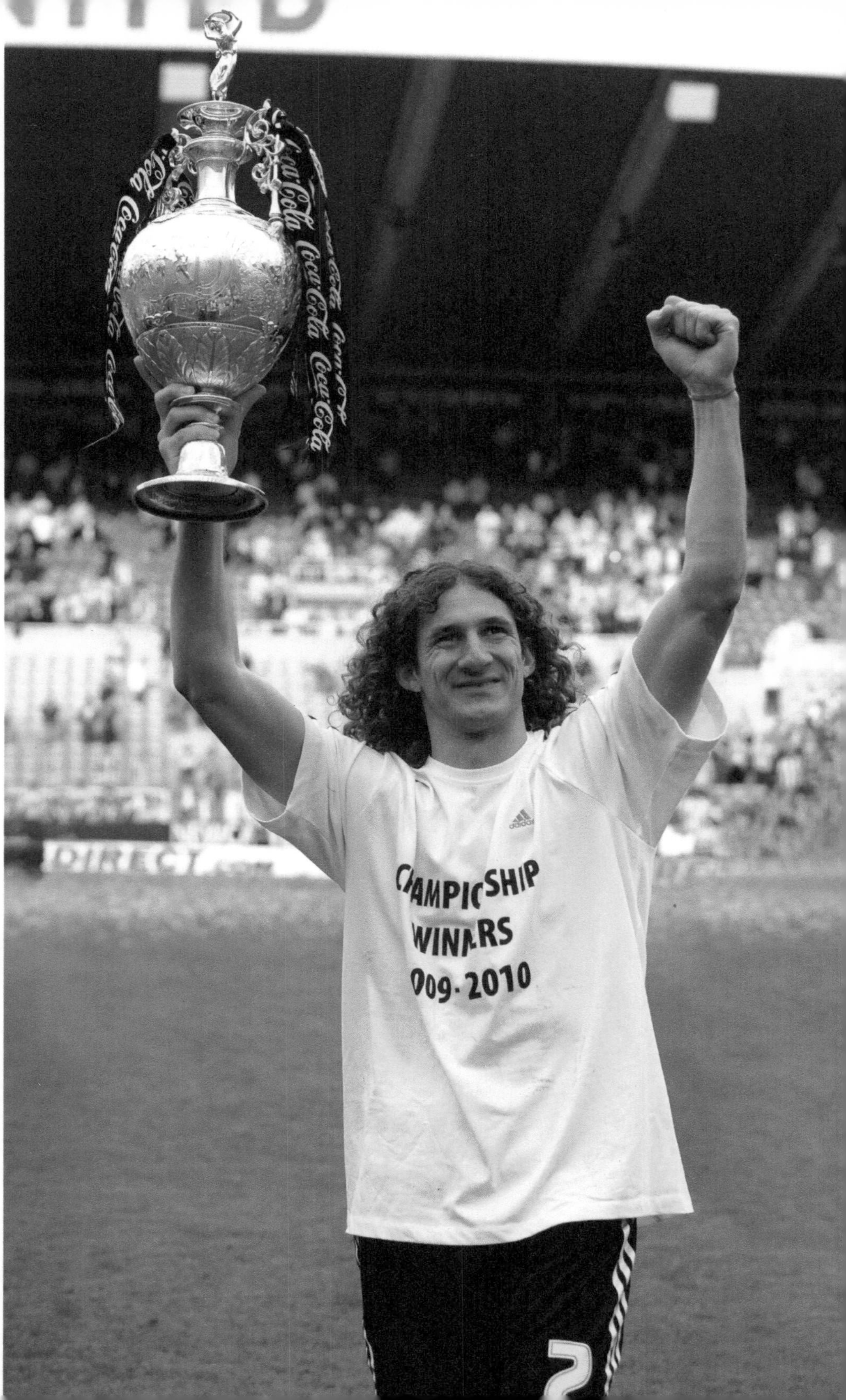

Fabricio Coloccini
Defender
2008–2016

For eight years, Fabricio Coloccini's trademark curly locks were an almost ever-present in the heart of the Newcastle United defence. The tough-tackling centre-back rode out the storm of relegation to the Championship after his first season on Tyneside, deciding to stay to help the club earn back its rightful place in the Premier League, turning down lucrative offers from top-flight rivals in the process.

The Argentine emerged from his season in the second tier a better, more consistent player, his style of play and dedication earning him a badge of leadership in the dressing room and cult hero status with the supporters on Tyneside. His inclusion in two 'Teams of the Season' in the space of three seasons – in the Championship in 2009/10 and Premier League in 2011/12 – are testament to the quality he brought to the English game.

Coloccini went on to rack up almost 300 appearances for the Magpies, most as captain, and featured in some of the club's most memorable matches of recent years, including the 4-4 draw with Arsenal at St James' Park, arguably the Premier League's greatest-ever comeback.

Newcastle 4-4 Arsenal

Premier League
Saturday, 5 February 2011
St James' Park, Newcastle
Attendance: 51,561

Newcastle	**Arsenal**
Harper	Szczęsny
Coloccini	Sagna
Enrique	Koscielny
Simpson	Djourou (Squillaci)
Williamson	Clichy
Nolan	Diaby
Barton	Fàbregas
Gutiérrez	Walcott (Eboué)
Tioté	Wilshere
Lovenkrands (Ranger)	Arshavin (Rosický)
Best	Van Persie

Managers

Alan Pardew	Arsène Wenger

Goals

Barton (2), Best, Tioté	Walcott, Djourou, Van Persie (2)

Before I came to Newcastle, Tottenham wanted to sign me. But at that moment, in the 2006/07 season, I was at Deportivo de La Coruña in Spain, and La Liga was the best league in the world. I said no because I wanted to stay in Spain for a few more years. But after that the Premier League started to grow up, to improve, and when Newcastle came to Deportivo in 2008 and asked to sign me, I said, 'Yes, let's do it.'

Jonás Gutiérrez had just joined Newcastle, and he was a close friend of mine, so that attracted me, and I knew the Newcastle fans were amazing. In Argentina we have amazing, passionate atmospheres at games, and I liked that. Everyone told me Newcastle fans were the best fans in England and, when I signed, I found out they were right.

I spoke with Kevin Keegan and he was very persuasive. He told me that they were going to sign big players and build a great squad, but nothing really happened with this and that's why he left soon after. We were relegated after my first season and that was very hard. We had lots of managers that season, and too many players, big players like Michael Owen, Mark Viduka, Obafemi Martins, Geremi and Damien Duff, but too many, and a lot of them were coming towards the end of their careers. When you have a lot of players it's hard to keep everybody happy.

Michael Owen had a lot of injuries, particularly with his groin. He played one or two games and then would get injured. He lived in Liverpool still, which was a little strange. One time we had to play away in a cup game, and I was at the training ground, parked up in my car, listening to music. I heard a strange thumping noise. I thought it was the engine so I turned it off, but I could still hear the noise. Maybe it was the music? So I turned it down. Then I looked out of the window and saw a helicopter – it was Michael Owen coming to the training ground from Liverpool. For us that was strange, I had never seen that in Argentina.

We were relegated by just one point, so I think we were unlucky as well. After we went down, I had offers from other clubs in the Premier League – Tottenham and West Ham were both very interested – but I said no because I felt like I had more to achieve at Newcastle and I'm very glad I made that decision.

For me, going down to the Championship was a good experience, playing in a different league in England and learning more. The fans were always there for us, whether that was in the Premier League or the Championship. The Newcastle fans are very special. Every week – home or away – they were there for us, and the year that we won the Championship was a great season. A lot of players were gone, but the players that stayed wanted to be there.

The manager was Chris Hughton and he was a lovely man. Jonás, José Enrique and I all played together, and we always tried to play good, passing football, but Chris would always be shouting from the sideline for us to play long-ball for the striker. We knew how to play, so we didn't change, and we were winning so it was okay.

Chris was replaced by Alan Pardew in December 2010, the season after we'd won promotion, and he was also a great guy. We always felt like we had his support. For some of us players from abroad, he understood that sometimes life could be a bit hard being away from home, and one season I had a personal problem with my marriage, and he gave me a few days off to focus on what I needed to focus on. When I went out on to the pitch I had an extra motivation – I'd do what I could for him as well, not just the team and the fans.

Alan was also the first manager to give me the captain's armband. When Kevin Nolan left, Alan came to me and told me that I was going to lead the team. For me to become captain was very, very special, especially considering I'm from Argentina, and the countries have a mixed history with the Falklands War and other things, like the 1986 World Cup! I felt very proud to be given the armband. It was amazing. I wasn't a big talker, but I tried to lead by example, showing the players how I thought things should be done. If I had to do talking that was okay, but I'd try to be what a captain should be in training and on the pitch.

My first game as captain was against Wigan in our first year back in the Premier League, a game that will always stick in my mind. We went two goals behind midway through the first half, with ex-Newcastle player Charles N'Zogbia scoring twice in two minutes. We came back in the second half and with 18 minutes to go substitute Shola Ameobi scored a diving header from a ball from Jonás Gutiérrez. Then in stoppage time I scored the equaliser, which was an amazing feeling. There was a corner, which came across to me at the far post, and I headed it past the Wigan goalkeeper Ali Al-Habsi.

I remember celebrating madly, and the fans going crazy too. I could hear my name chanted all around the stadium. They had a song for me, which was a little bit rude, and everyone started to sing it! Centre-backs don't often get songs – usually they're for the strikers because they score the goals – so for me it was special to have a song, but at that time I didn't know what it meant. My team-mates told me, and I thought it was very funny. Even in Argentina, the words were printed in the newspapers.

Another special match for me personally was the 1-1 draw with Tottenham in January 2011. It was my 100th appearance for Newcastle, and my birthday, and I scored my best-ever goal for the club. The ball was crossed by Danny Guthrie, and I was standing on the left-hand side of the box. I chested it down before hitting it right into the far corner. That one felt very special because usually I only scored headers. It was also special because Tottenham had tried to sign me before I signed for Newcastle, and again in 2010, but by then I was the captain, so there was no way I could leave.

At Newcastle, you never know what will happen in a game. I never thought about the score, even if we went a few goals down. We just always tried to do what we could, because we knew we could always turn it around. It was crazy.

No game sums that up more than the 4-4 draw with Arsenal in February 2011. We went one down within a minute when Theo Walcott scored, then Johan Djourou and Robin van Persie struck to put us 3-0 down with only ten minutes on the clock. Van Persie scored again to make it four, and at that point nobody would have given us a chance of coming back, but we did.

Even though we were 4-0 down, we still believed. We'd been in the game. Arsenal had very good players and every time they took a shot they scored. We kept going and managed to get a draw in one of the best Premier League comebacks ever.

In the second half, Abou Diaby was sent off for Arsenal, and that gave us a boost. Before we knew it we were back in it – Joey Barton scored two penalties, and Leon Best scored too, getting on the end of a cross from José Enrique to make it 4-3. Then Cheick Tioté stepped up to score a goal I'll never forget, right at the end. Cheick always tried to shoot from distance, and always the ball would end up in the stands, so when he received it at the edge of the box after Arsenal failed to clear a free kick, I expected that to just happen again. I was right behind him when the ball got to him and thought, *Oh my god, not again*, but he hit it perfectly and it flew in. I couldn't believe it. It showed a game is never over until it's over.

The only game in which I ever thought it was over early on was in 2015 when we got beaten 6-1 by Manchester City at the Etihad, with Sergio Agüero scoring five. When we were 3-0 down, I said to myself, 'Okay, this is over.' We couldn't get the ball! I played with Agüero for Argentina, and he was amazing. I remember people used to think that for a player to succeed in the Premier League he had to be tall and strong. I had a conversation with the kit man about him coming from Atlético Madrid. He said, 'He's going to be shit.' He thought he was too small for the Premier League, and that he looked fat, but I knew he was going to be a good player, and he showed that when he scored five against us.

Joey Barton, one of the heroes of the Arsenal comeback, was a big player in the dressing room. He was very funny and always playing jokes. During my first few months at the club, I turned up to training and Joey had put a picture of the Falkland Islands on my locker, with a Union Jack flag on it! I said I didn't really know much about the Falklands, but in reality I'm very patriotic, so I knew all about it. I just didn't want to have any confrontation.

Once, in training, we were doing a warm-up, running backwards, and Joey crouched behind me and made me fall over. I didn't think it was funny at the time – I was angry. I didn't speak English then. I talked to Jonás and said, 'Listen, tell Joey Barton that I'm not his friend. Is he wanting to fight?' Jonás said not to worry, that it was just a joke! I think it was because I was a new player, it was some kind of initiation. Once I found out he was just joking with me, Joey and I became really good friends in the changing room.

The 2011/12 season was a great season. For the first part of the campaign we were near the top, and we ended up finishing fifth. We had excellent players like Mathieu Debuchy, Sébastien Bassong and José Enrique. Our strikers as well were very good – Demba Ba and Papiss Cissé. Papiss scored one of the best goals I've ever seen on a football pitch against Chelsea. It was unbelievable. He was on the left and hit it on the volley with his right foot. I watched it fly over Petr Čech and I couldn't believe what I was seeing.

Hatem Ben Arfa was another fantastic player. He had everything, but I don't know what happened with him. Even in France, everyone said he was the next Zidane, but I always say that a player must have a lot of things, not just ability. A top player must have discipline and commitment.

At Newcastle, I'd always stay late at training with Jonás, because I enjoyed it. We'd go to the gym when other players would leave. That wasn't because the other players weren't professional, but for us it was easier as our families weren't living nearby. Jonás and I had a special bond, both being from Argentina, and we're still very close.

Sometimes Jonás would put on his Argentinian music on very high volume in the changing room, to the annoyance of the other players. I remember Steve Harper, who had been at the club for a long time, asking him to turn it off and Jonás laughing and telling him to shut up. It was very funny.

I was in the Premier League 'Team of the Season' for 2011/12, which makes me very proud. It makes me happier now than I was in that moment. It was nice then but now I've finished my career and I start to think about what I did at Newcastle, I can look back and see what an achievement that was. Our dream was to get into the Champions League but unfortunately we couldn't do it. There were so many good teams. We had good players as well, but the fans didn't like our owner, Mike Ashley, which made things a bit difficult.

I don't think it was to do with the amount of money spent that things didn't go better, but maybe because of scouting. There was perhaps not as much work behind the players that the club signed as there should have been. The network of scouts wasn't there that was in place at other clubs.

In 2013/14 I did come close to leaving. That was when I split up with my wife and my kids went back to Argentina, so it was very tough on me. Alan Pardew told me he wanted me to keep going with Newcastle. It was during the international break so he told me to take that time to go to Argentina, and then to come back and keep going with Newcastle. For me that was what I needed. Once a month or once every two months I went to Argentina and was able to be with my kids. Alan understood that and made sure I got it. I'm very grateful to him for that.

I made the right decision because I had some more great times at the club. When Rafa Benitez came in as manager in February 2016 and we were battling against relegation and he told me I could go to Argentina to see my family, I didn't feel like I could do that. We were not playing well and were bottom of the league – I was captain and felt like I should stay in Newcastle. That was very tough for me, but my club needed me.

When I eventually left, after we were relegated for a second time, I went back to Argentina because of my kids. I missed them. I also had the opportunity to go and play for my team in Argentina, San Lorenzo, where my kids were. It was difficult to leave but it was the right decision for me and my family.

During my time at the club, I played with some incredible players and was able to earn my place in the national team, even when we went down to the Championship. Agüero, who scored five against me in 2015, was amazing to play with, but the best I've played with was Lionel Messi. For me he's the greatest, not just as a player but as a person, too. Maradona will always be up there, but

Messi is so humble. I think this makes the difference. Maradona was our coach for a time as well, and he was different to what I was used to, a real character.

I was in Bolivia, coaching the Venezuela U20s at a tournament during the 2022 World Cup, so I watched the final on TV. I spoke with my kids on the phone after we won, and I started to cry, which was the first time I'd ever cried about football. I think everyone in Argentina cried that day. I texted Leo a message to say well done afterwards – I think he must have had millions of messages.

I look back now and have many, many happy memories of my time at Newcastle. I met so many lovely people during my eight years at the club – the kit man, the doctors, physios – everyone was amazing. I still stay in touch with some of my ex-team-mates like Jonás, Ryan Taylor, Mike Williamson and Rob Elliot.

Being at Newcastle was the highlight of my career. I felt loved by everybody at the club, and the fans. That's why I still have a house in Newcastle – I love coming back. I'll always have a bond and connection with this city and these people. It's a very special place.

FRANK CLARK

Frank Clark
Defender
1962–1975

From watching from the front row of St James' Park in the early 1950s to lifting the Fairs Cup in 1969, Frank Clark will always have a strong association with Newcastle United. Having signed from amateur club Crook Town, Clark went on to play 457 league and cup matches for the Magpies, becoming their fourth-highest appearance-maker in the process. Alongside the likes of Tommy Gibb, Bob Moncur and David Craig, Clark made up one of the toughest back lines in England, a defensive unit that was a huge factor behind their European triumph.

After controversially being given a free transfer by the club in 1975, Clark was quickly snapped up by Brian Clough at Nottingham Forest, where he went on to add to his collection of silverware with, among other trophies, the 1977/78 First Division title and a European Cup triumph in 1979.

Although Clark has fond memories of the 2-0 win versus Bolton Wanderers in 1965, a result that propelled the club back to the First Division after a four-year hiatus in front of almost 60,000 delighted supporters, for the match of his life Clark picks out a 6-0 League Cup demolition of Doncaster Rovers. Although arguably a less dramatic and ultimately less important victory, for Clark it remains a milestone match. The same will go for those 15,000 fans who made their way through the turnstiles at St James' Park on that Monday evening in 1973 – they could never have imagined what they'd soon be witnessing. After more than 400 appearances in black and white, 'Super' Frank Clark was about to break his duck ...

Newcastle United 6-0 Doncaster Rovers

League Cup, second round
Monday, 8 October 1973
St James' Park
Attendance: 14,865

Newcastle	Doncaster
McFaul	Book
Nattrass	Reed
Clark	Ternent
McDermott	Irvine
Howard	Brookes
Moncur	Wignall
Cassidy	Murray
Smith	Elwiss
Macdonald	O'Callaghan
Robson	Kitchen
Hibbitt	Moore (Higgins)

Managers

Joe Harvey — Bill Ridding

Goals

Robson (2),
Macdonald (3),
Clark

I was a Newcastle supporter all my life before I played for them. My mother and father took me to the games when I was young. I'd watch Newcastle one week and Gateshead the next, as they played alternately home and away, so I'd get to see a match every weekend. I used to sit on the wall around the track at St James' Park. In those days they didn't have fences, and at Newcastle there was a track around the pitch, with a very low wall at the bottom of the terraces, with the adults passing kids down over the heads of the supporters so they could sit on the wall and watch the game.

I spent most of that time seeing games from the front, until I was older and moved back on to the terraces. I can remember sitting there seeing players like Joe Harvey, Bobby Mitchell, Frank Brennan and, of course, my idol Jackie Milburn. Jackie was just a fantastic player and an even better human being. What a wonderful man. I got to know him quite well when I was playing in the team. By that time he was a journalist, but much too nice to be a journalist! He hated criticising people. He was just such a lovely man and I was lucky to know him.

I grew up in a village called Highfield about eight miles west of Newcastle and played for my school team. I started off as a centre-back, probably because I was usually the biggest player in the team. I also played for my local village side, which already had a couple of good central defenders, so they put me at full-back and that stuck. I was then signed by Crook Town, a top amateur team at the time, to replace a very accomplished England amateur international left-back who was already on their books but had suffered a serious injury and was forced to pack the game up. The position stuck and that's where I was for ever more.

Amateur football was very strong in the North East and I won an FA Amateur Cup medal and played for the England Youth and England Amateur sides. I assumed I'd be on most clubs' radars, and Newcastle had been trying to get me to sign for two or three years, but, when I was 15 or 16, they had a very poor reputation for looking after young players. It wasn't until Joe Harvey joined as manager in 1961 that it started to improve. The club was in a bit of a mess when he got the job; they'd been relegated to the old Second Division and he needed a clear-out to get them back to where they deserved to be.

I never had a burning ambition to be a professional footballer, so I stayed at school and did my A-Levels, with the aim of going to university to study chemistry. However, I didn't do as well in my A-Levels as I should have, so didn't get into university. I stayed in the North East and, eventually, in 1962 signed on a part-time basis for Newcastle, while working in the biochemistry department of the city's Royal Victoria Infirmary. I was working there full-time, training two nights a week and playing in the reserves on the weekend. Who knows, I might not have followed a career in football if my exam results had been different! My aim was to go to university to earn a degree. I hadn't thought much further ahead than that, but my decision was made for me.

The winter of 1962–63 was particularly severe, and football almost came to a stop for about two months. I was playing for Newcastle reserves in the first game since the shutdown, away to Liverpool, and I broke my leg in a tackle with Tommy Smith, or Tommy Smith broke my leg in a tackle with me! I was out for 11 months, during which time I decided to give up the hospital job and become a full-time footballer. I started playing again in January 1964, in the reserves, and got a couple of games in the first team at the back end of that season. The following campaign, 1964/65, I started as first-choice left-back and played every game as we won the Second Division, earning us a place in the First Division for the first time in five years.

We earned promotion with a 2-0 win on Good Friday 1965, which I remember very well. The thing I remember most was Wyn Davies playing for Bolton and being a real handful. He'd go on to have a great career with us. He gave us a torrid time until big John McGrath got a couple of tackles in and slowed him down a bit, and we went on to win the game comfortably. If you wanted someone to have a fight for you, John was the guy to go to. He was a big, tough centre-back, and very noisy, that was until his wife, who was about a foot and a half shorter than him, was around – then he was as quiet as a mouse.

Willie Penman scored the first goal in the first half, before Jim Iley scored the decisive second goal with a shot that bounced about five times before it nestled in the back of the net around the hour mark. Afterwards we couldn't really celebrate that much because straight after the game we had to fly down to London to play Crystal Palace on the Saturday, before coming back to face Bolton again, this time away, on Easter Monday. In the good old days, we were playing three games in four days.

It was an unforgettable weekend. After the game against Bolton, at home the supporters gave us a fantastic reception, and we went into the stands to acknowledge the fans. The captain, Stan Anderson, took his shirt off and threw it into the crowd. We all followed suit and threw our shirts into the fans, and, once we were back in the changing rooms, we got a right rollicking from Joe Harvey because that was the club's only set of shirts! One of the directors, Stan Seymour, had a sports shop, so someone had to race down there to get a new set before we went down to London. I sometimes wonder where those shirts we threw into the crowd ended up. I wish I still had mine! I was obviously delighted to be able to help the team earn promotion, playing constantly in the side.

In the summer before our first season back in the First Division, a local journalist published an article in the *Chronicle* about the upcoming campaign, in which he wrote: 'Surely even Frank Clark's mother doesn't think he's good enough to play in the First Division,' which I didn't think was particularly nice of him. It upset me quite a bit at the time; it was my first proper bit of criticism and I was really disappointed. But afterwards my mother said to me, 'Yes, I think you can,' so he was wrong, wasn't he! I went on to have a wonderful career in the famous black and white and became the club's fourth-highest appearance-maker of all time. Records like that aren't something I pay particular attention to, but I'm proud to have played that many games for such a fantastic club.

I didn't score in more than 400 appearances for Newcastle, because in those days full-backs hardly crossed the halfway line, not like today when they're expected to be playing almost like wingers. David Craig, who was on the opposite flank to me, and I thought our job was to defend. But that changed when we played Doncaster Rovers in the League Cup in 1973. Malcolm Macdonald was in the team then and he scored a fantastic hat-trick, one of many he got for the club, and Keith Robson got another two to put us 5-0 up.

I went up for a corner, which was pretty much the only reason I'd head over the halfway line, and even then I didn't do it that often! I was just outside the penalty area, waiting for the ball to come back out, and somehow it found its way to me from the left. Not even thinking about it, I hit it first time and couldn't believe it as I saw it fly into the back of the net! Unfortunately, I don't think there's any video evidence of it, because I'd love to watch it back.

The place erupted, it was absolutely incredible. The crowd invaded the pitch and raced over to celebrate with me – they were all over me! I got mobbed outside of the dressing room after the game as well; they wouldn't go home! I felt a bit embarrassed really. Later, when I was at Nottingham Forest, I played with Terry Curran – an ex-Doncaster player – and he told me Rovers couldn't believe what was going on, a pitch invasion for the sixth goal in the second round of the League Cup! I actually felt a bit embarrassed about it.

My team-mates were over the moon for me. It had become a bit of a standing joke. I used to get the mickey taken out of me for having never scored in so many games, but it was all good-natured. Malcolm used to give me the most stick, but when it went in he was all over me. He and I used to argue about him not working hard enough, and at the end of the argument he'd say, 'Okay, put your goals on the table.' He could lay down his 30 goals a season and I'd always have zero, so I'd never win the argument. Malcolm was a huge character in the dressing room, fantastic on the pitch but larger than life off it too. He opened a men's outfitters in Newcastle and I ended up being one of his best customers.

Joe was an excellent manager who took the club from a very precarious position in the Second Division to winning a European competition in 1969 – the Fairs Cup. He kept us in the top league after that and always brought in players that he thought would entertain the fans. He was aware of the need to put on a good show for the supporters. I wouldn't want to compare that team with 'The Entertainers' of the 90s – that side was all down to Kevin Keegan's philosophy – but Joe had a good eye for a player and never really complicated the game. He kept it simple and was a great all-round bloke. I can't remember what he said to me after I scored, but he probably laughed along with the rest of the players.

Unbelievably, I then went and scored my second goal for the club just a few weeks later in a Texaco Cup game against Birmingham. Big Dave Latchford was in goal and I hit a shot from about 25 yards with my left foot and it flew past him. It was great scoring two in such quick succession after such a long time without one, but it didn't go to my head. That one is on YouTube so there's definitely proof it happened!

I had 13 years at the club, and winning the Fairs Cup was definitely a highlight. I have a lot of very fond memories about it. Nobody expected us to qualify for it in the first place and once we were there nobody gave us a chance – the London media said we'd shame English football with our performances. We were the underdogs for every game so we went out and just enjoyed ourselves – and kept winning.

For us to win the Fairs Cup was an amazing achievement for a team that was written off from day one, especially considering we beat the likes of Feyenoord, Real Zaragoza, Sporting Lisbon and Rangers, and then, of course, Újpest Dózsa in the final, who were touted as the best team in Europe at the time. I can say with hand on heart that I valued that win on an equal level with claiming the European Cup with Nottingham Forest a few years later.

I had no choice in my move away from Newcastle. The 1974/75 campaign had been a bit of a disappointment really, especially coming straight after a season in which we got to the FA Cup

Final, where we played against Liverpool. We were hoping to push on with players like Macdonald, John Tudor and Terry Hibbitt, but it just didn't happen. I'd played most of the games and Alan Kennedy was coming through the ranks at the time and pushing to get into the team, so I played quite a few games as a centre-back to accommodate him.

Then, on the last day of the season, we lost 2-1 to Birmingham at home, and I was sat in the changing room with Keith Burkinshaw, who was the first-team coach, when Joe walked in and said, 'I've got some bad news for you lads: I've been pushed upstairs. Keith, you've been sacked and Frank, you've been given a free transfer,' which meant the same as being sacked. I couldn't believe it, it was an absolutely shattering blow to me. We had just moved into a new house in Whitley Bay. I went home after the game and found my wife putting some curtains up. I said, 'I hope you can take those down and move them somewhere else, because we could be on the move.'

To this day, I don't know why they did it. I assume it was a decision by the board who, in their wisdom, decided I was surplus to requirements. They tried to put out a story that I was injury-prone, which really annoyed me, but then I went and played 104 consecutive games for Nottingham Forest, so that proved that was a load of rubbish. That was the way of things in those days; they didn't give a toss.

The move to Forest came about after a phone call from Brian Clough. Someone tipped him off that I'd been given a free transfer and he gave me a ring. We arranged to meet at a hotel at Scotch Corner on the A1, about halfway between the clubs, and we went from there. My car broke down on the way, in the Tyne Tunnel. This was in the days before mobile phones, but somehow I got in touch with my wife, who let the hotel know I'd be late. They then passed the information on to Brian. Fortunately, he waited for me, and I walked in about an hour and a half late and the deal was done.

Newcastle appointed Gordon Lee the week after I'd left, and one of the first things he did when he got the job was to ring and ask me to come back! He was furious when he heard what they'd done, but it was too late by then. Even if I hadn't gone to Forest, I wouldn't have gone back after the way I'd been treated. My decision to move there was justified in the end; they did me a favour.

Things may have ended negatively with the club, but I've been a supporter all my life and still am now. Certain individuals at the club, who are now long gone, were responsible for kicking me out, but that definitely doesn't colour my affection for Newcastle United. I have only good thoughts and feelings about the club, and I always will.

LEE CLARK

Lee Clark
Midfielder
1990–1997 and 2005–2006

A dynamic midfielder who always gave his all for his beloved Newcastle, Lee Clark still holds a special place in the hearts of supporters on Tyneside. Coming through the club's youth system, he helped them achieve promotion in 1993, and was a vital cog in the Kevin Keegan machine that pushed for honours in the first few years of the Premier League.

Arguably Clark's most notorious moment was not in the black and white of Newcastle United, but in an anti-Sunderland T-shirt that he was photographed wearing before the 1999 FA Cup Final. Although playing for the Black Cats at the time, Clark was a die-hard Newcastle fan and still went to their matches when his footballing schedule allowed. Although the photograph printed by the tabloids of Clark in the shirt, with the phrase 'Sad Mackem B**tards' emblazoned on the front, spelled the end of his Sunderland career, for Newcastle fans it only endeared Clark to them even more.

Clark was one of their own, a lad from Wallsend who used to watch his beloved Magpies from the stands at St James' Park, and who went on to achieve the dream of every football fan by playing for the club he loved.

Newcastle United 7-1 Leicester City

First Division (second tier)
Sunday, 9 May 1993
St James' Park
Attendance: 30,129

Newcastle	Leicester
Srníček	Poole
Venison	Hill
Beresford (Peacock)	Whitlow
Robinson	Smith
Scott	Walsh
Howey (Kilcline)	Lewis (Gee)
Lee	Mills
Cole	Thompson
Kelly	Oldfield
Clark	Joachim (Grayson)
Sellars	Lowe

Managers

Kevin Keegan	Brian Little

Goals

Cole (3), Lee, Kelly (3)	Walsh

It was almost by accident that I ended up playing for Newcastle. When I used to watch the team in the early 1980s I'd be standing on the terraces at the Gallowgate End and I didn't understand how these guys got the chance to play for the club. I thought that was beyond someone like me, a kid brought up in Walker on the banks of the Tyne.

Even getting into football was an accident. I was in the infants at school, only six years old, and ended up playing in the school team with a load of 11-year-olds! The school coach, a man named Jim Horrocks, who was a great bloke and played a massive role in my football life, was the guy who gave me my first chance. I was just kicking a ball around in the school yard and he walked past and asked me if I had my boots with me, because the school team was short of a couple of players for a game that afternoon. The school was at the top of the street and my house was at the bottom, so I ran home and got my boots. I was a sub but got to come on, and I was absolutely tiny compared to everyone else.

From then on I started every game. That's when I got scouted for Wallsend Boys Club by a guy called Brian Clark, who also had a massive impact on my career. My teacher had to explain to him that I was only six, which he couldn't believe. The Northumberland FA had rules where if you were playing in a school's under-11s side, the youngest you could be was nine, so the school tweaked things a bit – every time I played I was someone else on the team sheet.

There were so many good players at Wallsend Boys Club at that time. Alan Shearer was a couple of years above me, and below me were players like Steve Watson, Robbie Elliott, Alan Thompson and Michael Carrick. I was a few years behind the likes of Steve Bruce and Peter Beardsley, but their pictures were on the wall to give us all motivation.

As things progressed, I was asked to go into Newcastle United's Centre of Excellence, the equivalent of the academy now, and started training there two or three times a week, playing friendlies. When I got to 13 or 14 there was quite a bit of interest in me, but it didn't matter which clubs were coming in for me, I was always going to sign for Newcastle. I got offered a long-term contract as a schoolboy and then a professional contract. I went on to make my debut at 17 in September 1990 and that was like living the dream for me – I knew how many lads would love to have had that opportunity. I'd done something that I never believed was possible, playing for the team I loved.

When I first broke into the team I hadn't passed my driving test so I used to get the bus in to the matches. I'd get on in Wallsend and travel to Haymarket bus station and walk to the ground from there to go and play. The bus driver would let me on without paying sometimes, especially if I'd had a good game!

That was just normal life for me and I didn't know anything different. I can remember the old days when I used to go and watch from the stands, with the likes of Keegan, Beardsley, Waddle and McDermott playing for the Toon. Over Christmas and New Year there would be no public transport so I'd walk from our house in Walker to St James' with my brother and my dad, stopping at every pub on the way. I was a bit of a chubby teenager because I'd get a Coke and a packet of crisps at every pub!

After struggling in the 1991/92 season under Ossie Ardiles, in 1992/93 we won promotion to the recently formed Premiership, largely down to the manager, Kevin Keegan. He had his first full pre-season with us, and from then on set such high standards. He made unbelievable signings, with the likes of Barry Venison, John Beresford, Scott Sellars, Rob Lee, Paul Bracewell and, of course, Andy Cole. I'd played with Coley in England youth teams, so knew him well. He was a quiet lad. People called it arrogance but it wasn't, he was very shy. At the start he didn't really know anybody and found it difficult to make conversations with others. Kevin had asked my opinion on him, and a little while later we were travelling to Swindon on the team bus when I got a phone call from the manager, who said, 'I've got a little surprise for you, I've got your mate.' I told him he'd made a great decision, and £1.25m proved a bargain in the end. I don't think Coley in his wildest dreams would have thought he'd have scored at the rate he did for us, but he was a perfect fit for Newcastle. Year on year Kevin knew what pieces were required for his jigsaw puzzle to come together and that's what he did.

We demanded high standards of each other and fought tooth and nail on the training pitch because we knew we had to work to get into the team, so the intensity of training was like a matchday. We weren't afraid to fall out with each other on the pitch because we were all determined to win. We didn't have this mentality that we looked after one another. If we felt someone wasn't doing their job in a game we wouldn't be slow at telling them. But it was never personal, and after the game we'd be back to being great pals again. We all wanted to win, and if it had to take a bit of a fall-out on the pitch to achieve that, then so be it.

We had a great social life together. We never did it in cliques, there was always an invitation for everybody to go out, whether that was just the lads or with girlfriends and wives too. We got on really well and that's still the case now. Whenever we bump into each other, those great friendships are still there.

That year we won our first 11 games, and getting 33 points out of a possible 33 really set us on our way, and we didn't look back from there. It came to the end of the season and we had the week of our dreams. On the Tuesday we went to Grimsby and won the league with a 2-0 win, so there was a fair bit of partying travelling back from there. We had a game in hand, which we played just two days later, against Oxford United. We were 1-0 down after the first half and even though we'd won the league, Kevin came in at half-time and gave us a real dressing down. We went on to win 2-1, with me getting a lovely goal from about 25 yards out.

We had the trophy presentation on the Sunday against Leicester. There was a real party atmosphere and the weather was unbelievable, with the sun shining and the stadium packed out. Everyone thought it was going to be one of those games where it's not played at any sort of tempo because you've already done your job. Leicester were flying, in the play-offs, but if results went against them, they could have been caught. But some of the football we played that day was incredible, it really summed up the season. It reminded everyone of what we were about: 6-0 up at half-time, winning 7-1 when it could have been double figures. I watched the highlights back recently and some of the goals we scored were unbelievable – the passing, the movement, the team ethic – we just blew them away.

I was playing the best football of my career at the time. I'd recently been named North East Footballer of the Year, North East Sports Writers' Player of the Year, and the club's Player of the Year. It was a great period for me and the club. There are other games I could have picked further down the line but this one had everything. When you think there was nothing really riding on the game from our point of view it makes it particularly impressive. We'd just been crowned champions. I'd been involved in those sorts of games before where they just end up in between a competitive match and a testimonial, but we had this mentality that we wanted to go out with a bang and that's what we did.

I got three assists that day and was involved in the movements that led up to another couple of the goals. Scoring goals is the best feeling but for me I used to get the same enjoyment out of making goals for people. I was really lucky with the calibre of strikers I played behind at Newcastle, and the two forwards that day were David Kelly and Andy Cole, who were very different types of players, but both had unbelievable goalscoring records that season and both got hat-tricks that day.

I always remember the chairman Sir John Hall was in celebratory mood. He'd had a few glasses of bubbly before an interview and I remember him saying on live TV that the Premiership teams needed to be wary of us, that we were coming for them and we were going to challenge the big boys. At the time most people outside of Newcastle thought, 'Here we go, here's an owner who has had too much to drink, spouting off nonsense,' but actually here was a man who was prepared to back what he was saying and put his money where his mouth was. He made a masterstroke when he brought Kevin in and backed him up with the finances to take the club to the next level. Obviously, we fell short not long after when we nearly won the championship, but we got into Europe and ruffled a few feathers in the process.

Kevin was all about the supporters. He always said the fans are the be-all and end-all of a football club. On our way back from Grimsby there were a few times we were travelling along on the bus and saw a load of black-and-white jerseys being worn outside hotels and pubs, so we got off and had a few beers with them. After the Leicester game we had the open-top bus through the city centre, which was just incredible. Sir John Hall had to have a word with Kevin to keep an eye on me – I'd had a few too many drinks before I got on the bus and he was worried I was going to go over the top! Travelling from the Gosforth Park Hotel and making it down to the Civic Centre took absolutely ages, it was bedlam. There were brilliant scenes. Some of the fans took up crazy positions. How they got up to the top of the lampposts and other places I'll never know. They were standing on the window ledges of bars a few storeys up, it was madness. When we eventually got to the Civic Centre and Kevin addressed the supporters, there were thousands of people hanging on his every word, it was amazing.

I was in and around the first team for around ten years in total and got to play alongside some unbelievable players. Faustino Asprilla was one of them – what a guy. He bought into what the club was trying to do but was a proper maverick. His debut in 1996 against Middlesbrough sums him up. We used to have a pre-match meal about 11.45am to give us a bit of energy, but not too much that we couldn't run around. As we came down for that meal Faustino was in the dining room and he was having a bowl of pasta with a carafe of red wine! We thought, well he's obviously not playing today, and when the manager named the team and he was on the bench we couldn't believe it – he'd just had half a bottle of red! He came on and produced some bits of magic and provided the cross for Steve Watson's equaliser, and we went on to win it. We knew then we were going to have a bit of fun with this guy. We loved him to bits. He could be frustrating because he could be the best player you've ever seen at one time, and then he'd do something crazy. But we had great laughs with him, and he produced some real special moments.

By 1996 I found myself out of the team a bit more, with David Batty coming in to replace me. He was an outstanding player and a great guy, but was a different type of player to me. The stats don't lie: my last game was in a 3-3 draw against Man City at Maine Road, and we had a cushion over Manchester United at the top of the league, and I felt it was a tough call on me to not play for the last nine games. Now is it a coincidence that we faltered over the last nine games? Obviously losing to Manchester United in the proverbial six-pointer had an impact, but I felt that we didn't have the experience they did. They'd won league titles and knew what it felt like to get to the final stages, and we hadn't. But I do feel that if I was still in the team, we'd have got more points than we did.

The following season, 1996/97, we lost the Charity Shield and our first league game, which I put down to a hectic pre-season. We went on a Far East tour to Thailand, Singapore and Japan, and it lasted a long time. We only arrived back in the UK on the Thursday and had the Charity Shield on the Sunday. It was a pre-season that had an adverse effect on us, in terms of the humidity and adjusting to the time differences. Manchester United blew us away, and then so did Everton in the league, but there were overriding factors.

I got back in the team and we were getting some results, but then it started unravelling with Kevin. When he left, Kenny Dalglish came in, and I hit some great form in the team, scoring three goals in three games. Before the following game, in the FA Cup against Nottingham Forest, Kenny had me in the office to say that I wasn't going to be starting, so he could bring Peter Beardsley back into the team after injury. I was never going to argue about Peter coming back into the team; he is, in my opinion, the greatest player to ever pull on a black-and-white shirt. But when it was at my expense, when I'd been playing well, I knew I had to do something else for my career.

The club offered me a new deal but I needed more than that, not just to be seen as the local lad who wouldn't kick up a fuss if he was left out. I got to the stage where I felt there had been some tough calls on me, that if I hadn't been the local lad but had been signed for a lot of money, those tough calls might not have gone that way, so I made the decision to leave. But that never extinguished the feeling and the pride I had of playing for Newcastle.

At the time I was thinking about leaving Newcastle, Paul Bracewell was assistant manager at Sunderland to Peter Reid. Paul had been a mentor to me so we had that existing relationship. I'd spoken to five or six different managers: Jim Smith at Derby County, who gave me my debut at Newcastle; Newcastle legend Frank Clark at Manchester City; Brian Little at Aston Villa; the late, great Tommy Burns at Celtic; and Sunderland was the last club I went and spoke to.

My first son Jack had recently been born and had never been away from the North East, so I found the thought of that quite daunting. We were settled and Sunderland seemed a perfect fit in terms of location, and they weren't in the same league as Newcastle, which was a big factor. I'd never have made that move if they were in the same league, and actually, once Sunderland did get promoted, it was a non-starter. I met Peter Reid and found he was a very passionate man, like Kevin Keegan, who could help me, and I wasn't disappointed. I loved the two years I had under him.

I had to hit the ground running and the fans then accepted me because of the level of performance I gave them, despite me being black-and-white! I never hid the fact I was a Newcastle United fan and would come back and watch the Toon, whether that be in Europe or in the league, if we didn't have a match. I went to St James' Park as often as I could. I wasn't going to change. I was a Newcastle fan and I'd made a professional decision. When you become a father and have young children, you have to look after them, and that's what I was doing.

I went to both the Newcastle FA Cup finals, in 1998 and 1999. For the game in '99 against Man United I got permission from

Peter Reid, who said, 'Don't wear any club colours,' which I didn't. I went down and took a black cab to Baker Street – there was a pub there owned by a Geordie guy, full of Newcastle fans and people I knew. When I got out of the taxi, this T-shirt with an anti-Sunderland slogan on was thrown over us. There were disposable cameras then, not phone cameras everywhere that you see today. People started taking lots of pictures and I remember my pals saying it could get me in a bit of bother, but I didn't hear anything of it until a couple of days before pre-season was about to start, when I got a call to say these pictures had found their way into the hands of the press and they were going to publish them! My agent had to deal with that, and once that had happened there was no way I could continue to play for Sunderland. You can't bite the hand that feeds you. Even though Peter was adamant I wasn't leaving and that I'd play in the first game of the season against Chelsea, obviously if you say derogatory things about the fans there's no way back, and I understood that. When you do something like that you have to accept the consequences.

I didn't wear the shirt on the pretence of trying to engineer a move, but it sped up the process. That season we'd wrapped up the league, but after going out of the League Cup to Leicester City I went to Peter's office. Andy Gray from Sky was in the office then too, and I told the gaffer that after getting promoted, going into the same league as Newcastle, that I needed to go. He said it wasn't possible – they wanted me to stay and were going to be making some big signings. But the incident sped up the opportunity, and that resulted in the move to Fulham.

Paul Bracewell was Fulham manager then so I joined him and did something I never thought I'd do – move away from the North East and down to London. It was a great decision because I had some fantastic years there. At Craven Cottage the players' tunnel leads into the cottage where the changing rooms, manager's office and family lounge are. There was one game where Chris Coleman was the manager, and I was captain, and refereeing decisions hadn't gone in our favour. My son Jack and Chris's boy were great friends, and were sat on the balcony over the tunnel. The boys weren't happy with the referee so got some sandwiches from the players' lounge and started throwing them at him! So the sons of the captain and the manager got a dressing down by some of the directors. It didn't look great.

A few years later I re-signed for Newcastle, which was something I just never thought would happen. If it had been left to me it probably wouldn't have happened, but it was down to the persistence of Terry McDermott, who I'd become really close to during his spell as Kevin's number two. I was out of contract – it was the first pre-season where I was training on my own, I didn't have a club. I was in talks with Southampton about potentially signing for them, as they weren't too far from my home in Surrey, and Harry Redknapp was there. But Terry kept persisting, telling me to come home and train with the team to keep myself football-fit. Eventually I took him up on his offer and then within a few days Graeme Souness took me into the manager's office and told me he liked having me around due to my mentality and my character. He asked me if I'd take up a player/coach role, with me being an emergency player for the first team while doing my coaching badges and working with the reserves. I thought, why not? I was looking towards the next stage of my career in terms of the coaching, but then by the second game of the season we were playing West Ham and I was named on the bench, and came on.

We drew 0-0 and then, not long after, Graeme had me in and told me I'd be starting against Blackburn, and we went there and blew them away, 3-0, and I ended up playing about 25 Premier League games that season. Graeme was sacked towards the end of that season and Glenn Roeder was brought in. When I'd been signed as a schoolboy they brought me into training with the first team, and Glenn was the captain at the time. He took me under his wing then, so to have him as my manager in the latter stages of my career seemed like it was meant to be. We went on to become very close friends. I went to Norwich with him as assistant manager, which was great, and I found it really tough when he passed away in February 2021. It's weird how things play out in your footballing life and go full circle – to start and then finish my playing career with Glenn, and then become close with him in the coaching world.

I feel unlucky when it comes to my international career. I played for England all the way through, captaining every single team from under-15 to under-21, and thought my chance would come when I was called up for the full squad for Le Tournoi in 1997 but spent three games as an unused sub. At that time there was a plethora of top central midfield players – Beckham, Scholes, Batty, Ince, Gascoigne, Redknapp, Wise, Lee and others – so perhaps it was just a question of timing.

I do get a bit frustrated with not having got a full cap, especially when a few years later Sven-Göran Eriksson was throwing them around like confetti. The two things that are missing for me when I look back on my career are that elusive full England cap and the Premiership title, which we should have won in 1995/96.

But I got to live out the dream of thousands of Toon fans, playing for my boyhood club at the highest level, so I know how lucky I am.

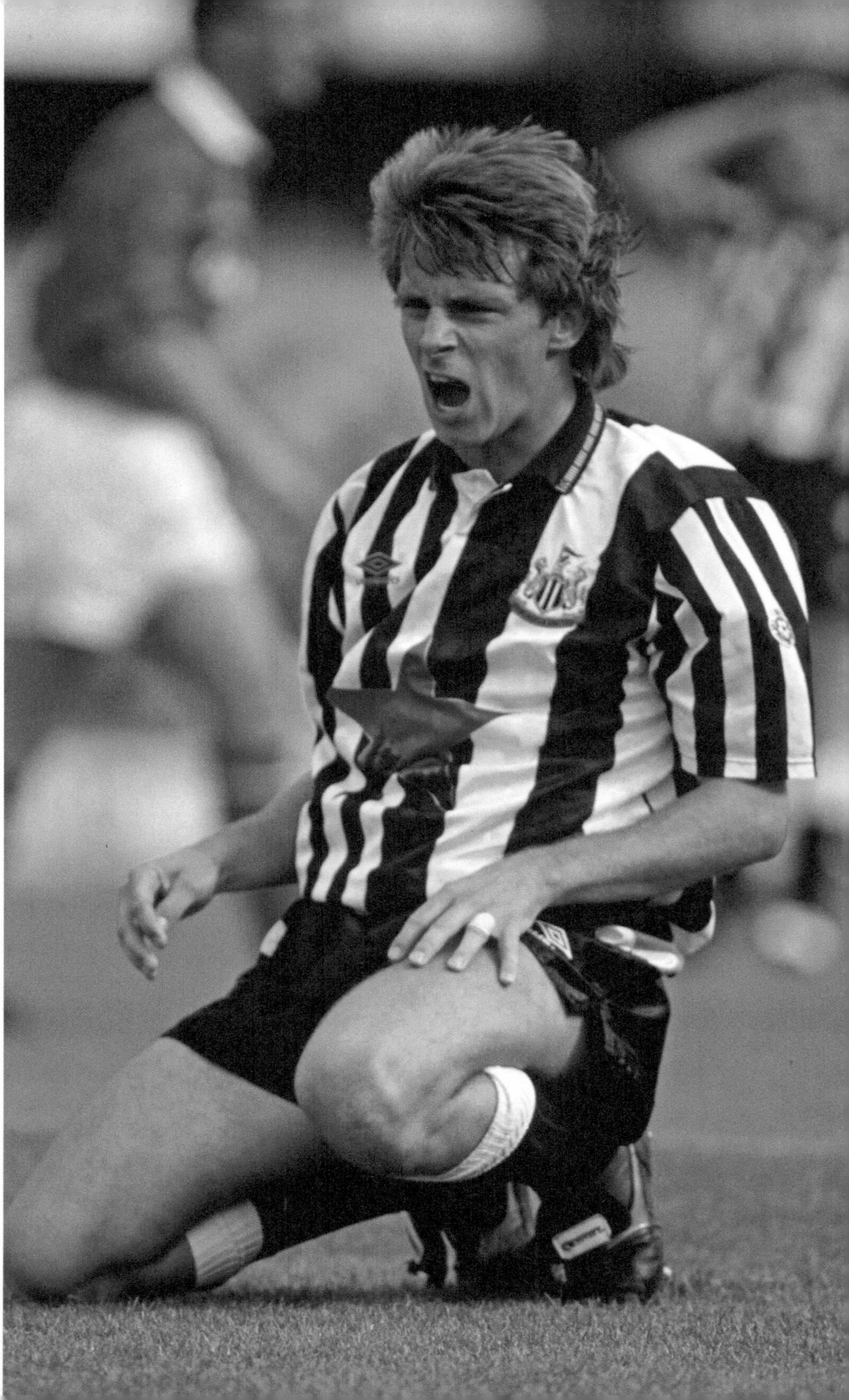

DAVID KELLY

David Kelly
Striker
1991–1993

David 'Ned' Kelly represented no fewer than 11 clubs during his nomadic playing career and had a tendency of never staying at any of them for very long. The Republic of Ireland international, part of Jack Charlton's squads at both the 1990 and 1994 World Cups as well as Euro 88, joined Newcastle from Leicester in a £250,000 deal in December 1991. His 39 goals in 83 appearances not only helped rescue the Magpies from relegation to the Third Division and the brink of financial disaster, but also fired them into the Premier League under Kevin Keegan.

Kelly barely had time to bask in the glory of promotion to the top flight before being sold to Wolverhampton Wanderers in the summer of 1992, but it's a measure of the mark he made during his time at St James' Park that the Toon Army continued to idolise him even after crossing the Tyne–Wear divide. Kelly was left speechless after Wor Flags unfurled a banner paying tribute to the crucial goal he scored to save Newcastle from the abyss, possibly one of the most celebrated strikes in the club's modern history, three decades later.

Newcastle United 1-0 Portsmouth

Second Division
Saturday, 25 April 1992
St James' Park, Newcastle
Attendance: 25,989

Newcastle	Portsmouth
Wright	Knight
Ranson	Awford
Neilson	Neill
O'Brien	Symons
Kilcline	Daniel
Scott	McLoughlin
Carr	Burns
Peacock	Anderton (Wigley)
Kelly	Doling
Sheedy	Powell
Brock (Quinn)	Aspinall (McFarlane)

Managers

Kevin Keegan   Jim Smith

Goals

Kelly

Seeing the tribute Newcastle fans paid to me before the Leicester game in April 2022 was a truly humbling moment, especially because I didn't know anything about it. My friend Martin Henderson, who I go to a lot of matches with, was in on it all, and we were sitting in the bar in the stadium before the match and he kept saying, 'Right, we need to go out, we need to go out.' I've watched guys warm up for thousands of games, so I had no real interest and wanted to stay in the bar, but eventually we went out and then I discovered it was for the unveiling of the flag. I was quite emotional to be remembered for something that happened 30 years in the past, and it obviously stuck in the mind of a lot of my generation. It was incredibly special.

It's weird because, when you look back at the 1992 team, and the type of players we had, we should never have been in a position fighting relegation because we had the makings of a decent side. We had good players and good staff, but just weren't able to maintain any sort of momentum. It was only when Kevin Keegan came in as manager that things started to turn around a bit.

John Hall hadn't long taken over the club and it was quite clear that it would be a complete disaster financially if we went down, there was no secret around that, and John told us players in no uncertain terms that it couldn't happen, we needed to do all we could to survive.

Considering previous results had been so poor, there was a lot of pressure on us going into the Portsmouth game, but Kevin was his normal self in the build-up to the match. He was always very good around the training ground and had good staff with Derek Fazackerley, who was a great coach, and Terry McDermott backing him up as his sidekick. As we got towards the match, we obviously knew the significance, but training was actually quite light and sort of jovial. I think Kevin was trying to take the pressure away from the players, albeit everybody knew the enormity of the occasion.

In terms of my winning goal, for several years afterwards I thought it was from outside the penalty area and didn't realise it was five yards inside the box until I watched it on YouTube! I should have known better because I never scored from outside the box. All my goals were either headers, tap-ins or goalmouth scrambles. For some reason, in my mind this goal was from further out and I'd smashed it into the top right-hand corner. It turns out it wasn't that good. It was still a decent strike, although at the time I thought the Portsmouth goalkeeper, Alan Knight, was going to save it. He was a good keeper and I feared he'd get a fingertip to the ball, so I was pleased to see it fly into the corner. It also came at a good time in the game, with only five minutes remaining.

Portsmouth were a strong team back then, with some very good players, but even at half-time when it was 0-0, the message from Kevin was 'don't panic, don't think that we're not going to win the game because we'll keep getting opportunities'. When you watch the highlights and the clips of it, we had a lot of chances to score so at no point did I ever think we weren't going to win.

That was our penultimate game of the season, and we then travelled to my old club Leicester on the last day to win 2-1 at Filbert Street. Those were the days before smartphones, so our supporters were listening to radios to keep on top of how our relegation rivals were faring, which meant every now and then there would be a rumour going around that somebody had scored. It didn't make any difference because we ended up winning, and, in fact, that victory over Portsmouth would have kept us up anyway, so it was as comfortable as it could be. I joined up with the Republic of Ireland for international duty straight after the game, so there was no time for any celebrations, not that avoiding relegation is any reason to celebrate.

My December 1991 move to Newcastle came about because I was at Leicester and, with Brian Little becoming my third manager in 18 months, he left me out of the team for three or four games. At that time the Foxes were a big club languishing in the bottom half of the Second Division, but I told Brian that, if I was going to be a substitute, I'd prefer to go somewhere else and try to play. I had nothing against the club, nor Brian, who was a really good bloke, and it was purely based on the fact I didn't want to play in the reserves. Then a couple of weeks later, Newcastle, then managed by Ossie Ardiles, came in for me – and the rest is history.

I liked Ossie and thought he was a really good guy. If you wrote down our squad on a piece of paper you'd think we had a good chance of success, but we just didn't win enough games and, before long, he was replaced by Kevin Keegan. When he first arrived it was as if the sunshine had turned up because we all know what type of character Kevin is. Right from the start he was so positive and relishing turning the club around.

I can remember John Hall and Kevin having a meeting when they'd both just taken over and they were talking about the Premier League, winning cups, European football, all that sort of stuff. Yet we were sitting fourth from bottom in the old Second Division and you're thinking, *Are these guys for real?* They just had that belief that once survival was sorted, the club would go from strength to strength.

Kevin simply tried to change the ethos of the group because it's difficult going into work when it's all doom and gloom, but under Kevin you were now looking forward to going into training and looking forward to the games, even though there was a lot of pressure on them. The turnaround the following season was amazing, and all of a sudden we reached the Premier League, and Kevin and John had delivered on their promises.

That summer of 1992 we recruited half a dozen players, really good footballers who changed the mood of the squad. A few out of contract had departed, leaving a lot of good young players in and around the team, such as Steve Watson and Lee Clark, then Kevin added some really senior professionals.

The first player he recruited was Brian 'Killer' Kilcline, captain of Coventry's 1987 FA Cup-winning team, who Kevin would later describe as his best-ever signing. Despite the nickname, Killer was honestly the nicest man in football and the most genuine person you'll ever come across. He was brilliant. Without being disrespectful, he wasn't the greatest player by a long stretch, but a super captain and superb person within the dressing room because he had this presence. Then there was Kevin Sheedy, another important signing, while Rob Lee and Barry Venison also came in. You're talking about people used to playing at a level far and above where we were at the time.

We started pre-season and, after winning a couple of games, I remember saying to Gavin Peacock, 'We've got a right chance this year.' We won the first 11 games and after that knew we had a fantastic opportunity of achieving something special.

Andy Cole came in towards the end of the season, in March 1993, and scored 12 goals in 12 games to help us over the line and win promotion. It was just a goal fest, and that side was the start of the team that became known as 'The Entertainers' because our attitude was 'if you score two, we will score four!' I remember Kevin telling Gavin not to bother running back and to stay in the opposing half, and I thought, *Well, this is licence just to be a lazy f****r.* I don't mean that in a negative way, he just wanted two people up front to attack when we won the ball back. It was basically score as many goals as you can.

Andy was 18 when he joined and came into a group of lads that were on the cusp of getting promoted, so he just blended straight in. He was a quiet boy, but you could see what a top goalscorer he was from the first training session, demonstrating he could score different types of goals. He had a fantastic career and moved on to bigger and better things, and having left myself two months after his arrival, I only played with him for a couple of months, but at least one of us scored in most of the games we played together, so that's a decent record.

As we topped the league, that made it easy for him to settle. It was like a roller coaster that everybody was riding and, regardless of the opposition, we were confident of victory. That was the general attitude of the squad, and playing up front with Coley for a couple of months was great. We also had Gavin Peacock, who was a really good player for us at the time, capable of playing in different positions at different times and always doing a good job for the team. We had a good squad of players.

We confirmed our promotion by beating Grimsby 2-0 in May 1993, which was ironic because they were the team that ended our 11-match winning streak at the start of the season. I'm told that when we went to Blundell Park our fans took up three of the four sides of the stadium, which doesn't surprise me because they're amazing supporters, although with both teams having black and white stripes as home colours it was difficult to know for certain.

I scored a scruffy goal and remember the fans streaming on to the pitch at full time to celebrate. I'm not a great lover of pitch invasions, simply from a personal safety point of view, so I just tried to get back in the dressing room as quickly as possible.

There was also a pitch invasion the previous season after we won at Leicester, and at Filbert Street the away fans used to be stuck away in one corner in a bit of a dungeon area. It wasn't very nice, and I took a calculated risk because, instead of running back towards the tunnel where everybody else was, I ended up in the away end in the stand with the supporters. I must have been there for a good five or ten minutes before I popped my head up and spotted a friendly-looking police officer, who kindly escorted me across the pitch and back to the dressing room.

There was a build-up to the last game of the season, in which we beat Leicester 7-1 and Coley and I both scored hat-tricks. Because we'd already won the league, we'd basically been on the beers all week. Training was reduced to twice a week because we had so many functions, with celebrations ongoing from the night of the Grimsby game until the end of the season. Everybody was out, the whole squad, people like John Beresford, Venison, Clarky and Pavel Srníček loved a party, but we still felt we could beat any team in the country at that time.

It was a brilliant time in my career but, due to circumstances, I never got the chance to play for Newcastle in the Premier League.

Once the season had finished, I was driving back down the motorway to Birmingham, where I'm from, when Kevin phoned and said we needed to have a chat, so I pulled into a service station on the A1 and said, 'Gaffer, are you selling me?' This was back in a time when mobile phones were as big as bricks, and he said he'd had a couple of offers for me and was going to sign a few new players so I wouldn't be happy about being on the bench. I said, 'Where am I going to then?' and he told me offers had come in from Wolves and Nottingham Forest – and the club had accepted Wolves' offer. He asked if I'd be happy to speak to their manager Graham Turner and I agreed I would, but only on the proviso Kevin told me who he was bringing in to replace me. He refused, as it was a big secret, so I said, 'F**k it, I ain't going then.' We had a bit of an argument, and I pointed out I still had 12 months left on my contract so I'd see him for the start of pre-season training, before putting the phone down in disgust. Kevin phoned me back about ten minutes later and said we needed to sort things out and it was then he reluctantly told me they were bringing in Peter Beardsley. My exact words were, 'F***ing hell gaffer, I'd sign Peter Beardsley instead of David Kelly!'

It was all sorted pretty quickly after that and my time with the Toon ended in June 1993. Kevin was right, I wouldn't have ever been happy to be a substitute; that wasn't for me. I just wanted to play and was obsessed with playing games. The same thing happened to me a few years later when I was at Sunderland when we won promotion and I left at the end of that season. It's just part of the system, and when teams get promoted they want so-called better players, and the rotation of players all those years ago wasn't like it is in the modern game. You did have players stay at clubs for a long time and get testimonials after ten years, but that's very unusual nowadays.

Not many players go to Sunderland after playing for their arch-rivals, but I'm lucky because Newcastle fans never held that against me. When I came on as a substitute in a Tyne–Wear derby at St James' Park in April 1997, I received a standing ovation from the Toon Army, even though I was wearing red and white. That was definitely unexpected. I wasn't happy with Peter Reid for putting me on the bench for a start and that's probably why I left a little later, but it was weird, as if it was a home player coming on. It was very strange, but much appreciated.

I scored the winner in my first derby game against Sunderland at St James' Park in March 1992, so I think that helped my relationship with the fans. I'm a West Bromwich Albion supporter who played for Wolves, so I know what derby day means. They're brilliant occasions. As a player you know how important they are, so I'm appreciative that I was able to score a goal in the derby. Whether it was a special goal or not, it's a special moment for the supporters.

NIKOS DABIZAS

Nikos Dabizas
Defender
1998–2003

As a teenager, Nikos Dabizas didn't have any great ambitions to be a professional footballer and it was only when he was 21 and playing in the Greek second division that his life changed when he was spotted by Olympiacos, arguably the biggest club in the country. The wholehearted centre-back helped them to back-to-back titles for the first time in a decade and played in the Champions League before finding himself on the radar of Newcastle manager Kenny Dalglish.

Dabizas moved to St James' Park in March 1998 for the modest fee of £2m, and weeks later turned out in the FA Cup Final defeat to double-winning Arsenal at Wembley. He was also part of the team beaten by Manchester United in the 1999 final and was in the squad as Greece pulled off a remarkable triumph at the 2004 European Championships, beating Cristiano Ronaldo's Portugal in the final in their own backyard. It was that tournament that proved the catalyst for Dabizas to leave Newcastle, due to concerns over a lack of playing time. He went on to join Leicester City before returning home and lifting the Greek Cup as captain with Larissa. After retiring as a player, Dabizas used his famous football intelligence to forge a career as a sporting director.

While at Newcastle, he proved himself useful in both penalty areas and there's one famous goal for which he'll be forever remembered by the Toon Army.

Sunderland 0-1 Newcastle United

Premier League
Sunday, 24 February 2002
Stadium of Light, Sunderland
Attendance: 48,290

Sunderland	Newcastle
Sørenson	Given
Haas	Hughes
Björklund	Distin
Craddock	Dabizas
Gray	O'Brien
McAteer	Solano
Schwarz (Butler)	Speed
Reyna	Jenas
Kilbane	Robert (Ameobi)
Phillips	Bellamy
Quinn (Mboma)	Shearer

Managers

Peter Reid   Bobby Robson

Goals

Dabizas

As soon as the ball hit the back of the net, all my team-mates were jumping on my back and I felt an instant desire to express my joy and my feelings, so my instinctive reaction was to rip off my shirt and show my hairy chest. That 30 seconds was an unbelievable sense of emotion running through my body. It was very special, to score the winner at the ground of your rivals. That goal was the icing on the cake of my Newcastle career and the moment that earned me cult status among the most amazing fans I ever had the privilege to play for.

I was blessed that for the majority of my career I played in front of such passionate home fans and, although there's a big difference between the size of the clubs, there are similarities between the North East derby and the Athens derby between Olympiacos and Panathinaikos due to that desire of the support. Athens is a big city of about four million people, whereas Newcastle and Sunderland are much smaller, but the intensity and the aggression between the fans and between the clubs is there and, in both cases, it's the biggest game of the season.

The difference is that in Greece there's a really nasty side to the rivalry, so much so that away fans aren't allowed to go to the stadium when those two play each other. That's not the best because you can't enjoy it on the same level. Imagine if I was lucky enough to score a winner at the Stadium of Light and there were no fans to celebrate with! What I like in England is that both sets of fans are there together, they're chanting, they can express their feelings and sing their songs. This is what football should be.

Newcastle fans were different as well because, unlike in Greece, it wasn't all about winning. As long as you gave your heart and soul, they'd support you even if the final result wasn't good. That's the most genuine feeling you can have as a player and that's what makes Newcastle United so special.

I remember the goal well because I had two or three big chances to score before I finally did. Let's just say I was up for it. We had a free kick from the right and Laurent Robert hit an inswinger across the goal. Alan Shearer ran to the near post and got a little flick on to change the direction of the ball. I was at the far post with Sylvain Distin. My marker was focused, watching the ball as it was travelling, which allowed me to lose him and get my head on it and direct it into the net. It wasn't a difficult goal, but it was a great goal because of the importance of it.

We were near the top of the league at the time after a great run of results – and scoring the only goal at the Stadium of Light was a big occasion. There's a longevity about the goal, and it's always the first thing that gets mentioned whenever I meet any Newcastle fan.

One of the first team-mates to celebrate with me was Gary Speed. Gary was the most respected and best professional I've met in my career and also the most balanced character in terms of his work ethic and his professionalism. Gary ticked every single box, and I still can't believe he's no longer with us. Gary was so friendly when I came from Greece because he'd joined the club a couple of months before me. We were relatively young in a new environment, and he was very supportive. He was a great leader and one of the key elements in our success during that period.

Sir Bobby Robson was our manager for this game, and he was so clever because he could squeeze every ounce out of a player, and you could exceed your talent under his guidance. He had that gift, that awareness of knowing what to say and when to say it in every single moment. He knew how to lift you when you were down and how to bring you down to earth when you were in danger of losing your balance. In general, he was a charismatic person and the fact he'd had success in the Netherlands, Portugal and Spain as an English coach is very unusual because the English culture is unique. It has a lot of positives, but also a lot of negatives in terms of how you approach the game, how you approach football. He was blessed with characteristics that made him very adaptable. He wasn't crazy and didn't do stupid things during games, but the way he man-managed the group, the media and a very demanding public was top-class. Sometimes, this is the most important part of being a manager. You need that tactical ability and that talent to read the game to be able to pick the best team on the field, but you have to be able to manage people.

Ruud Gullit had great tactical awareness, but the way he man-managed people was very poor. He was a very strong person, but he couldn't handle his emotions and his own ego. That was transmitted to the players. My only explanation for that is that he had a great career and was raised in the Netherlands where they have that superiority about their talent, about their own product and the way the game is being played. It's not bad to say the Dutch have that arrogance, which can be a positive if you use it in the right way, to believe in your style, but you have to try to marry that in the appropriate way to the club, to the fans and to the players. Ruud was a great player, but he couldn't handle that as a manager.

Alan Shearer was a strong personality as well, and a big name for the club. If you're sensible and wise enough, you don't go against a player with his history and his presence. Alan always wanted to do the best for himself, but also for the club, and when he and Ruud clashed it was always going to lead to one result. Ruud didn't use Alan in a positive way and tried to go against him.

Kenny Dalglish was the manager who brought me to St James' Park. I'd been offered a new contract at Olympiacos, with whom I was challenging for a second league title in a row and playing in the Champions League, but I decided I didn't want to continue in Greece and was keen to give it a shot in England. I was 24 and my agent told me that a scout from Newcastle was coming to watch me in the national team, so that was a great chance for me to perform. That was in November 1997, and they kept me on their radar for a couple of months, then in February they offered me a contract and I decided to take it, which was the best thing I ever did in my career.

My transfer fee was not by any means the greatest amount Newcastle ever spent, but it was a good fee for Olympiacos, and I think I proved value for money because I ended up staying for six years.

The first few months were difficult, but after that it was great. I didn't expect people to change or adapt to my culture or my personal way of living; it was up to me to change my way of life and become one of the lads. In Greece you don't go for a night out with six, seven or eight team-mates. Maybe a couple of us would go out, but in Newcastle we all went out as a team and that helped us become closer as we'd have a laugh together. I'd never drunk beer in my life, but trained myself to drink pints for those nights out.

I tried to take every single aspect of English culture and put it in my daily routine. I wasn't used to having food three hours before the game because in Greece it was always five hours, and I couldn't have something to eat between training sessions, but I started to change that so I was part of those special differences between Greek and English culture.

It was good that I could already speak English and was always part of the conversations in the dressing room and able to communicate with the fans. I changed my personality so I could be accepted and comfortable with the English culture. I enjoyed my life in Newcastle and still do when I go back to see friends and watch games.

Kenny was a very honest, straightforward man who always tried to protect his players and the club and would never make any negative comments in public. He'd have a go at you in the right place, at the right time, and I admired that about him. He was a leader, a winner who had that aura about him and was very self-confident. It was a shame when he was sacked only eight months after bringing me to the club. That was a big surprise for all the players and most of us were really sad for him to lose his job.

We had a great bunch of personalities in the team and that was the most important thing about our success. We had leaders and great talent in our squad, the likes of Alan, Gary Speed and Nolberto Solano, and flair players such as Laurent Robert and Kieron Dyer. We had that perfect mix of strong characters and youth.

Sylvain Distin was very athletic. I'm only 6ft 1in, so he's taller than me, but we had a good partnership because he is left-footed, and I'm right-footed, so that suited me. I only liked to use my left foot on the clutch when I was driving my car! Sylvain was faster than me and slightly younger, but I read the game slightly better. He had that desire and motivation to do well and that was a similar case with me.

We had Shay Given in goal behind us. He had a remarkable career and it wasn't easy, not just for Shay but for all the defensive players at Newcastle at that time because the majority of the play and the DNA of the club was about going forward and exciting the fans, which left us a bit exposed. It was always difficult on opposition counter-attacks, where we didn't have that defensive approach.

Shay wasn't the biggest for a goalkeeper, but he worked very hard and his career speaks volumes about that. I remember when I joined the club in 1998, he wasn't the best with his feet, but by the time I left he could kick the ball out of the stadium. It was an unbelievable turnaround and development of his weakness. He had a good relationship with Steve Harper and they were always pushing each other for the number one spot, so that brought the best out of Shay.

The week after the Sunderland win we played Arsenal at St James' Park in the game in which Dennis Bergkamp scored *that* goal, so in the space of a few days I went from heaven to hell! Whenever people ask me about that goal in March 2002, they think I feel bad about it. On the night it was really difficult because we lost at home and it was a goal I was involved in, but as time has gone on my emotions have changed. I view it completely differently now and feel lucky because I was part of a piece of footballing art from a genius. I say that I'm part of history, although not at the front of the stage, at the back, but I was there.

I hold my hands up high and you can only feel admiration for that. I don't feel bad or ashamed about the piece of magic Dennis provided that night. That's what makes football so unpredictable. I did my best to stop it, but for me it's better this goal was scored than if I brought him down, which I tried to do, but he pushed me away as I tackled him. It was a great moment of football. Dennis wasn't the most vocal person, so I never had the chance to speak to him, but I've since read him saying that he meant to do it. It doesn't matter if he meant it or not because the end product was perfect. It was great skill.

One of my other favourite matches for Newcastle was our 4-3 win over Manchester United in a seven-goal thriller in September 2001. It was a great game and a fixture with a lot of history because we had that 5-0 win against them a few years before. I wasn't there for that one, but knew all about it. As I've previously mentioned, we had a lot of flair going forward and I scored the goal to put us 3-1 up. After that it was immense pressure from Manchester United and one of the most difficult games I ever played because they had a great team, with players like Juan Sebastián Verón, David Beckham, Ryan Giggs, Paul Scholes, Roy Keane and Ruud van Nistelrooy.

They got it back to 3-3 but we managed to nick it late on with a deflected shot from Alan Shearer. It was a full house, which added to the occasion, and the way the scoreline went up and down and the changing of emotions made it very special. United had Roy Keane sent off after an altercation in the corner with Alan, who reacted very wisely because the most important thing for me is balance and handling your emotions. Roy was always a very fiery character and still is, so Alan was very smart as he didn't react when it happened. Football is all about mind games and Alan obviously lit a small fire – and after that the explosion came from Roy's side.

I was fortunate enough to play in two successive FA Cup finals during my time at Newcastle, but we were also very unlucky because at the time we were at the wrong end of the table and trying to avoid relegation. In 1998 we played against an Arsenal side who were going for the Premier League and FA Cup double, then a year later we were up against Manchester United's all-conquering treble-winning team.

There was a huge gap between us, so we were always the underdogs. I do believe we didn't have any kind of luck, especially against Arsenal when both Alan and I had great chances to score at 1-0 down. If we'd equalised with one of those then you never know what could have happened. Not taking that chance still haunts me because it would have been a great achievement to bring silverware back to Newcastle, but it wasn't meant to be.

My departure from the club was very amicable and it was only circumstances that led me to make the decision to leave. I'd picked up an injury in pre-season and when I came back to fitness wasn't a regular in the side. I was Greece vice-captain and it was always in the back of my mind that we had Euro 2004 coming up the following summer. I said to Sir Bobby that I needed to play and therefore it was important for me to go and find a club where I'd get those games. I didn't want to eliminate my chances of being part of the Euros squad.

I had offers from Portsmouth and Leicester and decided to move to the latter in January 2004. If the Euros weren't on the horizon, I'd have stayed and fought for my place, but that was the most important element in my decision.

As it turned out, I was injured for our first game against the hosts Portugal and after that found myself watching from the sidelines because the coach didn't want to change a winning team. It was still a very proud moment and great achievement as Greece, a small country with no great football tradition, went on to win the championship against Portugal. That glory helped take away the sadness that I could no longer pull on the famous black-and-white shirt in front of those amazing Geordie supporters.

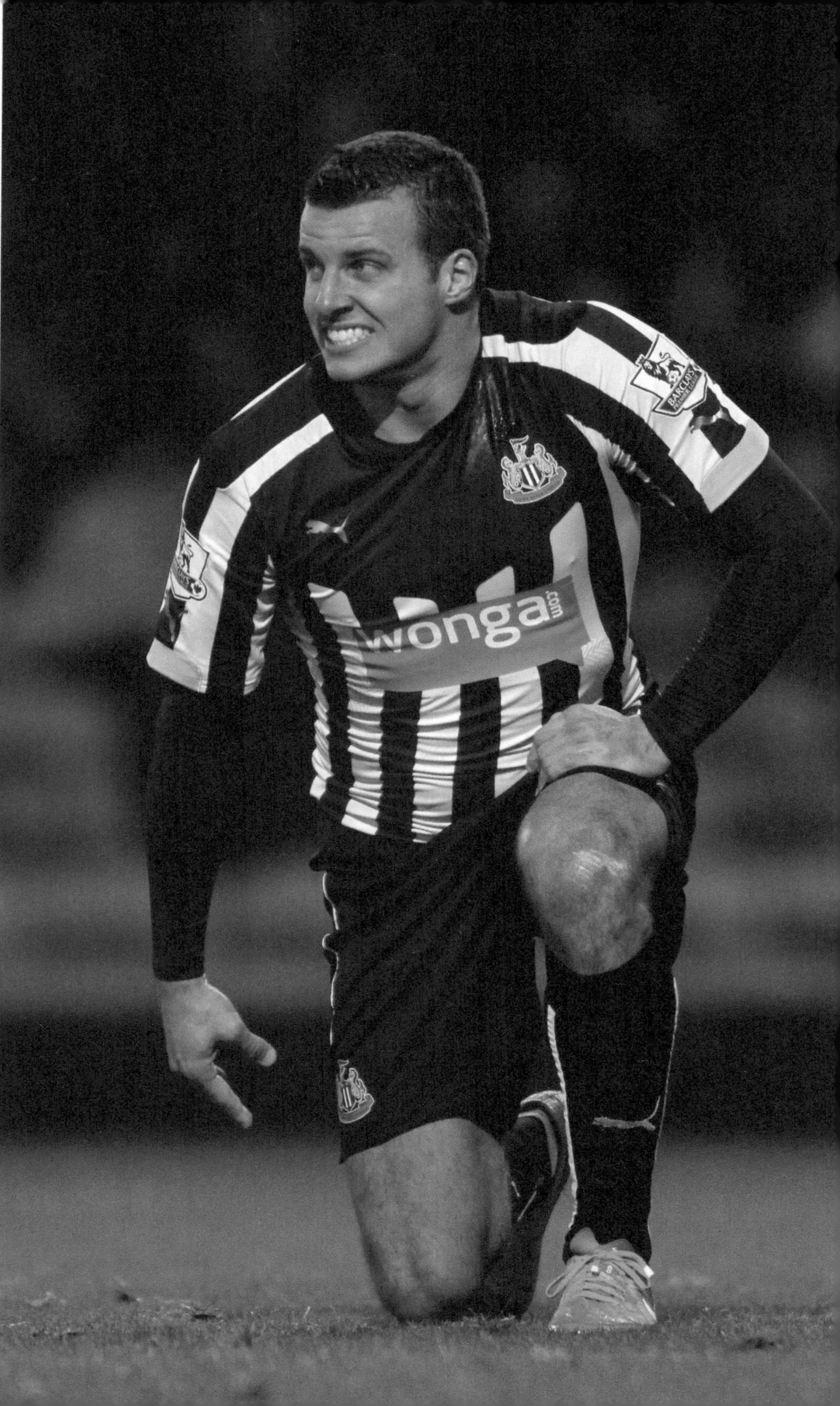

STEVEN TAYLOR

Steven Taylor
Defender
2004–2016

Steven Taylor was born in London but grew up in Whitley Bay among a family of Geordies and joined the Newcastle academy as a nine-year-old after being spotted playing for Cramlington Juniors. After being converted from a striker to a centre-back aged 13, Taylor, whose hero was former Arsenal captain Tony Adams, made his first senior appearance as Newcastle's youngest-ever European debutant after coming off the bench in a UEFA Cup tie against Spanish team Mallorca in 2004.

Taylor went on to play 215 league matches for the Magpies spread over a 12-year period, making him one of the club's longest-serving players in the 21st century. He was part of the team that won the Championship title in 2010, and earned cult hero status with his phantom injury in an ill-fated attempt to avoid a red card for deliberate handball during the infamous defeat at home to Aston Villa in April 2005 when team-mates Kieron Dyer and Lee Bowyer came to blows on the pitch.

It was the European nights under the floodlights of St James' Park that really got Taylor's juices flowing.

Newcastle United 1-0 Anzhi Makhachkala

Europa League round of 16, second leg
Thursday, 14 March 2013
St James' Park, Newcastle
Attendance: 45,487

Newcastle	Anzhi Makhachkala
Elliot	Gabulov
Santon	Yeschenko
Taylor	Ewerton
Yanga-Mbiwa	João Carlos
Haidara	Zhirkov
Tioté	Jucilei
Sissoko	Ahmedov
Cabaye (Gutiérrez)	Diarra (Shatov)
Anita	Boussoufa
Marveaux	Eto'o
Cissé (Campbell)	Carcela-González

Managers

Alan Pardew   Guus Hiddink

Goals

Cissé

Not everyone is lucky enough to say they went from watching big European games alongside their dad in the Sir John Hall Stand to actually playing in them, but I can – and that's why our dramatic stoppage-time win over a star-studded Anzhi side stands out in my memories. As a young kid, I used to love nights like this and will never forget the atmosphere, the roar and the excitement as we beat Barcelona 3-2 in the Champions League in September 1997 when Tino Asprilla bagged his hat-trick.

Now, 15-and-a-half years later, when Papiss Cissé's last-gasp header crashed into the back of the Russians' net, the roar that erupted around St James' Park was like nothing I'd experienced since that Barcelona night. It was an unbelievable feeling.

Going into the tie, we had the tag of underdogs because of the players in their line-up, which included Willian, who was eventually ruled out injured for the game, and the great Samuel Eto'o. I made my senior debut playing against Eto'o when he was at Real Mallorca, so it was like I'd come full circle. Did I ever think I'd play against him again? Absolutely not, but I ended up facing him when he was playing for Chelsea and then Anzhi.

The first leg on a freezing night in Russia ended in an uneventful 0-0 draw. That was a difficult evening because the game took place on an artificial pitch and a lot of our players had come back from injury or had suffered big injuries in the past, so were a bit nervous about playing on that kind of surface, especially in the cold conditions. Many of our team also wore Under Armour pants, which I'd never really seen before. It was different to what we were used to, so we had to deal with the conditions, and we did, but even back at our place we had to soak up a phenomenal amount of pressure and everybody played out of their skins because, as well as having a lot of talented players, the Russians were also a very physical side.

We were very mindful of being hit on the counter-attack, and keeping Eto'o quiet was one of our main focuses. We knew if we did that then we had a great chance of progressing. It was also my best performance in the black and white because we opened ourselves up a bit, particularly in the first half, and I made the most blocks I've probably ever had to in a single game. Everything just seemed to go right for me, and I had bags of energy.

Those European nights always brought the best out of me and I remember scoring my first senior goal against Celta Vigo when I rolled out my famous 'Forrest Gump' run around the pitch in celebration. That was something special, to get the winning goal at the Gallowgate End, unbelievable, and I didn't know what the hell was going on. I don't know why some players score and don't celebrate because, for me, the feeling that goes through your body is the best in the world.

I thought we deserved to beat Anzhi, but didn't expect it to take until the final few seconds for us to settle it with the only goal of the tie, scored with pretty much the last touch.

We had a very good squad that fought for each other, and Alan Pardew, our manager at the time, did a good thing by each week holding a French-themed day in the canteen because we had a lot of French players at the time. They mixed in well with the English and vice-versa, so it was never a problem for us as a team.

Under Pards, we finished fifth in the 2011/12 season and were top of the Premier League until December. The squad was phenomenal, with players of the quality of Hatem Ben Arfa, Cissé, Moussa Sissoko and Demba Ba. Sissoko was brilliant for us, a big powerhouse, and I remember one of his first games at St James' Park up against Ashley Cole down the wing, and he left him for dead. Then there was Yohan Cabaye, another Frenchman, who was like my quarterback when you gave him the ball, with Cheick Tioté sitting in front of us. We had a very good, tight-knit group.

Cissé scored two wonder goals at Chelsea in May 2012. I think he was frustrated and just thought, *I'm on the edge of the box, I'll smash this into the top corner.* He was on fire that year, everything he hit went in, like at Swansea when the ball seemed to come off his shin. He had a lot of ability and was a proper finisher.

One of the good things about Pards was that he was very relaxed and wanted the players to feel comfortable. He was a very good man-manager and just understood his players. He knew how to get the best out of certain individuals and personalities, especially with the Ben Arfas of this world, who a lot of managers would have found very difficult to deal with, considering his quality.

The manager had a very good relationship with Ben Arfa, who was one of the best players of my generation. Off the pitch, if he was late for team meetings, we'd accept that because we knew what he could deliver. We as players had to understand that we'd have to sacrifice Ben Arfa in certain games. It felt like we were down a man because he wasn't tracking back, but he was a game-changer, so we had to give him the licence to go and win the game. As a team we accepted that, and it worked for us.

I'd put Ben Arfa in a similar bracket to another of my former team-mates, Laurent Robert. Robert was also an incredible player for us who rose to the challenge of playing big games. Would either of those players train 100 per cent? No, but when it came to a matchday they'd deliver and that was the most important thing.

Pards' handling of Ben Arfa was very different from the infamous Graeme Souness–Robert bust-up that had marred one of our previous European campaigns when we were knocked out by Sporting Lisbon in the quarter-finals of the 2005 UEFA Cup. Souness came in and wanted to do things his way. It was April 2005, the morning of the second leg, and the press had printed some stuff Robert had said about him, so the manager stormed on to the bus waving copies of all the newspapers and ordered Robert to leave.

It was a horrible feeling having to go through that at the start of the day when we should have been relaxing, maybe taking a walk as a team and going through our set pieces. Later that night we lost 4-1, our cause not helped by Kieron Dyer and Titus Bramble picking up injuries, but I do believe if Robert had played we'd have won.

We could see even from the first leg in Portugal that they were vulnerable and we played very physically, in their faces and making a few more tackles to try to rough them up a bit. The Sporting players weren't used to facing that in their own league so didn't like it, losing to us 1-0, but winning on aggregate. During the game I felt we caused them a lot of problems, especially with the pace we possessed, but Robert was so important to us and sometimes with big names you have to bite the bullet and accept their quirks for the greater good of the team.

Losing that tie still bothers me because, with the squad we had, I honestly believe we could have gone on and won the whole competition. What made it all the more disappointing was that in our next game we had to play Manchester United in an FA Cup semi-final, which was far from ideal – and we also lost 4-1 in Cardiff.

That year really felt like the one that got away, never more so than when, after overcoming Anzhi, we were put out by Sporting's great Portuguese rivals Benfica 4-2 on aggregate in April 2013. We gave Benfica too much respect over the two legs and that cost us.

We also lost 3-0 at home to Sunderland in the Premier League that season and that was very painful. The derby game is always the first you look for when the fixtures come out in the summer, and if you lose you don't even think about venturing out into the city, and just stay indoors. Everyone in Newcastle eats and sleeps football, and even when you pop to the shops everyone, including the staff serving behind the counter, will give you stick after a bad defeat. I once headbutted a post playing against Sunderland and split both my eyes open, but there was no chance of me coming off, even with a bit of concussion, not a chance in hell.

Sir Bobby Robson was my first manager after I left school at 16 and bypassed the academy. I had a bit of a chip on my shoulder and didn't want to do the educational stuff or play for the academy. I wanted to be in the reserves, testing myself against the first team. My mindset was that if I got injured, broke my leg or something, then I'd go back to studying, but I wanted to give myself the best possible opportunity. I'd seen a lot of League Cup games down the years where Newcastle had played young kids and they'd fallen by the wayside and been forgotten about. I was determined that wouldn't happen to me.

Tommy Craig was the first-team coach at the time and he was unbelievable for me. He had me playing in the reserves with the Caldwell brothers, Steven and Gary, and there were about seven centre-halves ahead of me, but it was a great challenge because you're learning from them. What a lot of people don't realise is that when you leave school at 16 and are thrown in, you either sink or swim. You don't really get coached individually and I learned from people around me, like Jon Woodgate, Gary Speed, Shay Given and Alan Shearer. You have to learn quickly, learn how to win games; even in training it became very aggressive sometimes because it was competitive and there was always a forfeit for being on the losing side.

I remember a few of the experienced players would say to some of the younger lads: 'How many times have you been on the losing side?' There's a reason why that is. They just built your character up, and having leaders around the place was a massive help to me.

As for Bobby himself, you didn't want to let the guy down because he was an absolute legend. For me at such a young age, to be around him and to speak to him was very special.

There was a time shortly before I made my debut against Mallorca that I went into his office and he could see, not that I was angry, but that I wanted to be playing. I remember knocking on his door and the frustration on my face was there, but before I even got my words out he just started talking about family, about my mum and dad. The next thing I know, he's got his arm around me and we're walking around the corridor. A few of the lads said, 'I see you got your words out, Tayls.' I was devastated, thinking, *I don't know how he has just done that!* He just knew how to talk to his players and knew how to get everybody wanting to work for him. He could name any team and you wouldn't want to let him down. That's the biggest thing, if you speak to footballers, how many go out there and want to fight and graft for their manager. If they've had a bust-up with the manager or don't get on with their manager, it shows.

No matter how many big players we had in the dressing room, I never got intimidated. I was there to stay and wanted to stamp my authority and show that was where I deserved to be. As a young kid that's your dream, to rub shoulders with and be around those successful guys. I was around the best kind of leaders, on and off the pitch, just from the way they were, how they trained, their character and even how they dealt with bullying the referees and got in people's heads. They were the main traits I learned from the Woodgates, the Speedos, the Givens and the Shearers.

It was a big thing for me to work around those types of characters, and experiencing it every day and on matchdays, travelling to games and European nights, watching the build-up and how they prepared for matches, how they dealt with disappointment. That was a good platform for me to achieve my dream of playing for my hometown club and going on to have a 31-year career.

As a young player, the staff behind the scenes didn't want me to go on a particular Christmas party where we younger ones would have to sing *X-Factor* style for the first team. They knew there would be a lot of alcohol flying around and didn't want me to experience that culture, but there was nothing that was going to stop me from being part of it. Speedo and Shearer were among the judges and I sang Ronan Keating's 'When You Say Nothing At All' and won the £300 prize money from the karaoke competition, which I was delighted about.

Rafa Benitez was my last Newcastle manager. He was brilliant and we've always kept in contact to this day. I just wish he'd come in a bit earlier because, had he done, I think we'd have survived in the Premier League. Everyone bought into what he was trying to do and he brought the feel-good factor. We weren't really a team when he came in, but he got us playing like one again and back to basics.

Things had started to go wrong before Rafa's arrival when Steve McClaren was in charge and tried to change our style as he wanted us to play a more possession-based game. With the players we had, that kind of system never really worked. When people start over-complicating things, it causes problems.

That was the second time in my Newcastle career when we'd dropped into the Championship, the first being while Alan Shearer had his short spell in charge. I think it was unfair on Alan to expect him to take over a group that were struggling with so few games remaining. A lot of the players were discussing contracts and other things behind the scenes that were out of Alan's control. It was very hard on him and his assistant Iain Dowie, who were working with one hand tied behind their backs. Had he had a full season it may have been different. Who knows? I was gutted because Alan is an absolute legend of the game and at Newcastle. For the way he helped me when I was coming through as a kid, I'll always be in his debt.

Once we went down we got rid of the lads who didn't really want to be there, and probably needed that at the time because, for the two years before that, we had players who would come to Newcastle on big money. Michael Owen, in particular, came in for a lot of stick, but it didn't really bother me about him having a helicopter and landing it on the training pitch, because he could afford it. I came from an era where I'd turn up for training and there was a car park full of luxury cars and everyone had big houses, me included. You live within the means that you're getting paid, but you have to deliver as well – and the issue a lot of people had was with players in the squad they didn't feel were performing. It doesn't matter if you have a Ferrari or a BMX bike as long as you're delivering on the pitch. You're always going to put a big target on your back if you have a Ferrari, helicopter or a Range Rover, because the people criticising you are probably just jealous anyway. What did they want us to do? Turn up on a bike every day?

It was Chris Hughton who led us to promotion, and in my eyes he's another absolute Newcastle legend who never gets the credit he deserves for what he did in that Championship year and then stabilising us in the Premier League. As a guy, was he too nice? Possibly. He was absolutely loved by everyone in the team and the players wanted to do so much for him. Even the fans loved him as well. The ownership decided to let him go because they wanted to bring their own people in, but Chris should probably have been given more time, especially when you look at what he went on to do at Brighton.

Throughout my time at Newcastle there was always a lot of speculation about me leaving to join a so-called bigger club. That's natural, particularly when you're England Under-21 captain and playing at the European Championships. I'm a Newcastle lad and there was no way I'd have left. I had it good in the city and my family and friends were there. I could have earned a lot more money elsewhere, but the biggest thing for me was that I was happy and enjoying my football. I'd seen so many players leave Newcastle only to discover the grass isn't always greener on the other side.

It has often been suggested that my loyalty to Newcastle was a factor in me never winning a senior England cap, but I have to hold my hands up and say I was part of a generation where we had Rio Ferdinand, John Terry, Jamie Carragher, Joleon Lescott, all these top, top centre-halves. It was incredible for England to be producing this type of quality, but would I have had a chance? Absolutely not. I think you've got to respect and understand that these guys were some of the legends of the Premier League. Probably Woodgate and Ledley King would have been around that group as well, had it not been for injuries.

When I did finally decide to leave in the summer of 2016 to go to America with Portland Timbers, I'd been injured and wanted to play. I didn't want to be a bit-part player just picking up good wages, that wasn't me. I left on a high after a good 5-1 win against Tottenham, so it felt like the right timing. Newcastle offered me a one-year extension to my contract, but I wanted to go abroad and try something new. I loved my time in the MLS before coming back to England to play for Ipswich and Peterborough and then off to Wellington Phoenix in New Zealand, before moving to India, as it was the only league playing in a bubble during the Covid outbreak.

We never quite managed to get our hands on a major trophy during my time at Newcastle, but I have my winners' medals from the Intertoto Cup and the Championship, both of which

I'm immensely proud of. For me it was all about playing for my hometown club for as many years as I did, having my mum and dad come and watch me around Europe, and experiencing nights like against Anzhi, Sporting Lisbon and Benfica; phenomenal. The memories I have are unbelievable and the fans are unreal to me even when I go back now.

ALAN KENNEDY

Alan Kennedy
Defender
1972–1978

Alan Kennedy won it all – unfortunately for the all-conquering Liverpool of the late 1970s and early 1980s, and not Newcastle United. But Tyneside was where Kennedy's footballing career began and blossomed, as he stepped into the shoes of Toon legend Frank Clark at left-back, a position he made his own for six years.

Kennedy quickly became one of the best in the country, if not Europe, in that role, and was snapped up by Liverpool for what was a record fee for a British full-back of £330,000. Leaving Liverpool with a host of accolades and having scored the winning goal in the 1981 European Cup Final against Real Madrid, Kennedy had the chance to rejoin the Magpies in 1986, but turned it down in favour of a move to local rivals Sunderland, a switch he came to regret, with the Black Cats dropping to the Third Division within a season of his arrival.

Although grateful to the club and its fans for the start they gave him, Kennedy looks back at his time on Tyneside with some regret, and believes the blame for a lack of success lays squarely at the feet of the board.

Liverpool 3-0 Newcastle United

FA Cup Final
Saturday, 4 May 1974
Wembley Stadium, London
Attendance: 100,000

Liverpool	Newcastle
Clemence	McFaul
Smith	Clark
Lindsay	Kennedy
Thompson	McDermott
Cormack	Howard
Hughes	Moncur
Keegan	Smith (Gibb)
Hall	Cassidy
Heighway	Macdonald
Toshack	Tudor
Callaghan	Hibbitt

Managers

Bill Shankly	Joe Harvey

Goals

Keegan (2), Heighway

Getting to the FA Cup Final in 1974 was too much for some players. There was confusion in the squad as we didn't know what the line-up was going to be in the lead-up to the match. I didn't even know if I was going to be playing until the morning of the game, a couple of hours before kick-off, as we'd had a few injuries and the manager was waiting to see who would be fit on the day, which didn't help us. David Craig had been injured in the semi-final, so it turned out that Frank Clark switched positions to right-back and I came in at left-back.

I remember doing a TV interview before the match – every player had to do one and talk about what it was going to be like to play in an FA Cup final. I didn't feel comfortable with the interview. They asked me about one of Liverpool's players, Tommy Smith, and were saying how he was ferocious with his tackles; he does this, he does that, and how he intimidates players. I said something completely out of order: 'Tommy Smith? I've never really heard of him.' It was like a red rag to a bull, and what I'd said on live TV soon got back to the Liverpool dressing room, as Smith reminded me when he ran past me after setting up the third goal.

Liverpool started so well and had a goal disallowed for offside when Alec Lindsay smashed it in from the left side of the box. We were lucky because, looking back, it was well onside. Losing is losing, you can't get away from it, but going in at half-time at 0-0, Liverpool had given us a chance, but then they just upped a gear in the second half, and we couldn't cope.

The disallowed goal set the tone for the game, and they went ahead when Kevin Keegan got his first of the day, finding himself in lots of space and volleying home from the edge of the penalty area. Liverpool's captain Emlyn Hughes went very close from a free kick soon afterwards, before Steve Heighway broke through to make it 2-0 with a shot into the bottom corner past Willie McFaul.

The third goal was ridiculous, really. Smith, who I'd riled up before the game, was the creator, playing a one-two and finding himself in acres of space before his cross evaded our entire defence and Keegan tapped in at the far post.

Looking back, I was very naive and didn't take on board how big the game was. I didn't realise how big the pitch was and how good a surface it was and, consequently, got absolutely hammered. No player showed their real class for Newcastle that day. Terry McDermott was probably our best player – and he went to Liverpool a few weeks later. It felt like we didn't have any leaders, which was strange because we had some wonderful players at the back, Frank Clark being one of them, as well as Bob Moncur, a wonderful leader usually. Then there was Pat Howard and Willie McFaul, who was a great goalkeeper, but on the day it probably could have been six or seven.

To get away with 3-0 was a compliment to some of the Newcastle players who clearly didn't turn up. Even John Tudor and Malcolm Macdonald, two of the best forwards in football at the time, said, 'Well, let's give it to Liverpool,' and I didn't like it. But that was Newcastle to a T – if all our players weren't on form, they capitulated, and never played as a team; it was more of a collection of good individuals.

The old Wembley Stadium had those big sunken baths in the changing rooms. After the game we just sat in the bath, trying to console one another. But knowing we'd been beaten by a much better team was tough. We went back and had a parade a couple of days later, and I didn't want to be there. I just felt like saying sorry to each and every one of the supporters. I didn't want the blame attached to me. I felt very uncomfortable going round on an open-topped bus, having been trounced.

I went away and had a bit of a holiday, and thought then that things had to change. Gordon Lee came in as manager a season later and he shook things up a bit. We tried to play more as a team, but really we were still individuals. We got to the League Cup Final in 1976, but even then didn't have that much going for us. I was an individual playing on the left of defence, and never really had a rapport with the rest of the back four. We knew about the quality of our cup final opponents Manchester City, and it showed on the day. Peter Barnes scored their opening goal from close range, and we equalised through Alan Gowling, who had been brought into the club by Gordon Lee. They won it with quality – Dennis Tueart's amazing overhead kick that ended up in the back of the net.

On those two occasions I felt that Newcastle were glad to get to the final, and that was it. There were a lot of teams like Newcastle in the First Division, and on their day that team could beat anybody, but we only had our day every six to eight weeks.

I was progressing as a player, and had some lovely coaches like Dave Smith and Keith Burkinshaw, but they let me get on with what I was doing. Although they were coaching, they were letting me develop as a left-back, and Newcastle had it in their minds that eventually they were going to sell me.

I'm not saying you get greedy, but you start to think, *What can Newcastle do?* They were never going to win very much, they just wanted to survive in the First Division and consolidate what they had. They wanted to get players that cost very, very little and develop them into better players and sell them on. I didn't cost them anything, but they sold me for £330,000, which was a then-record fee for a British full-back. It was a lot of money. You don't know what goes on in the background; Joe Harvey, the manager, was a great guy, but I always felt his hands were a little bit tied. I felt they were just developing the team so the hierarchy could make a profit.

If you look at Newcastle's record in the 1970s and 1980s, they got to the finals of the FA Cup and League Cup, and that's as far as it went. That's what they were looking at – every so often give the fans something to shout about. But, on both occasions, Newcastle were outplayed, because other teams had better squads. We'd always give our all, but the quality wasn't there.

We finished fifth in the league in 1976/77 and everyone was going, 'Wow, Newcastle are right up there!' But where did we finish the next season? 21st! Many managers would try with new players coming into the team, like Malcolm Macdonald, Terry Hibbitt, John Tudor, Jimmy Smith – players that could play – but they really were buying players they wanted to sell on to make money. Then you see the likes of Liverpool and Nottingham Forest winning the

European Cup. The British clubs were dominating, but it wasn't us. When I joined Liverpool in 1978, we lost to Nottingham Forest in the European Cup, and that just spurred the club on even more to win the league that year.

The be-all and end-all when you get to a quality team is that you have to get to finals, that's what the fans expect. I don't think the Newcastle fans expected to get to a final every year, and that wasn't their problem, it was the board of directors and the people running the club. As I say, the players were decent, but if you pluck somebody from Scotland and pay £10,000 for him, that's the type of player you're getting. If you spend £100,000, you get someone better. Newcastle wouldn't often spend that kind of money on a player.

Leeds initially came in for me in 1978, but when Liverpool outbid them, that's where I went. Liverpool wanted to make a quick decision at the start of the 1978/79 season, and I joined the likes of Graeme Souness and Kenny Dalglish, who they'd also brought in. They'd sold Kevin Keegan and brought in Kenny, replacing quality with quality, whereas I don't think Newcastle looked to the future like that.

Unfortunately, Newcastle fans never really saw the best of me. They saw a youngster going on to the pitch, running hell for leather, getting the ball and making silly decisions, whereas at Liverpool it was structured. You were told who to pass to, where to stand, to do this and do that.

The make-up of the Newcastle team was that everything went through Malcolm Macdonald or Terry Hibbitt. But if they were marked, they couldn't do anything. We were reliant too much on 'Supermac', and he was sold too, to Arsenal. Even though we replaced him with Micky Burns, who was a bit of a different type of player, and Alan Gowling, we still had the same midfield players. I even went into the midfield a few times to freshen things up, but I was like a duck out of water because I was that inexperienced, and I didn't have people to tell me what to do.

The club was in transition after 1976, but we were still getting 50,000 fans through the gates every week. That was an awful lot of money they were receiving from the fans, and I'm not sure where it went, but it certainly wasn't reinvested into the team. They built a new stand but that wasn't the answer. Investment in the team was the answer. Newcastle always relied on local talent, even people like Paul Gascoigne and Peter Beardsley in later years, and I was just part of it in the 1970s. The same goes for Irving Nattrass, a young lad who came through in the early 70s – what a player. The board must have thought, *We have the best right-back in the country, the best left-back in the country*, and they sold them! It's madness really.

I had the chance to go back to Newcastle in 1985 after my spell with Liverpool, but I chose Sunderland instead. Their manager Lawrie McMenemy was the reason I signed for them. I spoke to Willie McFaul at Newcastle and told him I was choosing Sunderland, and he was okay with that. He went out and got John Bailey from Everton instead.

Looking back, I made a poor decision by going with the Second Division club instead of the First Division club. You should try to stay at the highest level you can, and I didn't do that. Consequently, it wasn't a successful year for me and Sunderland were relegated to the Third Division.

My time at Newcastle United was a learning curve – I didn't do anything wrong, but still got sold. As a footballer you're a commodity, and not much more, but it was the job I loved doing, I loved it more than anything. I never once went into a manager's office and asked for a pay rise. I wasn't bothered. I just loved playing football.

I always felt I was destined to be a footballer. Even from a young age I always had a ball at my feet. When I was a boy, we lived in a terraced house in a village in Houghton-le-Spring called Shiney Row. The best thing about it was Keith, my older brother by two and a half years, was just as keen to play as I was, and we used to go out playing together. We both had similar attributes in terms of kicking the ball naturally with our left foot, despite both of our parents being right-footed.

When we moved a mile down the road to a council house on a hill in Penshaw, the ball was forever running away from me down the slope. Sometimes we'd go down to Penshaw Monument and even then we'd take the ball. At home we'd kick the ball about in the garden, trying skills and attempting to get past each other. My poor father's greenhouse lost countless window panes as we played day in, day out.

It was literally what we lived and breathed: as soon as we got home from school we'd be straight out with the ball. It was always there, we were just constantly learning how to play. It's amazing to look back on our development – Keith brought out the best in me. I was just a young lad with a bit of speed who played on the left wing. He was more of a midfield player – he had a bit of finesse and a bit of quality about him, so we learned from each other.

Keith was snapped up by Newcastle, so it had done him good to work with me, and it had done me twice as much good because I ended up there with him. There was a scout watching me one school game and he looked at me and thought, *He has some talent*. When he found out Keith was my brother, he told me that something must run in the family, and it probably did.

After being scouted, I jumped from being a schoolboy into the big world of professional football. I got into the equivalent of the academy team, where I was put on the left wing, but somewhere along the line somebody suggested I was decent at defending so could go to left-back, and the rest is history, that was my position for life.

I served a one-year apprenticeship and had to make sure I performed to my very best between the ages of 16 and 17. If you don't do that, you don't make it as a footballer. Both Keith and I were built very differently to today's footballers, who are six-foot plus. He was much stronger and shorter than me, while I was taller. At that time you didn't need to be strong like today's Premier League players, you just needed to be fit. I started doing professional running, learning how to do the 100m sprint and other distances, which helped me to learn how to run properly, and fast, and built some muscle on my legs, which definitely helped my cause as I looked to progress at Newcastle United.

I had two great youth team coaches, Geoff Allen and George Herd, who were both former pros and helped me develop as a player, particularly going forward, which became part of my identity as a left-back in future years.

Keith ended up playing just one game for Newcastle, while I was lucky enough to get 158 league appearances in black and white. Frank Clark was the left-back when I started pushing towards the first team, and he was very defensive-minded. His job was to stop players getting through. I used to look up to him. He was the perfect person to follow – he was very clear in what his aims were. He was in his late 20s and maybe coming towards the end of his career, but he went on to Nottingham Forest and won the European Cup. He was proof of what you could achieve if you set your mind to it and was determined to keep in the team, even though I was pressing him all the time.

We had a couple of injuries and he filled in for people like Pat Howard and David Craig in other defensive positions, he was that talented. He was one of the best defenders I've ever played with. I used to watch him and it helped me really develop my game. The one big thing I learned from him was not to dive in. I was a young, tempestuous full-back and I often dived in at the feet of the player, thinking I could get the ball, whereas Frank was more measured. When you were playing as a forward, whether you were Steve Coppell or Mike Summerbee, you'd wait for the player to dive in and skip past him. Frank and the other coaches would turn their heads in shame when I slid in, so I quickly wised up. Frank would say to me, 'Stay on your feet,' and that really helped me.

I do feel lucky to have played for a club with such fantastic fans. The best example I can give of how good Newcastle United supporters are was that they were sat with the Liverpool fans for the FA Cup Final, and there were no problems or arrests. As players we felt very proud of the supporters, and countless times at St James' Park the fans won the game for us, even local derbies against Sunderland. You'd look at the size of the Gallowgate End and think, *We've got to win for this lot*, and, more times than we probably deserved, we did.

KEITH GILLESPIE

Keith Gillespie
Winger
1995–1998

When Newcastle manager Kevin Keegan sold star striker Andy Cole to title rivals Manchester United in January 1995, it sparked a very public uproar from the Toon Army. Keegan was forced to take the extraordinary measure of confronting angry fans outside St James' Park to explain his reasoning behind one of the most seismic transfers in Premier League history. Coming the other way as part of the deal was the little-known Northern Irish youngster Keith Gillespie. The flying winger quickly helped Keegan get the supporters back on side with a string of exhilarating displays as the team dubbed 'The Entertainers' came agonisingly close to pipping Alex Ferguson's men to the championship in 1996.

Gillespie went on to play 148 matches for the club, the best of which came when he tore the mighty Barcelona apart in a Champions League group fixture in 1997. Gillespie, who would later turn out for Blackburn and Leicester, among others, and won 86 international caps, was on the bench for the famous 4-3 defeat at Liverpool in April 1996. He then played a starring role as Newcastle fought back from 3-0 down to so nearly salvage a draw only to lose by the *same* scoreline a season later.

Liverpool 4-3 Newcastle United

Premier League
Monday, 10 March 1997
Anfield, Liverpool
Attendance: 40,751

Liverpool	Newcastle
James	Hislop
Wright	Barton
Kvarme	Albert
Matteo	Peacock
Bjørnebye	Elliott
McManaman	Gillespie
Berger	Batty
Redknapp	Watson
Barnes	Clark (Ginola)
McAteer	Beardsley (Ferdinand, Crawford)
Fowler	Asprilla

Managers

Roy Evans   Kenny Dalglish

Goals

McManaman, Berger, Fowler (2)   Gillespie, Asprilla, Barton

Everybody remembers the sight of Kevin Keegan slumped over the advertising hoardings at the end of our incredible 4-3 defeat at Liverpool during the thrilling 1995/96 season. I was sat right behind him, and it was such a feeling of utter disappointment because we put so much into the match – and it was one we deserved to win. We went 1-0 down, 2-1 up, then 3-2 up, and if you score three goals away from home you expect to get something out of the game, so to lose it was demoralising. The fact we were going for the title made it even harder to take.

People always talk about that Liverpool game costing us the title, but the big turning point that season was losing to Manchester United at home in March 1996 in another game we deserved to win. Peter Schmeichel was unbelievable in goal that night, he won man of the match, and Eric Cantona popped up and scored the only goal in the second half. I also remember us going to Blackburn towards the end of the season and being 1-0 up with four minutes to go and ending up losing 2-1, but, for me, it was probably the United game because, at that time, we were four points ahead, so had we won, the gap would have been seven. They triumphed and suddenly it was down to a single point.

After the Liverpool game, Kevin told us if we played like that for the rest of the season then we'd win more games than we'd lose. He was quite upbeat about it because I'm sure, deep down, he was hurting like we all were. Kevin was a very infectious character, and great at man-management. He knew we were disappointed but just wanted to get the positives out of the game, and there were positives. Anfield is a difficult place to go, and we scored three – but, unfortunately, conceded four.

That's probably the most iconic game ever shown on Sky Sports, so for that same scoreline to happen the following season was crazy. I don't think anybody expected it.

The second time, in March 1997, we weren't really challengers for the title. I know we ended up finishing second that season again, but we were never in it, whereas the previous campaign we were obviously out there in front. It was just another bonkers game, one of

235

two halves and completely different to the previous season because we were pretty poor at times and probably didn't deserve anything out of this one. We were awful in the first half and gave ourselves a mountain to climb by going 3-0 down. Steve McManaman, Robbie Fowler and Patrik Berger all scored in the opening 42 minutes, so we went in at the break starting to think about damage limitation because we didn't want to concede five or six.

When I scored 19 minutes from time, I didn't even celebrate as I thought it was only going to be a consolation goal to make the scoreline a bit more respectable, but Tino Asprilla scored with three minutes to go, and then our tails were up. A minute later we played a long ball forward, sparking a bit of a melee in the box and it almost just hit Warren Barton and went in. We thought we'd got out of jail, only for them to go and do exactly what they did the previous season and score the winner in the last minute, with Robbie Fowler burying a great header. It was totally demoralising to get it back to 3-3 from 3-0 down and then lose in the same circumstances as the previous year. Heartbreaking again but, because of how we played in the first half, we'd have got away with murder had it ended a draw.

It was interesting for me playing at Anfield as an ex-Manchester United player because their rivalry with Liverpool is the biggest in English football, so I always knew I was going to get a bit of stick from the crowd, just as a former Liverpool player would playing at Old Trafford. That's football and all a bit of banter at the end of the day. I remember signing for Blackburn from Newcastle and playing Sunderland in the FA Cup in January 1999; I got dog's abuse all game and ended up scoring the winner, so that was one way to shut them up.

People always go on about the goals we conceded under Kevin, but in the 1995/96 season we finished with the fifth-best defensive record in the league. It was clear we wanted to go forward and we gave our fans a lot of enjoyment, especially at St James' Park, where out of 19 home games we won 17, lost one to United and then drew with Tottenham on the last day of the season. The entertainment value was always there, and Kevin wanted his team to win, but wanted them to win in the right way. He got that message across to the players and that's why we played the style of football we did.

We had some fantastic players like David Ginola, Les Ferdinand, Peter Beardsley and Rob Lee, and, for most of the season, we had a pretty settled side because Ginola was on the left and I was on the right, Peter and Les were up front and then the midfield was Rob Lee and, until we signed David Batty, Lee Clark. Defensively we used pretty much the same back four of John Beresford, Darren Peacock, Steve Howey and Warren Barton, with Philippe Albert playing at times because he was coming back from injury. We didn't use an awful lot of players.

I didn't speak to my former Manchester United team-mates at all during the run-in and we really did have it in our own hands, but you must give them credit because they came back with an unbelievable burst of form. We'd come into the changing room after a game and check the other scores and just kept hearing they'd won 1-0 with Cantona scoring. They did that on quite a few occasions, and everyone will remember Kevin's rant after we'd played Leeds in the last week of the season. I feel particularly aggrieved because everybody talks about his rant – and nobody remembers I scored the winner that night!

We were on the coach on the way home, and I think somebody had spoken to their wife or partner and said that Kevin had gone on this rant. I didn't see it until I got home, and it was replayed on TV. The next day we were in training and Kevin was one of those you could take the mickey out of a bit, so we did, shouting, 'I would love it,' but everyone in that dressing room could see how much it meant to him, what it meant to manage Newcastle, having played for the club as well. He knew how special those fans are.

Alex Ferguson was maybe playing mind games and Kevin reacted to it, but there aren't many managers who would have come out with what he did. It just showed Kevin's passion, he loves Newcastle and is an absolute god up there. What he did in the five years he was there was incredible. When he took over during the

1991/92 season, they lost away at Southend towards the end of the year and, six years later, we beat Barcelona in the Champions League, in what would have been the match of my life had Shay Given not got there first. That rise was incredible, and even after getting promoted to the Premier League they managed to finish third in their first season. I joined in January 1995, and we ended up finishing sixth that year, but we were up there in the top three or four for quite a while and, in the following two seasons, we finished runners-up twice, so it was a special period for everyone connected with the club.

There was a bit of an uproar when I arrived because Andy Cole had gone the other way to join Manchester United, and Coley was a hero for the Newcastle supporters, having scored so many goals for them. I don't think there's any other manager who would have come out to address the fans on the steps outside the stadium as Kevin did. They were all having a go at him, and Kevin said, 'This is the way I see the club moving forward and you have got to trust me.' In the end, they were happy because they did trust him and, with the money he got for Andy Cole, he went and signed Les Ferdinand, who was incredible. Kevin was a great character who I absolutely loved working with, and I feel particularly aggrieved about the fact I only got a couple of years with him.

I didn't think for one minute the fans were on the steps because their unrest was about bringing me in, and I was always going to be under the radar a bit because of the Andy Cole situation and Newcastle letting their main goalscorer go to one of their biggest rivals. I was just at the beginning of my career so people wouldn't know too much about me, although I'd scored against Newcastle for United earlier in the season. It was better for me coming in under the radar because when you go to a new club you want to hit the ground running and there was more spotlight on how Andy was going to do than me.

It was difficult for me to leave Old Trafford because I was a Man United fan and was just starting to force my way into the first team. I was probably a bit unfortunate because of the European rule that was in place at the time, and, with me being Irish, I was classed as a foreigner. United really needed an English striker as Alex Ferguson had headaches every time we played in Europe because of the number of foreigners he had to pick from. There was Peter Schmeichel, Eric Cantona, Andrei Kanchelskis, Denis Irwin, Roy Keane, Mark Hughes, Brian McClair and Ryan Giggs. I think you could only have three foreigners and two players from Scotland, Wales or Ireland.

I saw it as an opportunity to go and establish myself at Newcastle, a fantastic club with a big-name manager like Kevin Keegan, who said that if he didn't get me then Andy Cole wouldn't have gone, so the final decision was mine. I just saw a chance to get regular first-team football because I had Kanchelskis in front of me at United at the time and he was a fantastic player. Six months later Andrei left the club to join Everton, and Alex Ferguson tried to buy me back, but Newcastle turned that down. I knew of the interest and some players would have gone and knocked on the manager's door and said they wanted to go back, but that wasn't for me. I was happy at Newcastle and that was the start of the 1995/96 season, so I wouldn't have changed anything.

Alex Ferguson also helped me get a nice pay rise as, having graduated from the Man United academy as part of the famous class of '92, we were all earning peanuts, £230 a week. When Alex was negotiating the deal, he told Newcastle I was on £600 and that he wanted them to double it! I never had an agent at the time, and it was only a little white lie, but he was obviously doing it in my best interests.

Kevin and Alex were very different in their management styles. Alex didn't do an awful lot on the training pitch and left that to his coaches, whereas Kevin was a real tracksuit manager and even joined in with training at times. His biggest strength was his ability to put an arm around your shoulder and his team talks. In 1995/96, if we'd won the previous week, which most of the time we had, he'd just pick the same team, and then would go around the dressing room and speak to players individually. You'd come away from those chats feeling like the best player in the world, wanting to run through a brick wall for him.

Everyone was totally devastated when Kevin stepped down as manager in January 1997. He brought me to the club and that was the same for a lot of other players, particularly the younger players from the Newcastle area like Lee Clark, Robbie Elliott and Steve Watson. They'd seen Kevin from when he came in and witnessed the rise of the club during his tenure. It was all because of politics behind the scenes that he ended up leaving, and I was very sad about that because I loved working with him. I loved his character, and he had great staff as well in Terry McDermott, Arthur Cox and Derek Fazackerley, who was the first-team coach before Chris McMenemy, whose dad Lawrie had managed Southampton and Sunderland. I've been at clubs where training can be a bit tedious, whereas Kevin and his staff made it an absolute joy every single day.

I was an old-fashioned winger who liked to get my head down, drop the shoulder, get to the byline, and put crosses in, and in Alan Shearer and Les Ferdinand we had two strikers who thrived on getting on the end of crosses. Kevin was great with me, because whenever I ventured too far back to help defensively, he'd tell me to get up the pitch. If ever I came in at half-time having not had the best of games but still trying to run at full-backs, he'd tell me to keep doing that. If nine times out of ten I lost the ball, then on the tenth I'd get a cross in and we'd score a goal. That's all you can ask from a manager.

Being a winger, you need pace, and I was fortunate that I had that and was always the quickest at school. I knew most of the time when I was up against a full-back that if I could get him isolated one on one and there was grass beyond him, then I could knock the ball past him and get on the end of it. It was a great asset to have, but obviously you need to have an end product as well, which I did. I never really came inside because I didn't have a left foot.

Les arrived the year before Alan and that season he was just incredible to play with, making bad balls look like good balls. Then the following year when Alan came and we had those two up front, it was the dream partnership. They were two similar players but scored a lot of goals, and I think it's a real disappointment for Newcastle fans that they only got to see them together for one season before Les left. Alan was an incredible striker, and his record speaks for itself.

David Ginola was my room-mate, and the other boys laughed at how a Frenchman and an Irishman ended up sharing together. I got to know him well, and he used to smoke in the room. Kevin knew he used to enjoy the odd cigarette, but that was just the Frenchman in him coming out. For six or seven months he was unplayable, absolutely amazing, and John Beresford, who played behind, used to do his running for him and then just give him the ball. I think the rest of us were quite envious of David at times because of how good-looking he was, as well as how talented he was as a footballer. He had it all.

Kevin was also great with me when my gambling addiction came out in *The Sun* newspaper, and he invited me down to his house. I had dinner with him and his family and we spoke about it and how we'd resolve it. Looking back, the club maybe should have done a little bit more because they advanced money that I was owed from my signing-on fee so I could pay my gambling debts, but then I was just left to my own devices again. They probably should have taken a bit more due diligence or due care to make sure it wouldn't happen again.

When it came out, there was an element of embarrassment attached to it. The players knew I liked a bet, but they'd not for one minute have known figures or how much I was gambling. Anybody who gambles and has a problem is going to be very secretive about it. There's a lot of boredom attached to it because, when I first signed for Newcastle, I lived in a hotel for six months, so we'd finish training about 12 or 12.15pm every day and then you're left to your own devices. The rest of the players may be going home to their wives and to pick their kids up from school – I was going back to an empty hotel room, which was quite tedious at times. That's pretty much how it really got out of hand because I'd moved to a strange city and was 19 years of age.

Newcastle is a great city and I always think if the football team is doing well, the whole place thrives. Everybody knows how passionate they are about their football team. I moved there as a teenager and then suddenly we were fighting for the Premier League title. We used to get 6,000 people down to watch training during school holidays and it was just a great place to be. It's very rare you get a stadium like St James' Park that's right in the centre of town. It just looms over everything and is an incredible ground.

We had a very sociable group of players and once every three to four weeks we all went out together for some food, and there was no excuse for anybody, you had to go. If you wanted to go home after that, you went home, but others would go on to a bar together. The only people who didn't go were Kevin, Terry McDermott and Arthur Cox, so you had the reserve team manager, the physios and youth team manager all involved. That's part of having a really good side and bonding together.

We always went to the same Italian restaurant on the quayside, called Uno's, so it could be anyone who mentioned that we needed another night out. Even when Peter Beardsley was captain and didn't drink, he'd still be there. The local lads would arrange a lot as well, people like Steve Watson and Steve Harper. I think it's important when you've got new players coming into the club, as we did that summer of 1995 with Les, Warren Barton and Shaka Hislop, the first thing you want to do is get them out because, when you're having a drink, you actually start to see their character and it's a good way of getting to know people. Philippe Albert, another fantastic player, came from Belgium and within two years he pretty much had a Geordie accent.

There was one time during a night out when big Pavel Srníček, bless him, dared me to down a carafe of red wine, which I did in about three mouthfuls. When we got outside, the air hit me and we were going to another boozer when I took off and started running down the road. I burst through these hoardings and fell straight down a manhole, so I had to get the physios to drag me out! I'd cut my neck, and, in the meantime, Peter Beardsley had gone to get his car to take me home. I went home with him and was sick all over the back seat. It was not my finest moment, but the next morning I saw Peter and apologised to him, and he was brilliant. I offered to pay to have his car cleaned and he said, 'No problem, anytime.' He was a great character too.

It was a sad moment for me when I had to leave Newcastle in December 1998. I was in the last year of my contract, having turned down the offer of a new deal because I wanted better terms, and they tried to sell me to Middlesbrough behind Kenny Dalglish's back. He didn't even know about it, but I failed a medical and rang Kenny to tell him, and he said, 'That's not bad news for me because you're still in my plans.'

Kenny lasted only a few more weeks before Ruud Gullit replaced him as manager, and Ruud didn't really speak to me at the start because I was still injured. I did eventually get into the side and played about six games in a row before they sold me to Blackburn because they didn't want to lose me on a free transfer at the end of the season and were happy to get some money. I was disappointed, but saw it coming because it had changed so much from when Kevin was manager.

Newcastle was without doubt the most enjoyable time of my career because you look back at the 1995/96 season and then the 1996/97 one when we qualified for the Champions League, those were special times. Newcastle was just such a special place to go and play football.

BARRY VENISON

Barry Venison
Defender/midfielder
1992–1995

'Former captain of Sunderland' isn't an ideal sentence to have on your CV when you move to Newcastle, but Barry Venison won over hearts and minds immediately when he landed on Tyneside, despite his association with their local rivals. Arriving on the back of six successful seasons at Liverpool, the Toon faithful quickly warmed to his commitment, leadership and determination on the pitch, so much so that he became a firm fan favourite and eventually went on to earn the captain's armband.

Venison, famed for his iconic mullet and outlandish dress sense, was a key piece of Kevin Keegan's plan as he looked to put together a team to challenge for the First Division title, and then to push on into the Premiership. It was a plan that worked almost perfectly.

Despite narrowly avoiding relegation the previous year, Newcastle won their first 11 matches of 1992/93 and went on to storm the league championship, with Venison an almost ever-present. The following year, Keegan, with Venison marshalling his defence, guided the Toon to an astonishing third-place finish in the Premiership, the club's highest in the top tier since winning the championship in 1926/27.

Scoring goals was never Venison's forte. In fact, in 133 appearances in black and white, he found the back of the net just once.

Newcastle United 3-1 Aston Villa

Premier League
Saturday, 25 February 1995
St James' Park, Newcastle
Attendance: 34,637

Newcastle	Aston Villa
Srníček	Bosnich
Venison	Charles
Hottiger	Staunton
Beresford	Ehiogu
Howey	Teale (Atkinson)
Peacock	McGrath
Lee	Townsend
Gillespie	Taylor
Beardsley	Johnson
Fox	Yorke
Kitson	Saunders

Managers

Kevin Keegan	Brian Little

Goals

Venison, Beardsley (2)	Townsend

My haircut always comes up in conversations with fans. It was a huge part of my career – I had a mullet for 15 years. What kind of an idiot has a mullet for 15 years?! It was probably in fashion twice in that time. Looking back, it's part of my identity now and I don't mind it. In fact, I loved it at the time. I used to get abuse every single game. At every single ground, I'd get hammered. It was part of the fabric of the game for me. Jesus, I spent enough money on peroxide to get it sorted so I had to embrace it.

All that banter brought me alive, it stimulated me. You can't shy away from that kind of thing. If you're shy and you get offended by people saying things to you, then you probably have to do what you need to do to stay anonymous, but to be bold, brash and forthright will always invite people to say things to you. That and the dodgy clothes too – I wouldn't put anything plain on, it had to be polka-dot or crazy-check, it was all part of the player I was at that time and I wouldn't change it.

Looking back on my career, I had my fair share of shots, and more often than not the ball went nowhere near the goal! For that reason, I'll always remember my only goal for Newcastle, against Aston Villa in 1995, and I have to admit I've watched it back a fair few times since – thank god for YouTube!

Usually when we were on the attack I'd be in our half as, at that time, I mostly played at the back, but in this game I was in midfield to help stabilise the team and keep things tight. As Keith Gillespie broke down the left and cut inside after about half an hour, I was coming towards the edge of the box. He picked me out with a perfectly weighted pass, which was going across my body. In training I'd try to cut across a pass like that, and sometimes they went in, so I thought, *Why not?* I caught it exactly the way I wanted and watched it fly in exactly where I intended. You can tell by my reaction what I was feeling – instead of running around like a little kid, I just couldn't believe I'd scored. It was a really lovely moment. Now I knew how Andy Cole felt three times a game! No wonder he was high as a kite all the time, feeling on top of the world.

I never felt scoring goals was part of my remit, and took great pleasure from doing the job I was given, which was either defending our goal or taking hold of the midfield and passing to players with ability like Scott Sellars and Rob Lee so they could go and do their stuff. But scoring was still a really special feeling. The fans were almost laughing with me, at me. We were laughing together as if we were all saying to ourselves, *I can't believe he's just done that.* The players, meanwhile, used to see me score in training. Striking a ball well was one of my assets, so they probably expected I should be scoring more than I did. I didn't expect it, but they probably did. Everyone had a bit of fun that day – they were all happy for me.

It brought consequences, though. Every time after that when the ball came near me at the edge of the box, the whole of St James' Park would shout 'shoot!' and Kevin Keegan was in the dugout shouting 'no!'. The goal worked well for me but didn't work well for the manager. Seeing as I never scored for the club again, it shows he was probably right.

Saying that, we played Chelsea away a few weeks later and the ball came to me in a very similar situation, and I thought, *Sod it, I'm going to hit it.* I scuffed it, and the keeper saved it, but Marc Hottiger tucked in the rebound. That was the sum total of the success of my shooting, but happened in the space of a few games.

Peter Beardsley scored twice against Villa to seal the win for us, after Andy Townsend equalised about ten minutes after my opener. I was a little disappointed that Townsend's was such a cracking goal, too – it took the shine off mine. He hit it first time about 25 yards out beyond Pavel Srníček.

Pav was a great lad, like a gymnast cut from stone, so supple and strong, a real athlete who pulled off some saves that he had no right to get anywhere near to. He was such a lovely guy, slightly crazy, mind – like most goalkeepers – he was a couple of tiles short of a full roof. Pav could be eccentric, and if you tried to chip him or do anything fancy against him in training then he'd be screaming at you – not that I ever tried to chip him! He could be intimidating because of his size, but he had a lovely warmth about him, and his slight eccentricities were just another part of his perfect make-up.

Peter Beardsley was our star that day against Villa — what a player. I spent a few years with Peter at Liverpool so knew exactly what sort of player and character he was and what he could bring to Newcastle United. I probably knew him better than anyone else at the club. He had so much maturity, experience and confidence, understanding his strengths and how he could beat players. He was given free rein at Newcastle, and there's not many people you can trust with that role, but he carried it really well. The magical side of his game was something we saw every day in training.

He certainly showed it in the win that day. Gillespie set him up for his first — Peter took a magical first touch before finding the bottom corner with his left foot. If his first one was good, his second was outstanding: I was involved as I shielded the ball in midfield, holding off a defender, before laying it back to Steve Howey. He knocked it on to Peter, who took on and beat two defenders like they weren't there, dummying it and then knocking the ball past Mark Bosnich. What a goal.

I'm not sure anyone realised quite how good he was going to be, but Kevin somehow was able to bring in the right players at the right time. He loved to bring in a big name, getting the headlines, and he did it with Peter.

Keith Gillespie set up my goal and one of Peter's, and he was a brilliant lad. He had ridiculous pace and was a great character, with a fantastic work ethic. The lads loved him. Scott Sellars is one player who doesn't get the recognition he deserves — an absolute genius with his left foot. He could change games, and though wasn't a big strong lad, would get stuck in. Work ethic was the most important thing, and they both had it, as did players like Rob Lee and Paul Bracewell. I did too and I think that's one of the reasons Kevin Keegan brought me in.

Before joining Newcastle, I'd been out for about ten months having had two Achilles operations. The Liverpool doctor actually told me there was a very good chance that I wouldn't play again, that my career was over. When I was out injured, Liverpool went out and bought a young lad called Rob Jones from Crewe, who did a tremendous job. My contract was up and, although they offered me a three-year deal to stay, I just knew that my opportunities would be limited because of Rob and the injury, and then I got a call that changed everything.

Terry McDermott rang me up and said Kevin was interested in me and wanted to meet. I drove up and met him, and Kevin being Kevin, he just said at the end of the conversation: 'Come on, let's do it.' He'd just saved Newcastle from relegation and was telling me about the players he was going to bring in and where he wanted to go with the club. He said he wanted to win the First Division, and that it was just going to get better. I knew I could be part of the rebuild of the club, part of his vision, and that really sealed the deal. Being born and bred in Stanley in the North East, I'd be going home, too.

My feeling is that he was looking for something that I was able to give him, at just the time he needed it. Newcastle were in the second tier, and he was looking to build a solid base looking forward, bringing in experienced players at the top of their game, and someone like me could affect not only the game but the people around me. He wanted a leader, and that's what he went for. Being able to lead and motivate players, and making sure that the right things are done on the pitch at the right time in the right areas, that's valuable. It's not as valuable as being an Andy Cole that scores 40 goals a season, but it's still valuable and every team needs people like that.

It was actually Newcastle where I started off as a youngster, which not many people know. When I was 12 or 13 years old I went there twice a week for schoolboy training. It was getting to the point when they'd be deciding whether they were going to sign me on as a schoolboy or not, and they said no. They rejected me, which as a young lad was absolutely devastating. I was heartbroken. Football was everything to me, and the only reason I'd go to school was so I could play in the school team.

After being knocked back by Newcastle, Sunderland took me on and that's where I got my apprenticeship and ended up turning pro. I became captain there at 19 years old and skippered them in the League Cup Final loss to Norwich in 1985, becoming the youngest captain to appear at Wembley, aged 20, which is crazy when you think about it.

In 1986 Sunderland had been relegated and I was coming to the end of my contract. I didn't have an agent, so decided I'd take matters into my own hands. I found out that you could approach clubs once it got to the January of the year that your contact was up. So, I wrote a letter to every top-tier club just to say that I was available, listed my experience and that I'd be free to move in the summer. Whether anybody read the letters or not, who knows? Kenny Dalglish, in all the years we've known each other, has never mentioned it, so it may have been a waste of time, but it made me feel as if I was being proactive and doing something for my own future.

During six seasons at Liverpool I won two league titles and an FA Cup. That's real experience – and that's what I think Kevin saw and wanted. I was still in my prime and could play in several different positions too, which I ended up doing at Newcastle. Kevin knew he was getting someone who was highly motivated and wouldn't accept losing. It was basic stuff, but every team needs players like that, and I'm just delighted he gave me the opportunity to be part of it. I thoroughly enjoyed every single game I played.

When I signed for Newcastle, the fact I'd played for and captained Sunderland was a little cloud as I was going through the process. I had to see if it was going to be a rain cloud, a thunder cloud or if the sunshine would take it away. As it was, the move couldn't have worked out better. We won the first 11 games of the season and straight away the fans could see my commitment, unquestioning, every game, every minute. The fact that we were flying helped, too. It doesn't get any better than that.

We ended up winning the First Division and I played in almost every game, 44 out of 46. We ended up sealing promotion by winning at Grimsby away in midweek in May 1993 – not exactly your Real Madrid, Liverpool or Manchester United, but it was so exciting for us. Andy Cole, who had been magnificent for us that season, scored the opener before David Kelly finished it off in the 90th minute.

I played against Coley for Newcastle before he signed from Bristol City. I'd never seen a player like him. I remember a lean, pacy forward, who had such quick feet in the box and was so sharp. He had so much ability. I could see it and Kevin could see it. Often after games Kevin and I would sit on the bus together and have a chat, and we spoke about this Andy Cole character after I'd played against him. Maybe that influenced his decision to sign him, who knows?

Andy didn't know what he had. When you watch games back and the number of teams that he split wide open with his pace … he scared the life out of them. He was razor sharp, like a scalpel. Even if we were under pressure at the back, we knew all we had to do was get the ball out and through to Coley and nine times out of ten he'd score, just like he did against Grimsby to help us win the league.

That win was probably one of the best feelings I've had in my life. Grimsby were the team that ended our 11-game winning streak earlier in the season, so that made the victory that little bit more special, too. When they came to St James', everyone expected us to thrash them, so losing was a big blow. That defeat was extra motivation and spurred us on to beat them and win the title.

Some of the wives travelled down for the game and joined the celebrations afterwards. There was nothing grim about Grimsby that Tuesday night, I can tell you! We had a game against Oxford United on the Thursday at St James' Park, and you can tell from our performance that we'd been celebrating rather well for the past couple of days. Jack Grealish thinks he's good at celebrating, but he'd be up against it to get into that Newcastle squad when it comes to enjoying himself after a title win.

Kevin wanted a big showing for the fans, to give them what they deserved, and we started poorly. We went 1-0 down and Kevin wasn't happy at all. We ended up turning it around and grinding out a win, but on the very last day of the season, the Sunday of that week, that was completely different. For that game he put us in our new shirts that we'd be wearing in the Premier League the next season. He wanted a big sunny send-off, with everyone getting together, entertaining and scoring goals, and that's what he got. Winning 7-1 against Leicester that day was amazing. He said to me before the game that he wanted me to play in midfield, and that was the first time I did that for him. It was a start that couldn't have gone much better really! That was a special week.

That title win was a reward for all the hard work, the intensity in training and the belief that was instilled in us by Kevin and Derek Fazackerley, the first-team coach, who was a huge part of that success. Kevin had so much belief in his players, and his belief was infectious. He uplifted everybody's ambitions and standards. He could get average players playing really well, could get very good players playing world-class football, and get them blended together. He was always looking on the horizon to where we could go. He'd say to us: 'You don't realise how good you are and how far you can go, and I am going to bring in more players to make this team, this club, better.'

So, after a full season with him it wasn't a surprise to hear him say that we were going to be pushing for the Premier League title. I knew when I heard him say it, he believed it. We knew we were better than a lot of the Premier League teams, but we didn't know if we could handle the pressure. Could we go to places like Manchester United and Liverpool and win? We showed ourselves, and everyone else, that we could. We left ourselves vulnerable at times, but we had so much enthusiasm, energy, ability and a knack for scoring goals that it made up for that.

When we went to Liverpool that first season back in the Premier League, I had a very special moment with the fans at Anfield. In the second half, Kevin brought me and Peter Beardsley off together and we got a standing ovation from the crowd. It was incredible. Seeing everybody there that I'd spent six years of my life with –

the coaches, canteen ladies, the security – it was great, but it was really good to go back with such a strong team, and to win 2-0 as well. The Liverpool fans nine times out of ten will welcome back players that have played their heart out for them, and though I'll never be Maradona, Pelé or Cruyff in terms of ability, in terms of commitment I'm up there with the best of them. I wanted to show them that the six years I had at Anfield are what really taught me the game – positioning, dealing with men, being humble in victory and pissed off in defeat.

One of the things that I was really good at was complaining like an old bastard; I was a world-class moaner! But that's one of the reasons I was in the Newcastle team, telling players to get back and mark up. I was a counter-balance to Kevin's free-flowing way of doing things. For me there was never a frustration with us always attacking, but I needed to instil sensibility in some players' heads, even full-backs. For example, John Beresford sometimes used to spend more time on the left wing than at left-back! Even Philippe Albert ... when I was playing central midfield, I used to spend more time filling in for him than I did anyone else, as he was off and running up the pitch, but that's why I was there, and I loved it.

Philippe really understood the game and could pass the ball short and long. He was phenomenal. The beauty about him was he could pass the ball out from the back and just keep pressing on, and Kevin encouraged him. He'd go forward, and the logical thing was that I'd slot in, and I was fine with that. 'You go on and express yourself,' and he could, and he did. He was a great lad and character to have around.

I'd played all through my school, youth and reserve days as a midfielder, and it was only when I was at Sunderland I changed position. My third game in they needed an emergency right-back and I obviously did okay and ended up staying there at Sunderland. I played a lot of games at the back for Liverpool and then for Newcastle.

I was moved back into midfield once Marc Hottiger, who was a great lad, came in at right-back. It didn't matter to me, I'd play anywhere. I was playing for one of the best teams in the country, so there was nothing to moan about in that respect. When I was right-back, there were loads of players ahead of me when it came to contention for England, but the move to midfield helped me get my longed-for caps for my country. After playing and captaining England at every level up to the under-21s before coming to Newcastle, I was made to wait for my full cap. Terry Venables called me up and brought me in for the win over USA at Wembley in 1994, aged 30, and then a 0-0 draw with Uruguay in 1995.

I was eventually given the armband at Newcastle, which actually didn't make that much difference to me as I didn't need it to be a mouthy so-and-so on the field, to be able to express myself as a player. Other than the coin toss before the game, it didn't change a thing. It was just Kevin's recognition of what I'd done for the club, and I was proud to wear it.

Whenever I'm in the North East, or when I meet Newcastle fans elsewhere, I always get a really warm welcome, and I think the reason for that's pretty basic. The type of player I was, was a good fit for Newcastle. I was fully committed, every minute of every game, I didn't back out, I always tried to lead by example and made sure I worked as hard, if not harder, than everybody else. There was a rawness to the way that I played and I loved a tackle, and sometimes a good tackle can lift the crowd as much as a goal.

After my first few games the fans realised that I was a genuine, hard-working player who was willing to leave everything on the field, despite having played for their big rivals. Hopefully I'll always be welcomed back in the same way.